Cheek by Jowl

ALSO BY EMILY COCKAYNE

Hubbub: Filth, Noise & Stench in England

Cheek by Jowl

A History of Neighbours

EMILY COCKAYNE

THE BODLEY HEAD
LONDON

Published by The Bodley Head 2012

2 4 6 8 10 9 7 5 3 1

Copyright © Emily Cockayne 2012

First published in Great Britain in 2012 by
The Bodley Head
Random House, 20 Vauxhall Bridge Road
London SW1V 2SA

www.bodleyhead.co.uk
www.vintage-books.co.uk

Addresses for companies within The Random House Group Limited can be found at:
www.randomhouse.co.uk/offices.htm

The Random House Group Limited Reg. No. 954009

A CIP catalogue record for this book
is available from the British Library

ISBN 9781847921345

Typeset by Palimpsest Book Production Limited,
Falkirk, Stirlingshire
Printed and bound in Great Britain by
Clays Ltd, St Ives PLC

To current neighbours

Contents

1   *Becoming Neighbours (1200–1699)*   I

2   *Terraced Neighbours (1700–1839)*   31

3   *Face-to-face and Side-by-side in*   56
     the Back-to-backs (1840–1889)

4   *Suburbia Grows Up (1890–1918)*   88

5   *Semi-detached Neighbours*   123
     (1919–1944)

6   *A Separate House for Every*   153
     Family (1945–1969)

7   *Detached Neighbours (1970–2010)*   181

8   *If Friends are Electric, are Virtual*   205
     Neighbours the Future?

Notes   226

Bibliography   252

Acknowledgements   258

List of Illustrations   260

Index   263

Cheek by Jowl

I

Becoming Neighbours (1200–1699)

Almost everyone has a neighbour, and nearly everyone is a neighbour. If you have a neighbour, you are a neighbour. Neighbours can enrich or ruin our lives. They fascinate and worry us equally. Soap operas followed by millions play with every lurid permutation of relationships in fictional neighbourhoods. One is even called *Neighbours*. Given, not chosen; neighbours come with each new home, and yet estate-agent particulars are silent about them. Some neighbours would not choose each other, and petty disputes over gigantic leylandii and noise turn nasty and feed the tabloids.

These stories have a rich history – as long as men have lived in shelters, they have clashed with those who live nearby. Neighbours star in two of the Ten Commandments; one of God's injunctions instructs us to not 'covet thy neighbour's wife, nor his manservant, nor his maidservants, nor his ox, nor his ass'. Coveting is undoubtedly bad, so Leviticus 19:18 asks us to 'love thy neighbour as thyself'. This concept of neighbourliness expects proximity to engender friendship, but such relationships can often be strained, and the neighbourly spirit withdrawn or poisoned.

The sweetness and strength of neighbour relationships is profoundly affected by the size, substance and separation of our homes. People packed in fetid tenements will behave differently to those who glide expansively through perfumed parlours. Neighbours separated by a linen sheet have a different relationship from those divided by a masonry wall. Demography, social class, affluence and ethnicity can all strain or strengthen neighbourliness.

Neighbours once relied on one another for material support
through hardship until the welfare state extended a bureaucratic
helping hand. The growth of home ownership in the twentieth
century arguably spurred people on to invest more effort in cultivating their neighbours because their property value was at stake.
However, the tendency towards a privatised materialism associated with home ownership may negate this effect. Static
neighbourhoods have become fluid and communities of proximity
have been supplemented in social life by communities of interest.
Hypermobility and instant communication technologies may have
extended the range of human contact at the expense of turning
some neighbours into permanent strangers. Cars push neighbours
apart, fracturing streets by divorcing one side from the other.
Groups of kith and kin can also be more geographically scattered
if they are mobile, so it is now rare for our neighbours to be our
relatives.

This book will show that, increasingly, neighbours form a
shrinking proportion of the people with whom we are in regular,
daily contact. Within this general trend the actual pattern varies
from person to person and across a life span. People might find
that they have more contact with neighbours once they retire or
if they become unemployed or incapacitated. The extent of
previous exposure to neighbours may affect responses to new
neighbouring situations. One woman who moved to a village
from a detached house in the middle of a field was disturbed by
the sound of 'neighbours banging away next door' (DIY, I
presume). The banging neighbours were actually very conscien-
tious. A fear of being regarded as bad neighbours had influenced
their use of space. Their third bedroom was directly above
the neighbour's sitting room and they did not use it. To try to
avoid disturbing her, three children crammed into another
bedroom.[1]

Privacy and exposure are constant themes in discussions of
neighbourliness. The research organisation Mass Observation
was founded in 1937 by a group of men determined to study

their own society as anthropologists. In their survey of 'People's Homes' in 1943, the team defined privacy as 'freedom from being overlooked by neighbours'.[2] The architect Walter Segal thought privacy was 'to be able to live one's own life without one's neighbours voluntarily or involuntarily taking a part of it', and he designed houses that helped to protect 'those little domestic secrets which the neighbour is so keen to discover'.[3] Neighbours can judge your taste in underwear by peeking at your washing line and your drinking habits by glancing into your recycling box. They might hear your arguments, how you discipline your children, what music you like, and your sexual exclamations. They have some access to your private face. Just like Cherie Blair emerging from Number 10 Downing Street on the morning after the general election in 1997, our neighbours might see our bed hair and nightwear; they could spot our curlers, aprons and rubber gloves. We could even witness a naked neighbour's damp dash to retrieve a bath towel. This uniquely intimate access can bring trouble when secrets are discovered. This book explores the delicate balance between people's determination to protect their privacy and their wish to cultivate contact with those who live close by.

Sssh! Listen. Are your neighbours in? Maybe you cannot hear them, but is that liver and onions you can smell cooking? Their car is outside. You piece together the evidence like James Stewart in *Rear Window*. I live on a terraced street. Our neighbours on both sides are quiet. I think one side is in now, the other not. My kids are hurtling around, so the neighbours will know we are in.

The construction and layout of some properties has prevented aural privacy. In 1688 a lodger in a house in London's Chichester Rents remarked that 'by reason of the narrowness of the said building which whatsoever is spoken at . . . any of the neighbours may be heard by the rest of them especially by them that are opposite on both sides'.[4] Similar comments were recorded from tower-block dwellers in the twentieth century. 'Things were bad for our neighbours upstairs', writes Barty Phillips, remembering a day when her mother was pressing sheets and they heard a voice from above say, 'That's funny, can you hear somebody ironing?'[5]

Both the layout of housing and the infrastructure that services neighbourhoods can affect neighbourly relationships. The significance of the physical arrangement of housing can be illustrated by a disconcerting thought-experiment. Imagine a terraced street with each dividing wall transformed into glass. How would we act differently? We may, for instance, become suddenly aware that our heads, when resting on the pillow, are a mere two-brick thickness away from our neighbours. The construction of our walls has a direct influence on our experiences. Detached houses give their inhabitants the freedom to be noisy without intruding on the lives of others. Terraced houses and flats usually require more consideration for relations to remain cordial. Each dwelling type (except the bungalow) has taken its turn to be the most prevalent, characterising its era. The Georgians built terraces, Victorians threw up back-to-backs and the semi-detached house proliferated in the 1930s. Houses eventually became directly connected to systems of water and sewerage, which saw less need for communal facilities like water pumps, toilet blocks and waste containers, where people met. Life became increasingly self-contained.

Walls do not simply separate interior spaces; gardens and land can be walled or fenced. In 'Mending Wall', the American poet Robert Frost dared to question the point of walls for neighbours without livestock. He wonders why we cannot demarcate symbolically. Wanting to know what was being 'walled in' or walled out, Frost warns that erecting a wall might even cause offence. His neighbour twice reminds him that 'Good fences make good neighbours'.[6] The neighbour had proverbial wisdom on his side. One tells us that 'a wall between doth best preserve friendship'. Another starts with warmth – 'love your neighbour' – but ends with caution: 'yet pull not downe your hedge'. A long-standing love of territorial markers is clear. We should bear in mind that the etymological root of the word 'fence' is in 'defence'.[7]

PLATE 2ᴀ

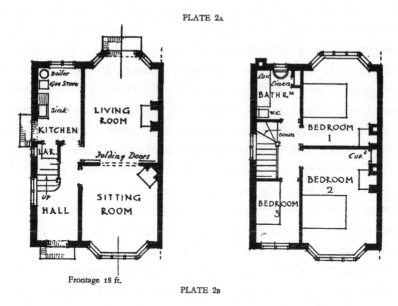

Frontage 18 ft.

PLATE 2ʙ

Fig. 1 From Ernest Betham (ed.), *House Building, 1934–1936*.

'A House . . . with a door . . . Windows . . . one, two, three, four'; this is my *Play School* childhood memory of houses. I drew a house – it stood alone – detached. The smoke from the chimney never blew over any neighbouring four-windowed boxes. This privatised, singular view of the house is not just child's play. The typical presentation of a house plan is with no occupants and the houses out of context, with their storeys side-by-side, sitting where the neighbour's house should be (**Fig. 1**). Presented this way, it is difficult to assess how other dwellings might impinge on the space around a property. Architectural historians tend to write about houses as aesthetic objects rather than as vessels for living that enable us to fulfil our human potential – or frustrate us from doing so. Houses are especially interesting elements of architecture because people live in them, near to other people; not because of the graceful inflection of a drip moulding or the observance of the classical orders. This book puts the people back in the houses and the houses back on the streets.

AT LEAST WITHIN HAIL

Medieval villagers farmed strips of common land, and the word 'nigh-bour' originally meant 'the man who tills the next piece of ground to mine'.[8] The meaning has evolved to signify people next door. Keith Wrightson has shown how in the sixteenth century it meant 'someone well known', but two centuries later the word was stripped of any notion of familiarity and rendered 'a mere indicator of residential propinquity'.[9] Samuel Johnson captured this mutation of meaning in his dictionary by blending 'one who lives near to another' with 'one who lives in familiarity with another'. To Johnson, being neighbourly was 'becoming a neighbour; kind; civil'.[10] Early-modern neighbours could be anybody in the parish, albeit they might live a mile from each other. The looseness and geographical vagueness in the terminology makes it difficult to uncover much about what it meant to live very near to somebody. The best clues come from nuisance and defamation cases, but these are skewed towards negative experiences.

Even in more recent times some biographers have been cavalier with the term 'neighbour'. Some have used it to mean 'from the same town', or even 'the neighbouring shire'. These writers sent me on wild goose chases, tracking down 'neighbours' who actually lived miles apart. In 1935 the writer Annie Swan defined neighbours as the people 'at least within hail'.[11] A rate collector from the mid nineteenth century thought neighbours were the people within the nearest five or six houses.[12] One of my own neighbours told me that 'a real neighbour is someone you can visit in your slippers' (he was wearing his at the time). Slippers sum up relaxed neighbouring. For my purposes, neighbours are those people who live either next door, opposite, in the nearest five or six houses, or possibly (at a stretch) on the same street, but no further. Neighbours live only a slipperable distance away.[13]

NEIGHBOURS DIFFER

Among neighbours we find all human emotions. Which relationships should I focus on? The *Daily Mail* might incline towards stories of cursing and conflict; fisticuffs or worse. However, I also want to show how neighbours fell in love, or set up businesses together; how they could erect barriers, or take them down. I will show how they liked, loved, laughed with, cared for and supported, as well as how they could hate, hurt and humiliate each other. There are a number of murders within these pages, perhaps more than street parties. I know the latter were more common, but they did not make the headlines. Love stories are under-represented too, but many couples have met as neighbours. The astronomer William Herschel married his widowed neighbour Mary in 1788.[14] In 1801, the novelist and philosopher William Godwin married his neighbour when his first wife, Mary Wollstonecraft, was ten years dead.[15] In his fifties Randolph Churchill, Winston's son, fell in love with a neighbour.[16] Captain W.E. Johns, the creator of flying ace Biggles, had separated from his wife, Maude, by the end of the 1920s. He became captivated by Doris Leigh, one of the daughters in the house next door. Johns hit a tennis ball into the Leighs' garden hoping to become acquainted with his attractive neighbour. His ruse was successful. Love all. Although they never married, Dol and her captain lived as Mr and Mrs Johns until he died in 1968.[17]

Naughty and illicit relationships between neighbours are the stuff of titillation. Such relationships attract salacious gossip. 'Don't make love at the garden gate,' warns one rhyme, 'love is blind but the neighbours ain't'. Some pre-modern partition walls were so thin that it would have been relatively easy to push a finger through them, creating a spyhole. Lovers could use this as a hole through which they could whisper sweet nothings. Historic relationships that were undiscovered usually remain hidden from us too. Please assume, therefore, that there were many more lovers than murderers, and I wish I could introduce you to more of the former.

Some people have problems with particular neighbours; some with neighbours in general. In response to the Mass Observation survey of 'People's Homes', one woman hinted at the importance of individual sensitivity when she discussed noise: 'It's hearing every footstep, and then the drill outside, it drives me mad, it does when you're nervy.'[18] Other people have noticed this. In her autobiography, Winifred Foley described the misery created by a neighbour in her post-war London flat. The Foleys had been warned that 'her downstairs' was troublesome, and had driven previous tenants away. To suppress noise, Winifred applied carpets and rugs to the floors, banned shoes and kept her children outdoors as much as possible. This was done to placate their irascible neighbour – 'an anonymous nuisance whom we did not know and had hardly even seen'. The strain of this eggshell existence depressed Winifred and made her hypersensitive too. Feeling 'trapped in a purgatory of noise', she yearned for a country cottage.[19]

While Jane Carlyle's husband, Thomas, was at home, Jane became more sensitive to neighbour noises because she knew how much they angered him. Like a guard dog, she grew protectively alert, ready to pounce on the source of Thomas's irritation. Her senses calmed in his absence. In 1852, renovations drove Thomas away, but Jane remained and wrote, 'I feel the dirt and disorder with my own senses, and not through his as well, it is amazing how little I care about it.'[20] In a review of Garret Keizer's *The Unwanted Sound of Everything We Want*, Jenny Diski wrote of her own struggles with noisy neighbours, and seemed to accept that, as an author who works at home, she was abnormally sensitive to noise. She describes her own responses to the 'sounds of other people' as 'horrid' and 'unsocial'. Like Thomas Carlyle, Diski made a soundproofed attic for escape.[21]

An eccentric early gay rights campaigner called George Ives pointed out that 'Men differ, and they always differed.'[22] We can extend this to neighbours too; neighbours differ, and they have always differed. The fact that all neighbour relationships vary means that patterns in neighbouring are difficult to trace. Indeed, they

may not exist in any meaningful way. All that we can really hope
to recover are the developments that might have affected the conditions of neighbouring.

THE PRESS OF PEOPLE

Literate medieval merchants and aristocrats left traces of evidence
about their neighbourly experiences. Sir Geoffrey Luttrell, the
patron of the Luttrell Psalter, was involved in property disputes
with his neighbours in the early fourteenth century. A little later
the Paston letters complain about the family's treatment by greedy
land-grabbing neighbours.[23] Enclosures began in the thirteenth
century; wastes, woodlands and commons were colonised to
create individual farms. Land that had been farmed in strips by
villagers was now turned to pasture. One person's improvements
could mean a loss of assets for his neighbours. Villagers could no
longer subsist independently by collecting firewood, grazing
animals and harvesting crops. They roamed, selling their labour.
The lack of access to land often forced them into poverty and
towards towns.

Permanent houses began to replace temporary wattle-and-daub
single-room hovels in the fourteenth century. As homes became
more permanent, so did neighbours. Medieval and Tudor cities
had tight and sinuous streets. Plots were deep and narrow. Buildings were often jettied out towards each other at upper levels,
and some dark dwellings wrapped tightly around neighbouring
buildings. Some constructions were extreme. When John Thatcher
of Watling Street in London built his house against Christopher
Nycholson's in 1549, he blocked a window and forced Nycholson
to enter his house through a tunnel that was less than four feet
wide.[24]

Ralph Treswell surveyed several London properties in the late
sixteenth and early seventeenth centuries, and his plans reveal the
ways that properties were subdivided, sometimes illogically, with
some people needing to walk through space rented by another.

One historian has described this as living in 'conditions of structural codependency'.[25] Labyrinthine routes to, and through, homes meant that neighbours would have unavoidably encountered one another as they went about their daily business.

Early-modern towns changed in a slow and piecemeal way, except when fire quickened the process. The increasing pressure on space meant all available plots were used. Infilling was a common form of urban development; the rear parts of larger, street-frontage houses were filled with smaller dwellings, often arranged around a yard, court or alley. By 1550, London's Ship Alley had been developed at the rear of four larger street-facing properties. Some of the dwellings were only one chamber big, or even just one cellar. These spaces then started to absorb increasing numbers of occupants. By 1630, Ship Alley was home to fourteen households. Eight years later the number had risen to seventeen, and by 1666 it had reached twenty-three.[26]

Fig. 2 Simplified drawing of the lean-to house depicted in *View of a fragment of London Wall, as it stood in the churchyard of St Giles Without Cripplegate in 1793*.

Temporary houses were banged up on to walls (lean-tos), and all types of buildings (including stables, coalhouses, barns, outhouses, privies and sheds) were converted into homes. This sketch of a building on the north side of the city wall in the churchyard of St Giles, Cripplegate (**Fig. 2**) indicates an infill shed-type house of the Stuart era, clinging to the side of an existing building. A survey of housing made in 1637 reveals the extent of this type of housing. In one such dwelling lived a carpenter, his wife and five children.[27] People lived ever closer as buildings filled available space.

The same survey revealed the number of households living in 'divided houses'. 'Doubling up' was a last resort for desperate families, especially common when housing was scarce and rents were high.[28] Larger houses once occupied by merchants were split to accommodate several families. Ralph Treswell's 1612 survey of the Maidenhead, a former hostelry on London's Cow Lane, revealed that it had been divided into many dwellings, some only a single chamber, and with various subtenants occupying spaces here and there.[29] Subdivision was increasingly common; sometimes the outcome of split inheritances, and sometimes done to maximise rents. Dividing in the Stuart era usually meant erecting a lath-and-plaster wall down the middle of the property, worsening overcrowding and placing strain on neighbourhood amenities and relations. Many families shared houses, often with a sprinkling of 'ancient widows' or 'aged parishioners' as lodgers to bring in a few more pennies. In Vintry Ward, one house was home to twenty-four families, and in the ward of Farringdon Within, fifty people lived over nine slaughterhouses. By the 1690s, nearly half of London's houses contained subsidiary lodger households.[30]

TH'OBSERVING NEIGHBOURS[31]

Over time, increasing numbers of English households have gained their own toilet, but in the fourteenth century toilets were often shared.[32] The London Assize of Nuisance dealt with the rancour when a man removed a privy that he shared with a neighbour. He

Fig. 3 How buildings could develop in a piecemeal fashion through encrustations and sag.

was ordered to return the privy so that his neighbours could 'continue to enjoy their easement as before'. In the summer of 1333, Londoners Joan and Andrew de Aubrey were at loggerheads with their neighbours over a shared privy. Their neighbour had removed parts of the enclosure, 'so that the extremities of those sitting upon the seats can be seen, a thing which is abominable and altogether intolerable'. At the same time he complained of a hole in the de Aubreys' floor, through which his 'private business can be seen'.[33] In 1542, two wealthy drapers, Henry Dolfyn and John Dymok, fell out over who would pay for their shared facilities to be emptied and cleaned. Dolfyn only had one opening into the vault, but Dymok had three. Neither could agree whose house the combined slurry would be carried through to be carted away. The authorities intervened and decreed that it should be shovelled through the Dolfyn residence, but that Dymok should pay all the charges for removal and making good.[34]

John Thatcher built his property against his neighbour's house, leaving no space for water run-off on his own land.[35] This sort of eavesdropping was regarded as trespass and would damage properties by undermining the structure and making interiors damp. This was not the only form of eavesdropping that bothered premodern neighbours. Eavesdropping was named because the person listening in to private conversations might need to stand under the eavesdrop of a house to do so (and so it could also be trespass). John Locke, a linguistics expert, has recently overheard the past to create an 'intimate history' of eavesdropping. His definition is a useful one:

> Eavesdropping is communication, and it has two features that make it unusually interesting. The first is that it feeds on activity that is inherently *intimate*, and is so because the actors are unaware of the receiver, therefore feel free to be 'themselves'. The second feature that makes eavesdropping so interesting relates to the way the information travels. It is not *donated* by the sender. It is *stolen* by the receiver.[36]

In 1964, a social historian of medieval England asserted that between 'kinship ties and economic co-operation comes neighbourliness, of which we know very little'. Nearly half a century later we know a little more, but our knowledge of medieval neighbourly relationships will always be limited by the sources available.[37] We can guess, however, that medieval neighbours had relatively little privacy, and knew a fair amount about each other. The insubstantial materials from which pre-modern buildings were made and the ways that they deteriorated meant that conversations within could be heard easily and could also percolate into buildings from outside. Most houses had no glass windows, allowing anyone nearby to hear domestic sounds. Neighbours were best placed to eavesdrop. In the fifteenth century, one man lay 'under the walls of his neighbours snooping into what is said in the house'. Eavesdropping was commonly linked with sowing 'discord between neighbours'.[38]

Most mundane sounds were never reported; only those that aroused attention appear in the sources. Peering through Tudor peepholes, Lena Cowen Orlin, the author of *Private Matters and Public Culture in Post-Reformation England*, found 'irrefutable evidence that in fact the occasions for surveillance, voyeurism, and accidental observations were many'. Some historians have dismissed these cracks and holes as fictions, invented to bolster the power of a witness statement, but Orlin makes a firm case for the lack of solidity in Tudor walls. She finds various sorts of peepholes – from latch-key apertures to sagging doors and rotting floors, shrunken panelling, burst wood knots and peg holes. We learn that any boundary 'could be breached by a defiant chink or cranny'. Privacy, according to Orlin, 'was not an object of the architecture of the period'.[39] We know about many peepholes because they were mentioned in ecclesiastical court cases centring on sexual transgressions in bedrooms. Diane Shaw explored an earlier period and found that neighbours 'eagerly ferreted out illicit activities', uncovering 'illicit sleeping together' in 1386.[40] Two sets of inhabitants in one Chester house lived separated by a 'broken wall and a painted cloth'. These flimsy partitions were intended to demarcate space rather than provide much privacy. Mr Conoway of Canterbury evicted a tenant from one part of his house because 'he was a bad neighbour and would ever be harkening and looking through holes in the walls to hear and see what the said Conoway did in his house'. Consequently, neighbours were in a privileged position to know about the routines, sleeping arrangements, habits, relationships and conflicts that were conducted in the household next door, above or below.[41]

Orlin introduces us to Mary Wallys from London, who took the opportunity to cavort naked in bed with her lover when her bookbinding husband was out of town – all overheard and then overseen (by lifting up a painted cloth) by Briget Upley, the neighbour.[42] In 1598, Margaret Browne of Hounsditch gave a statement to the Bridewell Court in which she alleged that her neighbour, Clement Underhill, had been 'making merry' with her lover, Michael Fludd, while Mr Underhill was otherwise engaged. Clement was seen to lie with her lover, and, at her bedside,

He pluckt upp her clothes to her thighes she pluckt them upp higher (whereby this deponent sawe not onlye her hose being A seawater greene colour and also her bare thighes) then he went upp to her upon the bed and putting down his hose had carnall Copulation with her and having so don he wyped his yard on her Smocke.

Meanwhile, Margaret had beckoned her husband, Henry, over to watch with her, as Fludd 'washed his yard'. The couple, effectively dogging their neighbour through a hole in the wall, presumably thought they were performing a social good by reporting the incident. Henry also testified, although in less lurid detail than his wife, claiming to have seen Fludd 'com from the said Clement of from her bed where she laye with his hose hanging about his legges'.[43] In Yorkshire in 1666, Elizabeth Tullett lived next door to Ottiwell and Mary Babb. Mary was having an affair with Ottiwell's brother, Richard, who lived with them. Tullett told the consistory court that through the 'wall betwixt them' she had seen Mary and her

brother-in-law commit 'very uncivil passages'. Mary and Richard
were seen to be acting as man and wife, and were spied 'in the
very act of adultery . . . in a very beastly manner'. Elizabeth watched
for a quarter of an hour, along with a couple she had invited along
for the show.[44]

These witnesses did not seem ashamed to have violated the
privacy of their neighbours. Tullett even reported the number of
sexual thrusts. Who could resist such glimpses of juicy naughtiness?
We should not, however, think of pre-modern neighbours permanently spying through holes to thrill the eye – as a modern glass to
the wall might please the mind's eye. Martin Ingram, an historian
of early-modern England, has pointed out that 'these spying cases
did not represent normal spontaneous, neighbourly behaviour but
carefully planned legally purposeful activity'. Watching, and
bringing other witnesses in to watch too, produced information
that was acceptable in court. People became especially observant
after prior suspicions had made them alert to transgressions. Neighbours were supposed to keep an eye on each other; it was part and
parcel of the neighbourly service.[45]

NOT LIVING QUIETLY TOGETHER

Cases of wife-beating rarely reached the courts in pre-modern
England. This was because it was an accepted method for men to
assert their domination over their wives. Neighbours appear as
witnesses in some of the few cases. Thomas Dey lived in West
Yorkshire. In 1383, a group of his neighbours reported him for
assaulting his wife, Alice. Perhaps their accusations were simply a
way to avenge themselves against a man whose other manorial
court appearances suggest that he was a nuisance neighbour (shortly
before the assault, he had been reported for dumping manure that
contaminated the communal spring).[46] When incidents do come to
light, it was often because they caused trouble to somebody else
besides the beaten wife. In 1639, it was related to a church court
that one drunken man had 'beat his wife about the street so as the

neighbours could not rest in their beds'.[47] A by-law required Londoners to observe that 'No man shall after the houre of nine at the Night, keepe any rule whereby any such suddaine out-cry be made in the still of the Night, as . . . beating hys Wife . . . to the Disturbaunce of his neighbours.'[48] Noise, not assault, was the offence here.

Wife-on-husband assault attracted more attention from neighbours. A Swiss doctor on a visit to England in 1599 observed that if a wife beat her husband their 'nearest neighbour is placed on a cart and paraded through the whole town as a laughing-stock'. The neighbour was punished for not having helped the man when his wife was beating him. Neighbours were expected to turn a deaf ear against the wails of wives but hearken to the moans of men and remind them that society expected them to keep order in the household.[49] 'Neighbours did not like the task of keeping order in other households, but they would do so when it was necessary.'[50]

Other tragic cases ended in the death of a spouse. In 1680, Margaret Osgood hacked her husband Walter to death and then dismembered him. Neighbours supplied titbits for the pamphleteers, one 'ancient neighbour' remarking that the Osgoods 'seldome went to bed without a storm of Oaths and mutual curses'.[51] Even the 'mediation and perswasion of several neighbours' had not prevented Margaret from burying her hatchet in Walter's head and strangling him 'with a Whip-Cord . . . whilst he lay weltering in his Blood'.[52] The assize session that heard the Osgood *guignol* also dealt with a drunken wheelwright who murdered his wife. William Trickler was 'heard to quarrel with her and also assaulted her with a spade, in so violent a manner, that some of the blowes were heard at a Neighbours house near to them'.[53]

'Living quietly together' was considered to be the best state for a married couple and indicated a harmonious relationship.[54] In 1685, Sarah Watson of Willoughby in Warwickshire was ordered to return to her husband George and instructed to 'continue with him, behaving herself as she ought to do towards him; and the said George is ordered to receive her and live quietly with her'.[55] George

Webbe, the Bishop of Limerick, revealed how a state of quietness could be achieved through 'an abstinence from whatever might disturb'. Essential outward signs of a quiet spirit were a quiet hand, a quiet eye, a deaf ear and a silent tongue.[56] Although Webbe did not pin all the blame on the wives when couples failed to live quietly, many others did, blaming it on a vicious, unquiet tongue.

The scolding, nagging wife could worry her husband 'out of his senses' and a bridle might be needed to silence her, or a ducking to punish her.[57] A medieval scold was a person who broke the peace through her quarrelsome nature, or who spread malicious gossip. In 1481, Margaret Akvede of Lincolnshire was accused of 'provoking controversy in poisonous fashion between her neighbours'.[58] A reputation for scolding could provoke suspicions that a woman was involved in witchcraft. Reginald Scot, trying to understand accusations of witchcraft in 1584, remarked how 'these miserable wretches are so odious unto all their neighbours, and so feared, as few dare to offend them, or denie them anie things they aske'. He decided that, rather than having magical powers, 'their cheefe fault . . . is that they are scolds'.[59] In 1566, half a dozen wives from the London parish of St Dunstan-in-the-West were described as 'being persons of evyll name and lyving & not worthy to dwell amongst honest neyboures' after they stirred up local conflict.[60] A dozen householders from Wellington in Somerset petitioned the Justices of the Peace in the mid seventeenth century, hoping to find some relief from a local harridan who could not resist scolding and fighting with her neighbours.[61]

Men were accused of being quarrelsome with their neighbours too, often under the umbrella of 'disturbing the peace'. In 1598, a quarrelsome man was described as a 'disturbator of his honest neighbours' and presented to a church court.[62] Some argumentative souls were accused of barratry, defined by William Hawkins as 'a common Mover, Exciter, or Maintainer of Suits and Quarrels . . . As where one makes it his Business to raise Dissentions among Neighbours, by stirring them to vexatious Law Suits; . . . or by spreading false Rumours and Calumnies, &c'.[63] This type of bad neighbourliness was included in Thomas Tusser's 'description of an envious and naughty neighbour' in 1573:

> His head as a storehouse, with quarels full fraught.
> His braine, is unquiet, till all come to naught.[64]

Barratry and scolding could be connected to eavesdropping, as the information gleaned could fuel the unquietness. One woman was described as 'a whisperer between neighbor and neighbor and a harkner at mens dores and one that maketh disaffection betwene neighbors'.[65] Good neighbours were 'not litigiously given'; they were quiet, amiable and harmless. Bad neighbours were lovers of disquiet who liked to stir.[66]

CONSCIENCE FOR YOURSELF, REPUTATION FOR YOUR NEIGHBOUR

Living quietly was the key to good neighbourliness, and the ability to do so was taken into account when people were asked to provide a character statement for a neighbour. Neighbours were best placed to judge a person's moral standing and sexual propriety because they had access to more information than people who lived further away. As a consequence, the word of a neighbour was often decisive in court.Compurgation was a defence used to clear the accused, whereby innocence could be established through oaths uttered by up to a dozen neighbours. Compurgation depended on a fairly static neighbourhood and required the accused to have already attracted the esteem of those nearby. It was used in the church courts long after it had been abandoned by common lawyers, but generally only in cases of suspected immorality where no firm ruling could be made in court. 'In these circumstances it made sense to establish a presumption of guilt or innocence by testing local opinion.'[67]

In court, neighbours were more credible as witnesses than friends, whose favourable accounts might seem biased or even perjured. St

Augustine had taught that conscience and reputation were two different things, 'conscience for yourself, reputation for your neighbour', and this was true of the early-modern period.[68] Reputation was cultivated through gossip. According to Melanie Tebbutt, the author of *Women's Talk*, gossip is 'talk about other people', and the behaviour and activities of neighbours have provided gossip fodder over the centuries. Gossip could dent, damage and even destroy reputations by spreading or confirming suspicions.[69] Neighbours judged each other and their opinions mattered. Gossip was on the 'spectrum of sanctions' used against disorderly neighbours.[70]

Gossipy nuggets, which might be gathered through observing or eavesdropping on the neighbours, could be twisted by calumniators bent on spreading malicious rumours. Some people fought back with defamation and slander litigation, which became more common between neighbours in the late sixteenth century.[71] The poet Thomas Tusser evoked the 'envious and naughty neighbour',

> His mouth full of venym, his lypps out of frame.
> His tong a false witnesse, his frend to defame.
> His eyes be promoters, some trespass to spye,
> His eares be as spyalls, a larum to crye.[72]

Most defamatory utterances were made outdoors, in the street or on the doorstep (see **Fig. 4**), whilst bystanders earwigged from their doorways.[73]

The threat of litigation might have curtailed these indiscretions but the thinness of pre-modern walls presented a challenge to privacy and an opportunity to snoop. In one case from 1611, a woman reported hearing her next-door neighbour call her a whore through the kitchen wall.[74] People who gossiped too much or defamed their neighbours were censured by the courts. It was hoped that both the gossipers and the gossiped-about would mend their ways and become better citizens. Some penances issued by church courts required naughty folk to confirm their misdeeds 'before the neighbours'. Actions like these were designed to reconcile communities.

Fig. 4 *The New Art and Mystery of Gossiping* (London, 1760?).

BETTER NEAR NEIGHBOUR THAN
FAR-DWELLING KINSMAN

An increasing individualism after the Reformation may have atom-ised communities.[75] According to Bishop Curle, a Puritan was 'one as loves God with all his soule, but hates his neighbour with all his heart'.[76] This did not always ring true at the parish level. Nehemiah Wallington was a puritanical wood-turner from London who did not hate his neighbours, although he did seek to reform them, writing instructional letters to help make them godlier. He wrote to one neighbour in 1640, criticising him for selling on the Sabbath and snoozing in church. The letter closes, 'and now neighbour, take this my admonition in love'.[77]

Protestantism redefined poverty in moral terms; paupers were deserving or undeserving. Rebuking a neighbour for loose morals was both an altruistic act of salvation and a selfish attempt to save paying more parish relief. This helps to explain the prying; neighbours wanted order next door so they did not have to help keep an illegitimate child or an abandoned wife. Some of the shunned poor left to join the ranks of landless labourers seeking work in the burgeoning cities. They would have lived there as strangers without ties. In the villages from which they migrated, people were often enveloped in a collective memory – they shared childhoods or family affinities going back generations. The migrants might have found it liberating to be free of such links. In towns it was easier to be anonymous, or to reinvent oneself, but at a cost to neighbourliness.

Despite the gossip, defamation and increasing individualism, the historian Keith Wrightson has discovered that early-modern neighbours still supported each other and co-operated for the good of the community. He has found evidence from the sixteenth and seventeenth centuries that 'abundantly demonstrates the vitality of the concept of neighbourliness' both as an ideal and as a realistic practicality. Wrightson observes that neighbourliness promoted co-operation and helped people to overcome isolation 'in a relatively fluid society in which individuals and independent nuclear families were little cushioned by kinship ties'.[78]

Neighbourliness was clear in the lending of tools, domestic paraphernalia and food. In 1688, London servant Dorothy Harding was 'wont frequently to go in and out to Borrow somewhat or other, as other Neighbours may do'.[79] Tusser provides the rhymes again:

> Lending to neighbour, in time of need
> Wins love of thy neighbours, and credit doth breed.

Craig Muldrew has linked early-modern neighbourliness with creditworthiness. Neighbours were entwined in credit networks that relied on trust and the Christian duty to lend money to poorer neighbours in need. Tusser warned that 'who quick be to borrow, and slow be to paie, their credit is naught, go they never so gaie'. People did not just exchange small sums of money; they could also guarantee a neighbour's loan. This carried a risk. When the economy looked shaky, judgements about creditworthiness became more important.[80] Advising his readers to shun the 'naughty neighbour' whose 'credit much like, to the chance of the dyce', Tusser notes that his 'friendship is counterfet, seldom to trust'.[81]

Neighbours also gave without expecting repayment. They gave each other time, and practical and emotional support. The word 'gossip' stems from the 'godsibbs' who attended a woman in childbirth. Many of these women were neighbours. Their invitation was a 'significant rite of passage', which indicated 'acceptance within a network or community'.[82] Being present when a neighbour was born would have encouraged a person to invest emotion and material support in the new life as the child matured. The parish relief system was not a reliable support for most of the indigent poor, so many people depended instead on the kindness of neighbours.[83] In the late seventeenth century, nonagenarian Elizabeth Shatton gathered rags to make money and her meagre income was enhanced by 'help from neighbours' and a modest pension.[84]

A link between witchcraft and neighbourliness was mooted in the 1970s by Keith Thomas and Alan Macfarlane, who both thought that guilt resulting from the denial of charity to the poor might have prompted accusations. Some contemporary pamphlets identified witches as old women who had been rebutted when they sought relief amongst their neighbours.[85] In some cases people lived for years as neighbours to women suspected of witchcraft before going to the authorities. Misfortune might have triggered accusations towards those who were already under suspicion. Neighbours who were considered to be marginal, strange, annoying, scolding, slandering, lonely, or non-conformist were more liable to accusation than popular, involved and helpful neighbours.[86] The subjects of gossip and those who were outside the gossip loop may have been singled out. It is likely that some people might have added their own voice and accused an annoying neighbour of witchcraft simply

to have them removed, or to teach them a lesson, without actually
believing their own testimony. Only a tiny minority of bad neighbours were ever accused of being witches, but it was an important
facet of the neighbour relationship that was unique to this era of
English history.

HERE'S TALK OF THE TURK AND POPE, BUT IT'S MY NEXT NEIGHBOUR THAT DOES ME THE HARM

A Southampton hatter we know only as Baggs endured nuisance
neighbours between 1611 and 1613. First a foot of water flooded his
cellar when one neighbour diverted a watercourse. Two years later
the bakehouse next door was deemed 'so Rotten and Rewinous as
it is daylie and suddainelye like to fall downe verie dangerouslye'
and the town jurors ordered demolition.[87] Nuisances are breaches
of neighbourly obligations, and nuisance laws and rules regulate
neighbourly relations. Nuisance cases involve the damage caused
by another's use of property, whereas negligence cases concern the
conduct of the defendant.[88] There is overlap, and historically some
lawyers have tried to subsume nuisance within negligence. Baggs
was a victim of negligence and nuisance that affected the use of
his property. Damage in nuisance cases can be interpreted quite
widely and can include loss of sleep. The judgement that guides
nuisance cases is 'reasonableness'. Was it reasonable to flood Baggs's
cellar? Was it reasonable to leave him fearing structural collapse?
Clearly not, but in other cases reasonableness is harder to measure.
Is it reasonable to hammer at particular times? How much smoke
is reasonable? These are questions neighbours have asked each other
and the courts for centuries. The medieval Assize of Nuisance was
used to deal with building conflicts between neighbours, such as
drainage, and the positioning of windows, privies, jetties and walls.
Unlike modern planning tussles, which generally occur before
construction, these were usually judged after work had been carried
out, or deterioration had occurred. In the early-modern period the
London viewers were responsible for visiting properties to resolve

neighbour disputes. Most of their caseload involved boundaries, party walls and gutters.[89]

Natural light was exceptionally valuable in an era before gas or electric lighting, and people were frustrated by neighbours who blocked their 'lights' by building structures that stopped daylight from penetrating their rooms. Denial of light to windows that had been there for 'time out of mind' (usually interpreted as a few decades) was serious. In 1351, Londoners Geoffrey and Maud Aleyn complained that some neighbours had obscured their windows and open apertures and won their case by proving their historic enjoyment of the light.[90] When Cardicon Thomas of London built a house on the back of Edmund Bolsworth's house in Shore Lane it darkened Bolsworth's windows. In typical Solomonic judgement, the viewers suggested that Thomas whitewashed his wall 'from the first storey up . . . to give reflecon or light to the said Bolsworth's house'.[91]

As plots grew tighter and properties darker, legal opinion became increasingly divided. Lawyers quibbled in the seventeenth century over the legal permutations arising from different quantities and configurations of windows. One advocated that the need to build adjoining and infilling properties could outweigh the historic right to light. Neighbours should put up with a bit of darkening so that other people could have a house. This debate is endemic to construction and will never be properly resolved, despite nineteenth-century attempts to create complex charts and diagrams to show acceptable angles of light, allowing for the differing needs of workers such as watchmakers.[92] Meanwhile, in the early-modern period the infill continued, and many more houses were darkened.[93] The darkness caused by obscuring one window in 1678 was thought to leave the householder in 'danger of being robbed'.[94]

The nuisance viewers were also challenged by reports of dodgy guttering. In 1350, a fishmonger's widow called Maud le Leche was reported, along with three other neighbours, for allowing water to fall on the property of a skinner who lived next door. The neighbours who blocked Geoffrey and Maud Aleyn's windows also hijacked their lead gutter. Into it they tipped their sewage, which then floated through the midst of the Aleyn house. This was one way of getting to know the neighbours' business. The case was far from unique. In 1314, Alice Wade rigged her privy up to the gutter that ran under her neighbour's house, and it often blocked, leaving her neighbours 'greatly inconvenienced by the stench'.[95] In 1536, the viewers ruled that any windows on the north side of one house must be glazed and rendered unopenable with iron bars to 'keep them continually closed, so that there be no water nor filth cast out' into the neighbour's gutters.[96] Nuisance gutters did more than just smell. In 1604, it was recorded that a rotten wooden gutter on a Southampton house 'doth putryfe & rott' the neighbour's timber frame.[97] Samuel Pepys had little luck with his neighbour's water in 1660. In November, 'a great deal of foule water' flooded through the partitions between the houses. The previous month, he stood in a 'great heap of turds' that had worked its way into his cellar from the neighbour's house of office, and pondered the best location for a window 'in lieu of one' that another neighbour had 'stopped up'.[98]

Houses in courts usually had little or no private land. Dunghills were heaped up wherever they could be contained, sometimes against the neighbour's house. Rain saturated these stinking piles, encouraging damp to penetrate indoors and creating the potential for flooding. A London innkeeper heaped dung against his neighbour's wall in 1677 and the moisture from it soaked through the wall 'to the great damage and the Annoyance of her house'.[99] In the early seventeenth century, Manchester man Charles Worsley was ordered to remove coal and timber from a neighbour's wall 'by w[hi]ch her walle ys rotted downe and her lighte stopped'.[100]

Nuisance records from the period show how neighbours could annoy each other through the smells and sounds of their work. Complaints usually resulted from excessive hours, noise, smoke or filth; when activities went beyond reasonable expectations. In 1377, a London armourer built a forge made of earth and timber next to a neighbour's house. He sledgehammered armour plating and shook the neighbours' walls, ruined beer and wine in their cellar and filled their home with smoke from his short chimney. It was argued that goldsmiths, smiths, pewterers, goldbeaters, grocers, pelters, marshals and armourers should be free to work as long as they adapted their premises accordingly and that in this case the anvil was positioned away from the kitchen next door. Furthermore, the defendants argued that the plaintiff's house was quite new and was higher than the house it replaced, with windows facing the forge, causing smoke to infiltrate.[101] The seventeenth-century hate list of neighbouring trades included coopers, founders, tanners, skinners, tallow-chandlers, coppersmiths and dyers.[102]

Insomniac leisure annoyed neighbours too. Biographies of a seventeenth-century college head, John North, reveal that an 'early enthusiasm for playing the organ came to an end when his lubrications upset a neighbour', who retaliated with a cacophony.

> His under neighbour was a morose and importune master of arts; and one night the doctor could not sleep; and thought to fit himself for it by playing upon his organ. The bellows knocking on the floor, and the hum of the pipes made a strange din at midnight, and the gentleman below that never heard it so before could not tell what to make of it; but, at length he found it out to be his neighbour's organ. And thereupon, to retaliate this night's work, got out of his bed and, with his two couple of bowls, went to bowls by himself. This made a much louder noise than the organ, and the doctor was as much at a loss to know what that meant, but, suspecting how the case stood, he left off.

Thereafter North devoted his life to 'cerebration and arachnophilia' and he did not touch his organ at night again.[103]

By the early seventeenth century, most people seeking redress for a nuisance would take legal action, because the process was relatively simple. Tenants (not just freeholders) could bring actions against their neighbours. *Aldred's Case* (1608) laid down the new doctrine when a Norfolk man sued his neighbour for erecting a pigsty next to his house. The smell was considered unhealthy (diseases were thought to arise from miasmatic stenches) and so the sty was deemed to be a damaging nuisance. Thenceforth, if it could be proven that a person's home was rendered significantly less habitable, healthy, quiet or light, then legal action could succeed.[104]

FISHING THY NEIGHBOUR'S POND

Neighbours frequently faced peril together. Proverbial wisdom warned them: 'when thy neighbour's house doth burn, be careful of thine own'. Urban authorities intermittently reminded citizens of their obligation to reduce the risk of fire, but records reveal that some citizens did not heed these orders. In Manchester in 1618, William Barlowe's chimney was 'verye daungerous and hurtefull' to his neighbours. In the same year, neighbours of a nearby property feared the consequences of fires being lit in a room without any chimney. Fire was one of the greatest enemies, consuming homes and entire neighbourhoods.[105]

Theft was another bedevilment. Some of the most valuable possessions were taken by neighbours from land. In 1461, the Paston family found Waryn Herman to be a troublesome neighbour. Margaret Paston wrote to her husband that he 'hath dayly fyshid hyre watere all this ye[a]r'.[106] In describing seventeenth-century Myddle, Richard Gough immortalised Reece Wenlocke. The Wenlockes were a family of petty criminals who lived by the brook in the Meare House. William Higginson lived next door. One day Wenlocke built himself an oven, and Higginson's servant, guessing that the neighbour would 'teare his master's hedges to burne the oven', planted gunpowder in a branch and jammed it into the Higginson hedge. Sure enough, the bait was taken, and the top of the new chimney was blown off, setting Wenlocke's house ablaze.[107]

Neighbours were ideally placed to steal from each other. They did not look out of place on the street and knew when the coast was clear. In 1675, a man called Stevens was found guilty of breaking into the house in which he lived (to make it look like an outside job) and stealing £30, some plate and jewellery.[108] Four years later, an even more audacious burglary was committed by a neighbour who accessed a chamber in Clement's Inn through the wall from next door. Knowing that 'a considerable sum of money' lay just beyond the party wall, a 'young Gentleman and a servant to a Poulterer' moved their bed, removed a portion of the wainscot and 'at convenient times, when they knew their Neighbour' was out, 'fell to work on the Brick-wall', digging through until they reached the room. After breaking open a closet and a trunk and gathering their booty, they carefully tidied up all the debris and pulled their neighbour's bed back into place 'close to the wall . . . so all seem'd cleverly performed'. Returning home, the neighbour was perplexed; his door was 'double lockt and all the Chamber to appearance sound', but he eventually peered behind the wall-hanging behind his bed, and found the breach.[109]

Wives, the property of their husbands, could also be stolen. The fear of the smiling, priapic neighbour is embodied by Leontes in Shakespeare's *The Winter's Tale*. He suddenly reacts with deluded jealousy, thinking Hermione has been unfaithful with Polixenes.

> . . . There have been,
> Or I am much deceived, cuckolds ere now,
> And many a man there is even at this present,
> Now, while I speak this, holds his wife by th'arm,
> That little thinks she has been sluiced in's absence,
> And his pond fished by his next neighbour, by
> Sir Smile, his neighbour . . .[110]

A neighbour can know when a husband's back is turned. John Marketman, a ship's surgeon of West Ham, returned from sea in 1680 to find that his wife had been 'over lavish with her Favours to a Neighbour of hers', a shoemaker called George Bonah. Mr Marketman felt angry, betrayed by someone he thought to be 'one of us'. His wife initially decided to stay at a neighbour's house. When she returned, John stabbed her to death.[111]

Privacy was caught in a legal contradiction. Statements from prying neighbours were accepted in court as admissible evidence, while eavesdropping on neighbours was an offence. The arrangement of buildings often denied privacy, but people wanted to hold on to whatever seclusion they had. A sixth of all Assize of Nuisance cases from the fourteenth and fifteenth centuries concerned privacy in relation to door and window positioning.[112] The viewers devised all sorts of schemes to screen windows but keep some light coming in, so that people could not see into a neighbour's grounds. In 1341, a London widow called Isabel Luter was particularly keen to safeguard her privacy and complained about five neighbours whose windows allowed them to see into her garden or property. One was singled out because 'stench from his cess-pit penetrates her tenement' through his window. The fishmonger John le Leche had a lead tower on the wall adjoining Isabel's, 'upon which', it was stated, 'he and his household stand daily, watching the private affairs of the pl[aintiff] and her servants'.[113] In 1549 Londoner William Lambkyn was ordered to board the windows of his Suterhill Street house to stop him seeing into Peter Grene's land, yet he could do this with the boards set away from the house, so that some light came in. Grene was given permission to build upright by Lambkyn's wall, as long as it was not done in malice.[114]

Society was in flux. Towns needed to accommodate more people, spaces were infilled and houses were darkened. People in flimsy houses, pockmarked with peepholes, found it hard to get away from their neighbours' noises, excrement and dirty laundry. Their circumstances made it hard to be private. Sometimes, perhaps in times of tension during the Reformation and the civil wars, the things people knew about what went on next door quickened anxiety and raised suspicion, leading to accusations of defamation, nuisance or witchcraft. Was neighbourliness crumbling? Were neighbours constantly at each other's throats? No – they just had a lot of contact, and some of it was inevitably malign. Many could not even enter their own space without first walking through their neighbour's property. Lives were entwined.

2

Terraced Neighbours (1700–1839)

Most urban houses built between 1700 and 1839 were terraced. They were fitted around the snaggletooth remnants of past buildings. By the time Victoria settled on to the throne, there was a terraced house for every stratum of society. The freshly stuccoed grand terraces of London's Belgrave Square were occupied by aristocracy (when they were not at their country seats). At the other extreme, humble back-to-backs were cobbled up to accommodate the northern poor. Worse still, perhaps, were the cottages of Bermondsey, constructed from chips of wood from the nearby wharves, in violation of the 1707 Building Act.[1]

The filling of gaps in the urban fabric continued along eighteenth-century streets. No new residential streets were cut in Leeds between 1634 and 1767, and the urban historian Maurice Beresford attributed the total absence of social segregation before the development of the city's west side to this building pattern. All types and classes of people were shoehorned into the city centres and connected through networks of neighbours. The expanding class of Georgian merchants and professionals occupied the grander houses fronting the street, but they were not detached from their neighbours. Beresford likened the owner-occupiers who lived along Georgian Briggate in Leeds to village squires, who 'might feel that the absence of privacy implied by having close neighbours [behind them] had its compensation in the knowledge that they contributed to his rent roll'. Tenants in the frontage houses would not have enjoyed such a payoff for their loss of privacy when new homes were put up behind them. Narrow footway tunnels gave access to the yards and backside houses.[2]

The German journalist Heinrich Heine toured England in 1831 and noticed that English families, unlike tenement-loving continentals, wanted a whole house to themselves.[3] Whether he lived in a 'palace or pile of chip-boxes', an Englishman must, according to caricature, 'when he goes out, be able to lock the door and put the key in his pocket'.[4] However, poorer householders would be lucky to occupy a whole house. About a tenth of London houses were divided at the start of the eighteenth century, and that proportion increased through the century.[5] Divided living was associated with poverty. An eighteenth-century serjeant-at-law, William Hawkins, included the division of a house 'for poor people to inhabit' in a list of common nuisances, because 'it will be more dangerous in Time of Infection of the Plague'.[6] A house that might have been built originally for a single merchant family could contain several different types of occupant, with the poorest (although not necessarily the smallest) families occupying the cellars and the garrets. In his *Report of the Diseases of London* published in 1801, Dr Robert Willan pointed out that although families living on the upper (but not the top) floor were 'better accommodated', they did 'suffer from contiguity and from their friendly attentions to those above them or to the tenants of the cellars'.[7] In these conditions it could be difficult to work out who your neighbours were. Were they the household in the room beyond the thin partition, or the household who shared your room? Neighbours were everywhere.

Demand for housing was not always met by supply. In some areas people crammed into dark and dank cellars in court dwellings. By the end of the Georgian period, these were identified as the worst type of unsanitary dwelling, and a contemporary estimated that an eighth of all Liverpool's citizens lived in cellars. They were concentrated around work sites such as the Old Dock, and averaged more than four inhabitants. Cellar occupation by a separate family to the main house continued into the second half of the nineteenth century, even though it was banned in 1842. This closeness must have strained neighbour relations at times by depleting resources, and creating noise, dirt and ideal conditions for the spread of disease.[8]

COMMON PRIVIES

The chaotic divisions of space that characterised urban living made privacy elusive. The historian Lawrence Stone has argued that 'a growing desire for physical privacy' developed amongst the middle classes in the mid eighteenth century, but that for poorer members of society, a lack of space meant that 'privacy was neither a practical possibility, nor, one imagines, even a theoretical aspiration'. It was also elusive in richer houses with servants around.[9] Recent studies have revealed a more nuanced picture: Amanda Vickery has shown how people living in houses of multiple occupation protected their own secret things using lockable boxes, trunks, chests and closets.[10] Vickery has also shown that landlords could show 'proper respect for the lodger's threshold' even when their lodger was suspected of stealing from them.[11] Another historian has analysed the pattern of building in London after the fire of 1666. Solid structures were built on a regular building line, meaning that individual houses were 'inconspicuous' and 'one's next-door neighbours were permanently excluded from one's own field of vision'.[12]

Most households shared facilities such as water sources, privies and spaces to contain waste. The social reformer and tailor Francis Place described eighteenth-century court dwellings, some 'so narrow in parts that the Mopsticks of the poor inhabitants rigged out from their windows to dry their clothes, met in the middle of the space between the houses'. Some local improvement acts included rules to prohibit the hanging of laundry across streets.[13] Place approved of the new houses built from the end of the eighteenth century because 'the privies are not within the houses, one privy common to a number of families in a large or lofty house was a great inconvenience and a horrid nuisance, there was always a reservoir of putrid matter in the lower part of the house.'[14]

Locating the privies outside meant that more could be provided, and more distance could be put between their contents and living spaces. A 'common necessary House' served people who lived in Old Round Court off London's Strand in 1738. Most of the neighbours had a key to it, but it was often left unlocked.[15]

Neighbours were obvious witnesses in cases of infanticide, because they often shared privies and would notice swelling bellies, bodily fluids and small corpses in the privy. In March 1718, the London neighbours of Jane Plintoff were suspicious when she stopped looking pregnant. The baby's body was not found until May, when the shared house of office was emptied by the night-soilman. Crouching on the privy in 1815, Matthew Prendergrast heard pained sounds from beyond the partition that 'separated one necessary from the other'. He then heard an infant's cry and the sound of something dropping into the cesspool, followed by 'a snuffling'. Prendergrast looked over a railing to the yard next door and heard a sound that he took to be the floor of the privy being wiped. Before long, Catherine Tewner, who had spent the day mangling, was identified as the mother. Tewner did not deny her baby had fallen into the privy, but claimed to have been unable to prevent its fall. Neighbours verified that Tewner had been pregnant and that she had made no secret of the fact. Her next-door neighbour said she 'never knew a better tempered or humane girl'. Tewner was found not guilty of concealing the birth.[16]

It was ruled in 1709 that windows could not be changed to overlook a neighbour's property 'if before . . . they could not look out of them into the yard'. This judgement includes the enigmatic statement, 'for privacy is valuable'.[17] Partitions between properties were often flimsy when houses had been crudely subdivided. Misdeeds and confessions could be heard through the thin walls. Neighbours in a Gosport court heard a murder in 1827. The statements, from a woman who lived in the house where the murder occurred and a woman who lived in the next house, both tell a very similar story pieced together through snatches of overheard sounds. The woman from next door was 'well acquainted' with the voices of the two people present at the murder. One of these, Betsy Clark, lived in the house, and the other, John Sullivan, was a regular visitor. The murdered man, a Bermudan called Alexander Stroud, was heard throwing open the sash window and calling for the watchman. The next sound heard was 'a noise exactly like a man falling down heavily'; then silence. One neighbour, who had her bedroom on the same floor as Clark's, explained that 'the head of my bed comes to the foot of hers, and there is only a thin partition between the rooms'. Sullivan lived elsewhere, and his landlady did not hear him come home on the night of the murder. He finally returned at six in the morning, when she 'heard him come up the stairs and go to his room which is over mine'.[18] The case shows how the sounds neighbours heard allowed them to place people quite precisely.

The account of the trial of James Bannan in the Old Bailey for murdering his wife, Mary, in 1769 reveals the access some people had to the activities that took place in their neighbours' houses. On 30 July, neighbours of the Bannans heard a violent skirmish, something they were accustomed to living near the couple, who 'did not live happ[il]y together'. Elizabeth Dodd, who lodged with the Bannans, saw the attack. Mary emerged 'in a very bloody condition' and sat under the window of a neighbour's house. Dodd and Frances Turner from the house next-door-but-one washed Mary's face, before she returned to her husband. A little later Frances visited the couple and witnessed James punching Mary to the ground. Frances, who usually saw her neighbour two or three times a day, reported that she had 'seen him ill treat her several times' previously. Dodd's husband, Thomas, had seen it all before as well. Supposing that James had beaten Mary, he just 'went through the passage and went out about my business'. Clearly, he considered the assault on his landlady none of his business. The Bannan's servant, Barbara Aston, described the fight as 'a usual thing, I took no notice of it'. When asked why she never intervened, Aston responded that she feared receiving a blow that 'would have knocked my old carcase to pieces'. Each witness except

James skirted questions about Mary's drinking, but Elizabeth Dodd
was keen to point out that Mary had been 'very peaceable with
the neighbours'. Before beating his wife to death, James Bannan,
who described his wife as a drunken scold, told her to be quiet,
fearing the lodgers would refuse to pay their dues. He was cleared
of murder, but found guilty of manslaughter.[19]

Neighbours could be asked to give evidence in divorce libels
because they were in a position to know intimate details of married
lives. In *John v John* (1824), it was reported that Mrs John had been
heard indulging herself 'in criminal amours' with her doctor's
assistant. The house she lived in was once large, but had been
divided into two tenements by a 'thin partition' through which
'nothing could be kept from the neighbours'.[20] In 1767, Dorothy
Arnold of Devereaux Court, off the Strand in London, sought a
divorce from her husband John, on grounds of cruelty and adultery.
He had 'contracted an adulterous conversation with diverse lewd
women' and had assaulted and threatened Dorothy, keeping her
confined in one room. A next-door neighbour provided some details
of the Arnolds' lodgers. Another neighbour, James L'Argeau, who
'used frequently to dine and sup' with the couple, reported seeing
Dorothy swollen and cut. His wife, Jane, claimed to have seen the
Arnolds rising from separate beds on different floors of their house,
and heard John say that he would not eat with Dorothy, 'such a
bitch as she was'. On the day the Blackfriars Bridge was opened,
Jane heard Dorothy 'call out murder'. Hurrying round, she found
her neighbour bloodied and bruised. On another occasion she
thought she heard a pot of beer being hurled at Dorothy, and later
saw her wet. Mrs L'Argeau's deposition is much more fulsome than
her husband's, suggesting she was witness to more of the mael-
strom. She even saw a woman, Margaret Wood, settle into the
house once Dorothy had been driven out, and could state that
Arnold and Wood shared a bed. Dorothy was granted a divorce
and alimony of £20 per year.[21]

Some people did not like the way their neighbours could hear
their personal business. The essayist Charles Lamb lived with his

sister Mary, who sporadically suffered from mental illness. In 1800, the Lambs were set to move to Southampton Buildings in Holborn, which Charles believed would be the perfect place for the siblings to be anonymous.

> It is a great object to me to live in town, where we shall be much more *private*; and to quit a house & a neighbourhood where poor Mary's disorder, so frequently recurring, has made us a sort of marked people . . . We can be nowhere private except in the midst of London.

The Lambs would move a further eight times before 1823, but returned to Southampton Buildings more than once.[22]

Each of these stories reveals a lack of privacy, or at least an ease of overhearing. Many of the sounds made were calls, shouts and exclamations, which we might expect neighbours to be able to hear. However, some of the witness statements show that neighbours knew very private details, such as when somebody was in bed, and who they were in bed with. Lodgers and those they lodged with got the most access. Some sounds were filtered out by the hearers, who thought them none of their business. The accounts left by women are generally more elaborate, indicating that they were either more observant, or more often at home than the men.

GOOD NEIGHBOURS, AND TRUE FRIENDS, ARE TWO THINGS

In the spring of 1811, William Hazlitt and Samuel Taylor Coleridge, both friends of the Lambs, found themselves neighbours in Southampton Buildings. Coleridge had recently fallen out with William Wordsworth and was lost in opium. The new neighbours 'sat up together in the small house, Hazlitt puffing on his pipe while Coleridge ranted against the Grasmerians'.[23] This arrangement was a little uncomfortable for both men, who had a history of sniping at each other. Hazlitt painted Coleridge's portrait in 1798, and during the sitting Coleridge was seething inwardly, jealous of Hazlitt's nascent talent. These feelings intensified and culminated in Keswick in 1803, when Coleridge and Wordsworth both helped Hazlitt flee (he had assaulted a local lass and her neighbours had threatened to duck him). Hazlitt was shunned in the aftermath of the incident; this rankled with him, and animosity brewed. Luckily, the men were only neighbours for a short time.[24] A few years later, Hazlitt savaged his former mentor in print, calling him 'the dog-in-the-manger of literature'. It nearly ruined Coleridge's reputation.[25]

Less famous neighbours got on more famously. A Leeds cement-maker called Joseph Aspdin established a partnership with his neighbour, William Beverley, as 'patent Portland cement manufac-turers' in 1824. Their business lasted for thirteen years.[26] Bookseller Thomas Davies died in 1785 and was 'by his own desire' buried in the vault of St Paul's, Covent Garden, 'close by the side of his next door neighbour, the late Mr Grignion'. The two lived adjacently on Great Russell Street. Thomas Grignion had died the previous year and Davies had witnessed his will.[27]

An ideal clergyman was a neighbour to the whole parish – ready to listen to anyone who sought his help, or to mediate in neighbour disputes. Clergymen were also neighbours in the sense of living next to others. Gilbert White, the naturalist and on-off curate of Selbourne, was close friends with Farmer Hale, who lived on the other side of the street. Hale witnessed White's will.[28]

Hale and Davies were not unusual; many people witnessed a neighbour's will. Testators might even nominate former neigh-bours.[29] A legal case to determine the legitimacy of a will in 1828 hints at why neighbours were a good choice. They saw the will-maker regularly and therefore would be in a good position to verify the soundness of his mind. One witness was shown to have been 'well acquainted with the deceased', and another was an opposite neighbour for five years, 'with whom he used often to gossip'.[30] Trust between neighbours was shown in many ways, not least by their habits of lending possessions and leaving keys with each other.[31] Tools and paraphernalia like bellows, ladders, buckets, shovels and umbrellas were borrowed.[32] In 1828, a costermonger lent his donkey to a next-door neighbour when he found more lucrative (but illegal) business coining in the donkey's shed.[33]

Many eighteenth-century neighbours cared for each other, just as their predecessors had done. In 1794, Francis Place's landlady accompanied Place's wife while their second child was born. Francis was invited to 'sit in the room of the first floor'.[34] Noting that the young poet Thomas Chatterton was looking peaky in 1770, Mr Cross, a neighbouring apothecary, offered him a meal but was rebuffed. Chatterton's landlady also tried to feed him, but he assured her that he was not hungry. Chatterton died soon afterwards of unknown causes. He was seventeen.[35]

By contrast, an historian researching early-eighteenth-century London pauper houses found little evidence of neighbours helping each other. Noting that few families 'seem to have expected their neighbours to provide childcare', Jeremy Boulton detected an unwillingness to burden neighbours. He wondered if the 'current literature may sometimes paint too rosy a picture of the supporting networks of neighbours employed by the poor'.[36]

Friendly societies and benefit clubs were not specifically made up of people who were direct neighbours to each other, but they did start to fulfil some neighbourly roles. The societies were groups of men or women (but not both) from a particular place, and were organised to help the members in times of need. In the articles of the Bedford Friendly Society (established in 1826), the society is stated to be 'for the purpose of relieving its members in cases of sickness, accidents, and bodily infirmities; and in case of deaths'. This was mutual aid, not charity. The members developed a community, shared a group identity and met together, often in a pub. These societies were limited to the more respectable and more permanent members of the community, excluding itinerants. During the nineteenth century, they faced mounting competition from the commercial insurance industry. The strengthening of neighbourhood bonds was a collateral benefit of the societies. One historian considered why a bachelor would pay into a society, and decided it was to ensure 'that his community thrives and continues . . . it makes sense for him to contribute toward the expense of burying the neighbour's wife. Doing so, he insures his own belonging and connects himself to a coherent collective identity.' The societies were therefore a more formalised way of doing what neighbours had done before. Additionally, by tying people to a place, they ensured that they put down deeper roots in their community.[37]

DANGER IS NEXT NEIGHBOUR TO SECURITY

Nefarious neighbours were privileged to know the whereabouts of valuables and when they were unguarded. When gold and silver items were taken from John Dew's London house in 1717, Diana Pearse was accused of their theft, 'she being a neighbour and knowing where the key was used to be laid'.[38] Joseph Byford masterminded the burglary of his neighbour's house in 1823. At his trial it was stated that he 'knew her habits' and was able to find the key to her back door.[39] In Leicester in 1758, blind octogenarian William Thompson broke into his next-door neighbour's house at night and took seven guineas. He had been there when his neighbour had received the money and was 'suppos'd to have heard where the money was put, and night made no difference for a blind man'. Thompson was seen hiding his booty by his neighbour's sister, 'through a crack in the wall between their houses'.[40]

Being a landlord carried the risk that lodgers and tenants might leave with more than they brought. Dorothy George, the redoubtable historian of the eighteenth century, claimed that 'an enormous number of cases' heard at the Old Bailey centred on tenants who had pawned the furniture from their furnished room. Victims included Mrs Swinney of Shallow Street, London, who regretted letting a room in 1756 after her lodger fled with the bed. Some of the stolen items were found to have been pawned and the lodger was discovered in a neighbour's house, hiding behind a curtain.[41]

Judith Godfrey, who lodged in a house in Whitechapel, had her goods purloined by a neighbour who lived beneath her. On 6 August 1805, Margaret Weaver was found with six yards of Godfrey's calamanco in her pocket, and a pair of her stockings tucked into her bosom. Weaver was not the only person to stash a neighbour's stuff this way. In 1814, James Stock kept an old iron and rag shop in Holborn. His shop was opposite the shop of Thomas Palmer, a shoemaker in Baldwin's Gardens. On the night of 25 March, Stock broke into Palmer's premises and stole fifteen pairs of shoes and a pair of boots. Apprehended by a watchman who had heard 'a comical noise', Stock was found to be carrying a bundle of footwear, and had more shoes 'in his breeches and his bosom'. The shoes had the names of Palmer's customers on them and could be easily identified. Stock was sentenced to death. Palmer got a new neighbour.[42]

Two especially sad cases heard at the Old Bailey in the 1720s reveal the dangers that could lurk next door. In 1722, fifteen-year-old apprentice James Booty of St Brides was found guilty of 'assaulting and carnally knowing' a five year-old girl who lived next door and played with his master's child. The incident came to light when the little girl developed venereal disease. Two years later, another five-year-old girl, living in Aldersgate, fell ill with the same complaint, and the source of her infection was found to be her next-door neighbour.[43] In an environment of lending and borrowing, of overhearing and overseeing, familiarity and trust formed between neighbours. Sometimes this was abused.

IT IS NOT AS MOTHER SAYS, BUT AS NEIGHBOUR SAYS

People accused of crimes would often ask neighbours to provide character statements in court, rather like medieval compurgation. Accused of coining, Hopeful Hore pinned all his hopes on 'divers Neighbours of very considerable Credit, to prove his Reputation and Honesty' and managed to secure a not guilty verdict. Mary Wilson was accused of clipping coins, and despite incriminating evidence against her, some neighbours gave such 'manifest' testimonies 'to her Credit' that she was acquitted.[44] Two neighbours living in different tenements within the same Holborn house fell out in 1716. Edmund Dawson accused Eleanor Quinby of stealing his cabinet (actually just a 'Square Pastboard Box') and money. It was suggested in court that Dawson had framed his neighbour in revenge for her previously having him arraigned for assault. Quinby's other neighbours attested to her good reputation, one 'having known her for 20 or 30 Years', and the jury acquitted her. A few years later, William Richards from the same parish, accused of a warehouse theft, was acquitted after several of his neighbours attested to his good reputation.

When Elizabeth Carter was accused of assaulting a man in 1742, one neighbour provided her with an alibi, stating that 'she brought a Bit of Meat, and sat down to eat it, being a Neighbour' at the time the offence took place. Others gave her positive character references, one saying she had 'never saw an unhandsome Word come out of her Mouth', and another declaring her 'a good Neighbour and an honest Body as far as ever I heard'. When Ann Russell stood accused of picking pockets in 1781, her landlady vouched that Russell had been in bed at the time a watch was snatched, and that she was below in the kitchen. A co-lodger, who had the room next to her, where they lay separated by a 'thin partition', stated that Russell was in bed; and could not have committed the crime. Russell was acquitted.[45]

In 1768, Elizabeth Greaves was accused of stealing and pawning shirts and waistcoats from a current neighbour (he had left some shirts with her to 'be ruffled'). An ex-next-door neighbour of hers gave a glowing statement at her trial. Describing Greaves as 'brought up . . . honest and sober to the greatest degree', he implied that she came to be in court because she now 'lived in a gossiping place'.[46] When called, neighbours would often stress the good neighbourly qualities of the accused. Providing evidence in a murder case in 1755, a neighbour of the accused claimed to 'live within a few doors of her, and have been conversant with her, and know her general character and behaviour. She is a person of as humane a disposition as any woman I know, one that has relieved poor people in our neighbourhood.'[47]

Supportive character witness statements did not always get the

accused a verdict of innocence. Defending himself against an accusation of consenting to be sodomised in 1750, waterman William
Huggins 'call'd a great many of his neighbours, who gave him the
Character of an Industrious Man in his Calling'. They talked of his
family, his business, his faith, and described him as 'one of the last
Men they should have suspected as to such Practices, and should
more readily have credited his Familiarity with Women'. Nonetheless, the jury believed the case against him.[48]

WHO COMMENDETH HIMSELF,
WANTETH GOOD NEIGHBOURS

A conduct book writer, focusing his advice on the 'polite lady', advised
her to 'never affect to be at the top of fashion' as the drive to 'outvie
her neighbour' is at the heart of fleeting and trifling fashions.[49]
Comparisons were inevitably made, however, and satirised. In James
Gillray's 'Farmer Giles and his Wife showing off their daughter Betty
to their neighbours on her return from school' (1809, **Fig. 5**), Gillray
tramples on tasteless, ostentatious, newly rich yeomen farmers.
Gormless and graceless Betty thumps out a simple tune on a square
piano. Her other 'accomplishments' litter the room – a needlepoint
on the table, an eclectic sampler (which includes the motto 'Evil
Communications Corrupt Good Manners') and a hackneyed painting
of 'Cheese Farm'.[50] The Giles family have invited their neighbours
to be impressed, but they are simply not seduced by this contempt-
ible faux-aristocratic display. They sneer behind a fan, sit somnolently
or twiddle their thumbs. The Gileses' hangdog hound feels the morti-
fication of the moment and wants the carpet to eat him up.

Sitting together with one's neighbours in the evening exchanging
arch and stilted banter was a pastime familiar to Jane Austen and
her contemporaries. Austen was a keen observer of the social life
around her. Mr Bennet's rhetorical question in *Pride and Prejudice*
goes some way to sum up the view from the wealthier houses:
'For what do we live, but to make sport for our neighbours and
laugh at them in our turn?'[51]

Fig. 5 James Gillray 'Farmer Giles and his Wife showing off their daughter Betty to their neighbours on her return from school', 1809.

Jeffrey Whitaker was a schoolmaster in a Wiltshire village. There was not much to do, so he spent several evenings with the Ballard brothers, whose houses flanked his, even though he disliked them. His descriptions of the neighbours are negative. In March 1739, 'Mr Ald. Ballard laid a bed all Day at pipers' (probably the local pub), then the following day 'Mr Ballard continued at pipers till Mr Froud and myself got him out and try'd to the utmost to reconcile him and his wife.' When the brothers died in 1740, within three days of each other, Whitaker penned catty epitaphs in his diary. One brother was described as 'a facetious Companion Given to Drinking and idle company' and the other was remembered as 'stubborn and perverse in his temper, Tyrannical in his Family, Arbitrary in the neighbourhood, and when he drink'd, Quarrelsome in Company . . . despising others and much given to Law.'[52]

A collision between different expectations of privacy and neighbourliness was exemplified by an 1831 case in Lower Broughton (Salford). When Mrs Yates moved in, she informed her neighbours that 'she should not visit the ladies of Broughton, and that if they called on her, she would not return their visits'. This attitude provoked extreme interest in her motives and habits. She was seen 'walking in the garden with two servants holding an umbrella over her head', an action judged 'extremely ridiculous'. Her neighbours threw stones through her parlour window and their servants held wine-funnels to their eyes through which they stared at her and insinuated she was a prostitute.[53] This case reveals the curiosity aroused by newcomers; especially ones who refused to play the social game and standoffishly rejected the values of neighbouring.

In an era of slow and limited communications, neighbours were a source and subject of news. Whitaker keenly follows the news of his neighbours, especially when they were threatening to take his family to court, or when smallpox was circulating. Dislike and mistrust did not prevent him sharing their evenings. Although they did not see eye to eye, they were social equals in a very limited rural pool and spent time together out of necessity.[54]

Female neighbours were thought most likely to gossip. Erasmus Jones, the self-styled *Man of Manners* (1737), warned that 'Long Conversations flag, they languish at an Hour's End', and that women especially run out of material quickly, and fall to 'comment upon Neighbours Failures' as a perennial topic.[55] When the Georgian diarist and shopkeeper Thomas Turner met with an 'Old acquaintance' who was a neighbour's servant maid, he worried that their meetings would be 'a most delicious and Savory morsel for the Gossiping Part of my Neighbours to Chew & Band about from House to House'. The woman was just a friend, but Turner knew that his motivations would be twisted in a chain of gossip.[56]

NEVER EASY APART: KEATS, HIS FANNY AND OTHER LOVERS

Two men whose experiences with neighbours affected them deeply but in contrasting ways were both born in 1795. One, Thomas Carlyle, was long-lived. We shall meet him in the next chapter. The other, John Keats, died tragically young and full of love for his neighbour, Fanny Brawne. His wan ardour was mirrored by her alluring vivacity. They first met in 1818, and the Brawnes moved in next door to Keats the following year. Keats and Fanny became engaged, but 'her presence came close to intoxicating' him, and soon Keats's tuberculosis meant that their meetings needed to be rationed. Instead, they exchanged yearning letters. Keats's letters reveal the anguish of a man tantalised by living adjacent yet separate lives. 'How illness stands as a barrier betwixt me and you!' he complained in February. When she passed by his window one March day, Keats gushed that he was 'fill'd with as much admiration as if I had seen you for the first time'. His notes mention sounds they both might have heard – 'Did you hear the Th[r]ush singing over the field?' he asks. Imagining his lover in a black dress, Keats writes, 'if I were a little less selfish . . . I should run round and surprise you with a knock at the door'.[57] He died the following year aged just twenty-five.

What was it about poets? In his youth, Byron had fallen in love with his neighbour in Harrow, a cousin, Mary Chaworth.[58] Another poet, Thomas Hood, addressed his verse of unrequited love to a 'Miss Lindo' who lives 'Over the Way'. The undeclared suitor watches his neighbour as she reads until her candle gutters. He dreams of her in bridal white and he plays the flute to attract her attention. Even though Miss Lindo surveys the street, she is blind to him – 'she does not seem to know she has a neighbour / Over the Way!' To his chagrin, one day he watches 'a young man very fond of calling' and soon 'all is over / Over the Way!'[59]

Romantic neighbour relationships can be beset with difficulties. Edward Chapman was the publisher of both Dickens and Thackeray. In 1840, as a shy bachelor, he visited his uncle Michael on the Market Place in Hitchin. He was transfixed by Mary Whiting, a daughter in the Quaker family next door. Communication was forbidden, and Chapman had to woo her through a hole in an upstairs wall. They eloped in 1841.[60] In his *History of Myddle*, Richard Gough recounted the sad tale of James Wicherley, who courted his neighbour, Miss Crosse, who was his social inferior. Wicherley fell trying to reach his neighbour through some outbuildings, broke his leg, and died.[61]

Stories of neighbours in tragic trysts were devoured by the reading public. In 1706, a Dorchester woman's entanglement with a neighbour steered her fate. Mary Brooks doted on her neighbour and gave him gifts, including her virginity. Her shenanigans scandalised the community. 'They were censur'd as not living within the Bounds of Modesty, and the young Man hath been since accus'd as the chiefest Instrument of her Ruin.' Mary's reputation in the neighbourhood was so besmirched that when her parents let it be known that they wanted her married, and backed this with a 'considerable Fortune', no Dorchester men came forward. A splay-footed grocer called Thomas Channing from out of town 'was persuaded to take her for a Wife'. Shortly after the wedding, Mary was back in 'the Company of her belov'd Neighbour'. When Channing threw up a dish of rice-milk, it was suspected to have been poisoned by his wife. A neighbour's dog, having eaten Channing's vomit, was also 'taken with the same Distemper'. Channing died and neighbours provided damning testimony. Mary resolutely asserted her innocence, but was executed by strangulation and then burnt in a Roman amphitheatre on the southern edge of Dorchester in front of thousands of spectators, three months after giving birth to a baby boy.[62]

In 1818, Maria Stent, a butcher's wife of Arabella Row in Pimlico, had fallen in love with Samuel Seaton (or Sweeting, depending on which paper one took), a married man who lived next door. They ran away abroad together, leaving Henry Stent distraught. Mrs Seaton, pregnant with her fifth child, broke down, and died, as did her newborn baby and another of her children (if we believe some of the newspapers, she died in Henry Stent's arms). The papers polarised hard-working and kind Mr Stent with his 'miscreant' neighbour. Seaton was said to have spent eighteen months trying to seduce Maria, and 'had been gradually sapping the foundation of her honour' whilst being outwardly friendly and hospitable to her 'unsuspicious' husband, 'whose doors and whose house alike

[were] open to his obtrusions'. Until the elopement, 'the greatest possible harmony subsisted' between the families. The story came to the attention of the press because Henry Stent had repeatedly stabbed his wife when she returned to him, hoping to reconcile their differences after Seaton had deserted her. Nonetheless, Stent was described as 'a fine and indulgent husband, a sincere friend, and an honest and humane man', as well as 'a man very much respected by his neighbours'.[63]

Mrs Hutchinson, the wife of a Bethnal Green brewer's clerk, was 'seduced' by Mr Burford, her neighbour, in the late 1780s. Burford knew that Mr Hutchinson 'had no opportunity of being at home in the day time'. As women 'are frail', Mrs Hutchinson could not resist 'the arts of wicked and profligate men'. The Hutchinsons' servant claimed to have seen Mr Burford 'take some liberties with her mistress; she had seen him put his hand in her bosom, and make very free with her petticoats, she had likewise seen them together in the parlour, in the very act of criminal conversation'. Shortly after this illicit intercourse, Mrs Hutchinson and Mr Burford ran away together. Mr Hutchinson took Burford to court 'for a criminal connection with' his wife, and was awarded £200 damages.[64]

Love between neighbours was complicated at best and fatal at worst. Relationships could develop without suspicion under the guise of normal neighbourly transactions. Loving neighbours had an unusual opportunity to become intimate. The eventual revelation of infidelity, if allowed to become known, would challenge the discretion and prurience of the neighbourhood networks. Sometimes it was just not socially acceptable to love thy neighbour.

THE TOWN IS COME TO THE DOG KENNEL

'No man can live longer in peace than his Neighbour pleases. For an ill Neighbour, with his Scolding, Noise, Complaints, Law-Suits, and Indictments, may be very troublesome', wrote James Kelly in 1721.[65] Jeffrey Whitaker understood this, living next to the bullying and litigious Ballard brothers.[66] The inescapability of bad neighbours gnawed at people's nerves and temper. Even the genial curate Gilbert White found some of his neighbours' foibles grating. Their pigs perambulated his garden and some 'unsightly outhouses' had to be 'treed out' to stop them spoiling his view. When smoke from Farmer Spencer's charcoal-making penetrated his house one night, White muttered darkly in his diary.[67] In Oxford, Samuel Johnson was reported to have reprimanded Sir Robert Chambers for gathering snails and throwing them over into his neighbour's garden, rebuking his 'unmannerly and unneighbourly' behaviour. Chambers argued that his neighbour was a dissenter, so Johnson changed his tune – 'if so, Chambers, toss away, toss away, as hard as you can'.[68]

More serious than snail wars and the odd rootling pig were the interruptions to seemly life imposed by living next to a whorehouse, especially if the walls were thin. In 1802, Elizabeth Denman lived with her sister, in a 'house entirely for the accommodation of infamous women of the town' just off London's Chancery Lane. Their home was described as 'containing such disgusting and abominable nuisances that all the neighbours united in getting rid of them'. The Edges, who lived next door, organised a clique to try to expel the sisters from the neighbourhood, and 'in consequence of this', Elizabeth Denman 'conceived a spite against Mrs Edge' and spat in her face. She was sentenced to a month's imprisonment.[69]

By the eighteenth century, nuisance law had matured. Although the Assize of Nuisance was not formally abolished until 1833, it had become moribund during the late-medieval period and given way to actions to recover damages.[70] In 1705, Lord Holt clarified the position of the law on nuisance, explaining that 'every man must so use his own as not to damnify another'. Deciding against a defendant whose privy had collapsed, sending waste into a neighbour's property, Lord Holt argued that '. . . as every man is bound to look to his cattle, as to keep them out of his neighbour's ground, so he must keep in the filth of his house of office, that it may not flow in upon and damnify his neighbour'.[71] Some lawyers were unclear about the difference between nuisance and negligence. In his *Introduction to the law relative to trials at Nisi Prius* (first published in 1760), Sir Francis Buller detailed 'injuries arising from Negligence or Folly'. His opening statement went:

> Every man ought to take reasonable Care that he does not injure his Neighbour; therefore where-ever a Man receives any Hurt through the Default of another, though the same were not wilful, yet if it be occasioned by Negligence or Folly, the Law gives him an Action to recover Damages . . .

The judge Sir William Blackstone used his *Commentaries on the Laws of England* to guide his readers to consider nuisance as any annoyance that 'worketh hurt, inconvenience or damage', and private nuisances to be specifically 'any thing done to the hurt or annoyance of the lands, tenements, or hereditaments of another'. It was negligent to not scour a ditch, and when the ditch flooded it could cause a nuisance to a neighbour.[72] Recourse to law was costly, and by this period cases were generally brought to seek damages from a nuisance-maker. This would effectively stop a nuisance, because each repeat occurrence was considered to be a fresh offence incurring costs. Only a very wealthy or very stubborn nuisance-maker would persist.

With more and more people cramming into the cities, the opportunities for conflict over sensory nuisances increased. There are numerous examples of window-blocking, having dangerous or smoky chimneys, allowing water to damage neighbouring properties and storing lolling or unwholesome dunghills against a neighbour's property.[73] Blackstone explained how pigs and other 'noisome animals kept close to another house' could be regarded as a nuisance because 'the stench of them incommodes him and makes the air unwholsome'.[74] In the 1730s, a distiller called Lewis Smart kept several hundred pigs on Tottenham Court Road. He was found to be causing a public nuisance. His nearest neighbours sickened, their servants quit, their linen discoloured on the line and their silver tarnished. Local property prices fell, on account of a smell that, it was said, 'drives thro' the walls of the houses'. The defence argued that the area was blighted even without his piggery, being the location of nightsoil pits, a dump and a ditch.[75]

New trades developed in the industrialising towns. Some were noisy, some smelly, and some smoky. Several were all three. Trades were often set up next to homes, and cities extended outwards towards the filthy establishments that had once been on the outskirts. In 1757, the case of *Rex v Burrell* heard that dogs in kennels were fed stinking horsemeat, the stench of which infected the nearby air. In defence it was noted that 'the town is come to the dog kennel'. The law generally took account of who was the first occupant and gave them more rights. As we have seen already, claiming ancient rights to light gave a person more protection from window-blocking. Blackstone developed this idea, explaining that a person who builds up against an existing wall has no right to compel the neighbour to demolish the wall, 'for there the first occupancy is rather in him, than in me'. And so, if 'I fix my habitation near him, the nu[i]sance is of my own seeking, and may continue'. However, being in a place first did not allow businesses to be excessive in their creation of smells, dirt or noise. The kennel was judged to be a nuisance.[76]

The mid eighteenth century saw a growth of clauses in leasing contracts in some areas – prohibitions that prevented occupiers from engaging in certain trades or activities. Many restrictions were designed to prevent fire, but several incidentally kept the air more salubrious. Nuisance trades were zoned out of some residential areas – usually the more desirable areas where wealthier people lived. The stinking trades carried out by dyers, brewers, soap boilers, sugar refiners and skinners were prohibited from taking some leases. Smiths, tallow-chandlers and other trades likely to 'annoy the neighbouring . . . inhabitants' were excluded in a clause in 1724.[77] Other areas were less restricted. At the close of the eighteenth century, Richard Harwood's *Plan of London* shows Bermondsey proliferated with tan yards and was also the location of a large 'Glue Manufactory'.[78] If they got really offensive, smelly establishments could be tackled as a public nuisance, and any action taken would have improved lives for those nearby.

Neighbours in College Street in West Camden were often disturbed by the antics of Henry Kirkham. In May 1833, Kirkham 'made divers loud offensive and alarming noises . . . beating and hammering with pokers hammers and other Instruments . . . and screaming, groaning and making other noises and also heating melting and dissolving divers large quantities of brass'. His neighbours also complained of the smells and effluvia from his house. Ten neighbours were listed, who were also disturbed by his habit of 'deliberately exposing himself naked in a most indecent posture situation and practice to divers liege subjects both male and female'.[79]

During the period many towns gained Local Acts, and henceforth many nuisances were dealt with by the improvement commissioners. They were not dedicated to the control of neighbour conflicts, but where they were effective, they would have ameliorated some of the worst excesses of neighbourhood nuisance.[80] In May 1832, the Hastings Improvement Commissioners dealt with Rev. William Wallinger's overflowing cesspool and addressed the 'smell coming out of a number of air holes' near a row of buildings. The commissioners also established early planning regulations, requiring permission to be sought before work was carried out on extensions, gratings, steps and other developments.[81] The 1835 Municipal Corporations Act brought these various specialised authorities under tighter control outside London.

Some legal rulings of the early nineteenth century reveal inconsistency in the application of nuisance laws. In a public nuisance case heard in 1805, the judge directed the jury that a sulphurous smell must be 'generally dangerous' to those nearby and not merely unpleasant. However, eleven years later, another jury were guided to consider inconvenience as well as 'injury to health' when deciding whether to oblige a Preston farrier (Mr Harris) to stop causing a nuisance to a cheesemonger (Mr Thompson). Some years earlier,

Harris had built a cowshed on the street (described by *The Times* as 'composed of respectable houses and inhabited by respectable people'), eight yards from Thompson's back court. One day this shed was topped with a chimney and hammers could be heard within. The shed had spawned a smithy, which enveloped the cheesemonger in smoke and annoyed his family with noise. Linen needed rewashing and windows were kept shut on the hottest days. Others nearby were also inconvenienced. In his defence, Harris argued that smoke and sounds were issued on a much grander scale from steam engines and foundries in the neighbourhood, and asked what his neighbour expected, living in a manufacturing town. Despite hearing his defence argue that people 'must not hope to enjoy in Manchester or Preston the same good air as on the site of Lancaster-Castle or the top of Skiddaw', the verdict was for the cheesemonger.[82]

In the poorest areas nuisances were least likely to be tackled, as those nearby would not have the money to take their neighbours to court. After the cholera outbreaks of the early 1830s, an impetus to clean up poor areas saw the authorities concern themselves more energetically with potentially unhealthy accumulations and stenches, and any successes would have improved the lives of those nearby. Reports revealed the terrible state of some residential areas. Nevertheless, the people of England had to wait a while longer before any statutory measures would address nuisances systematically.

LOOK TO THYSELF WHEN MY NEIGHBOUR'S HOUSE IS ON FIRE

Fire insurance companies thrived after London's Great Fire of 1666. Nicholas If-Jesus-Christ-Had-Not-Died-For-Thou-Sins-Thou-Hadst-Been-Damned Barebon developed a successful scheme under his trading name Nicholas Barbon.[83] In the eighteenth and nineteenth centuries, homes displayed plaques embossed with the name of their insurer so that rudimentary engine teams would know which buildings to save. Blandford Forum in Dorset was almost entirely destroyed in a conflagration of 1731 (which began in a tallow- and soap-boiling establishment), and was rebuilt by the Bastard brothers over the next three decades.[84] Fire was a lively concern, especially when walls were thin. In 1828, George Cockburn, a London stationer, was charged with assaulting his next-door neighbour, Mary Timothy. Cockburn was worried that the gas lighting next door might burn his house, there being 'a very thin partition' separating the two properties. The Timothys claimed that Cockburn's recent appointment as constable had gone to his head, and that he was inclined to be petty. Whenever the Timothy baby cried, 'Mr Cockburn made a noise, in imitation'.[85]

A few cases of arson were examined in which the accused appears to have set fire to their own home while pretending that the fire had come from a neighbour's house, in order to claim on fire insurance. In some cases, their behaviour gave them away, such as being fully dressed at night or removing precious items first. In 1811, Edward Phillips was found guilty of arson after turpentine chips had been used to set fire to the partition with his neighbour's house on the High Street in Shadwell.[86]

Some neighbours committing arson were motivated by malice and revenge. In 1742, William Ford of Rotherhithe was made an order of the court after he was declared to be 'not in his Senses' when he set fire to his own and several neighbouring houses. Ford had previously been heard to threaten arson, and had behaved suspiciously.[87] Londoner Susanna Garner was accused of setting her terraced house on fire in 1769. One witness suggested it could have been an act of revenge against her neighbour, a tallow-chandler called Mr Wells. The witness claimed that at the time of the arson attack Garner had been lamenting the loss of a child, and was reported to have said that 'the stink of Mr Wells' tallow was the death of her child . . . she would be revenged'. Many of Garner's neighbours gave evidence in court, but Henrietta O'Brien's was most curious. O'Brien recalled hearing Garner say that 'she never saw such a place as Charles Street, there were no neighbours'. She took this to mean that

Garner had no friends on the street, and was isolated. Perhaps Wells was not the only intended target.[88]

In 1700, the streets of England had been mixed. The rich in the grander street-frontage houses rubbed shoulders with the poor, who lived in smaller properties 'in their backsides'. There was some small-scale industry in every settlement, and many citizens, rich and poor, lived next to butchers, bakers and candlestick-makers. Gradually terraces were built to more efficiently accommodate the growing population. The terraced house created a new form of neighbourliness, where neighbours had a similar income and status. The poor generally occupied homes in mixed areas where proto-industrial development boomed. By 1840, a poor man was more likely to be a neighbour to a factory or foundry than a rich man, who could afford a lease in an area with restrictive clauses. The poor, with more cause for grievance, lacked money to seek redress against nuisance neighbours. Belgrave Square and Bermondsey, although separated by only a few miles, were worlds apart. Neighbouring expectations differed.

3

Face-to-face and Side-by-side in the Back-to-backs (1840–1889)

The Georgian terrace-building boom quickened under Victoria. Large swathes of the industrial Midlands and north were covered with small terraced houses. Most were within walking distance of the factories, mills and mines that provided employment. Fields made way for new streets of houses that backed on to one another – 'back-to-backs'. Three of the four walls in a back-to-back house were shared with neighbours. This meant that every room was next to at least two, and often three, rooms in other houses. These houses packed people in and eroded privacy (see **Fig. 6**).

'Through terraces' (seen in the panoramic opening credits of *Coronation Street*) are often wrongly named back-to-backs because their backyards adjoin each other. The real back-to-backs were fetid little boxes. Leeds had the most – 49,000 in 1886, representing over 80 per cent of all housing in the city. Birmingham had 40,000 in the 1840s, but it became illegal to build them in 1909 and they were eventually cleared, leaving only a handful of survivors, which are now managed by the National Trust as tourist attractions for those members seeking a respite from aristocratic luxury and cream teas.[1]

Back-to-backs were more basic than the Georgian terraces, having few facilities, which were usually shared. Each room was tiny and dark. They were generally rented out by private landlords, whose tenants, in turn, might also sublet to lodgers.[2] In his *Report on Sanitary Conditions* (1842), Edwin Chadwick shone a light on this type of housing. He showed that it was harder to be a

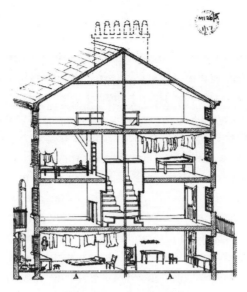

SECTION OF BACK TO BACK HOUSES

*In positions A A on the walls (taken out to shew interior)
the fireplaces are which are carried up, and brought
above the roof, as shewn in dotted lines.*

Fig. 6 Diagram from a Manchester and
Salford Sanitary Association report.

good neighbour in these properties and compared them with
'advantageously situated' families, who were 'better neighbours,
and with each other better friends'.[3] Shortly afterwards, Friedrich
Engels documented squalid back-to-back living in Manchester. He
noticed spaces that had been infilled with court and alley buildings. He saw privies without doors and pig pens littered around
an 'unplanned and chaotic conglomeration of houses, most of
which are more or less uninhabitable.'[4] Overcrowding was a
feature not just of the new industrial centres; it was also common
in the old commercial districts. Various types of worker, including
costers, market workers, porters and dockers, all needed to live
'near their bread'. Commuting was not an option.[5] In *London
Labour and the London Poor* (1861), Henry Mayhew described
'dilapidated though extensive' court and alley dwellings, 'wherein
are huddled more people than one could count in a quarter of
an hour, and more children than one likes to remember'.[6]

LITTLE HOUSE WELL FILLED

Demand for housing too rarely leads to its provision. The press of people increased in many places during the nineteenth century. In 1883, Andrew Mearns's book *The Bitter Cry of Outcast London* drew attention to conditions in working-class areas in the east and south of the city.[7] He showed that many families lived in one room each, with neighbours on all sides. This was exemplified by Little Collingwood Street, a narrow lane in Bethnal Green. The census for 1851 showed extreme overcrowding, and the official figures tended to under-represent true numbers because tenants and landlords conspired to conceal subletting. Phoeby and Joseph Damels and their five children lived with a dependent elderly woman in one part (likely to be only one room) of number 1. Mary and Joseph Tarrant and Joseph's father lived in the other part of the house. Number 2 was no less crowded, being occupied by a family of seven, the Scots, and a blacksmith and his extended family. Number 5 contained the Foulmin family of eight and the six Johnsons.[8] In such conditions, how could one tolerate a neighbour's child whose caterwauls disturb the sleep of shift workers, or not hate the coster who lives next door and leaves his barrow in the tight entrance to the street because he has nowhere else to put it? Yet people usually did live and let live, and many formed supportive relationships out of necessity, sharing meagre resources and helping each other through crises.

The convulsive intrusion of Victorian infrastructure projects is depicted by aghast Parisian Gustave Doré in his picture 'Over the city by railway' (1872). Many railway lines were cut through dense residential communities to the new termini. These displaced thousands and exacerbated crowding nearby. Jerome K. Jerome was forced to move from Alpha Place to make way for the Great Central Railway's new line to London, and a jobbing engineer, Thomas Wright, and his wife found themselves looking for a new home when the City and Suburban Railway Company cut a line through their street.[9] Improvement projects and Parliamentary Acts intended to remove insanitary houses added to the shortage.[10] A statistical report on the census of 1851 revealed trends in density of populations across England. In 1801, English people had lived an average of 153 yards from each other. By 1851, this distance had fallen to 108 yards. The spaces between houses also decreased. The figures were most stark in London. Average proximity in 1801 had been twenty-one yards, but by 1851 it was just fourteen.[11]

The poorer citizens crammed into back-to-backs, whilst wealthier Victorians enjoyed suburban developments and moved into villas where home was separate from work. The author John Claudius Loudon lived with his wife in Bayswater in a suburban villa he had designed himself. His three sisters lived next door.[12] He saw 'proximity to neighbours' as the best advantage to suburbanites that was denied to rural dwellers, though only if one chose 'a neighbourhood where the house and inhabitants are all, chiefly of the same description and class as the house we intended to inhabit, and as ourselves'. It would be awkward to be an isolated rich household in a slummy area or an ill-shod family in a refined milieu, feeling a pressure to spend beyond their means to fit in.[13] Frederick Willis, a hatter, placed his family in the latter position. In his memoirs, Willis described how he lived in cringing class-conscious isolation among 'worthy people' on Burdock Road in London, feeling 'not of them' and perceiving that their 'neighbours had the same feelings about us'. Their only friends in the neighbourhood were the family of a French musician, the bohemian Gerrards.[14]

DIFFERENT STROKES FOR DIFFERENT FOLKS

The nature of neighbourliness was believed to differ between cities. A radical newspaper cast Sheffield as a city

> . . . full of feuds. No party tries to convince – each aims to be at and to damage the other. The whole town is akimbo. Every man has his elbows in his neighbour's side, which produces a permanent state of ecstasies and vituperations.

The description concludes on a surprisingly upbeat note; this discord 'implies life, activity, pluck'.[15] The trade unionist William Newton gave a speech at the London Metropolitan Board of Works in 1875 in which he contrasted provincial towns with London. People in the provinces enjoyed 'a complete community of interest . . . Everybody knows everybody else within the town', whereas in London, 'there is no such thing' and each 'man scarcely knows his next-door neighbour, and one manufacturer has little to do with another'. His comments were made in support of his campaign to unite the fragmented governmental structures of the capital so he probably exaggerated for oratorical and polemical effect.[16]

London suited one nameless woman (the wife of a clerk) because its society was free of the 'envy, hatred, malice, and all uncharitableness, so rife in a small neighbourhood'. She found herself free of interference, but did recognise that this came at the expense of some 'neighbourly interests' and friendship too. The author did not doubt that friendships existed in the capital, but thought that they were

> few and far between. People associate more at arm's length, and give
> their hand more readily than their heart, and hug themselves within
> their own domestic circles. You know too little of people to be deeply
> interested either in them or their fortunes, so you expect nothing . . .
> An acquaintance may depart London life, and even this life, or be sold
> up and disappear, without the same surprise or making the same gap
> as a village circle.[17]

There were references in court cases to people who did not know their neighbours by name, or even by appearance.[18] However, that does not prove a widespread and general lack of neighbourliness.

Childhood reminiscences about neighbours are different to those of adults. Children tend not to notice nuisances, and they often make friends easily. This may be why many people believe that neighbours were friendlier in the past, when they were young. They might not know the occupation of their neighbours but they remember generosity or miserliness. Recalling the streets of his boyhood in Farnham in the 1860s, George Sturt disregarded his nearest neighbours on East Street. On one side was Mrs Bolland, who ran a fruit and red herring shop – 'if our ball went over the palings into her backyard . . . it would be thrown back sooner or later'. Even less was remembered about the tavern on the other side. It was screened from George's house in such a way that none of the Sturts noticed when it burnt down one night. Opposite George, and of more interest than herring and beer, was the elderly spinster Miss Nichol, who sold toys. Further 'Up-street' and 'Down-street' were other shopkeepers, 'Tom Eyre the rubicund grocer' and 'Pullen the Barber'. Supreme among them in George's esteem, thanks to his generosity, was Tom Hackman, who planted a 'truly pleasant memory' when he gave George a red and yellow tulip, cultivated in his garden. 'So far', says George, 'I have told of nothing much more than a hundred yards away from my own home', which is where, in his opinion, his neighbourhood stopped.[19]

Another child's-eye view of Victorian neighbours was left by Eleanor Farjeon, who in maturity penned 'Morning Has Broken'. The Farjeons moved in 1886 from one end of London's Adelaide Street to the other.[20] Eleanor seemed most struck by her new garden, and how easy it was for neighbouring children to play with each other. On one side were the huge musical family of Lutgens, and on the other side lived the Leveaux family (with children Freddy, Monty, Bibsy, Violet and Daisy). Eleanor savoured the fruits of their pear tree, whose boughs overhung her garden. The Leveaux family moved away and were replaced by siblings Alice and Eddie Franc. Eleanor was relieved that she could stop pretending she liked the 'horrible doll' that Daisy Leveaux had given her. She describes adjusting to the new neighbours: 'It was not long before we were appearing circumspectly through each other's front gates, and less circumspectly over the dirty wall at the end, where their "rockery" gave you a leg down.' Like George Sturt, she remembered her neighbours selectively. She had fond memories of Mrs Franc, with whom she read German literature every week, but Mr Franc was a cipher.[21]

ONE TOILET FOR TWENTY HOUSES

The streets were populous and the limited sanitary infrastructure was strained. It was common for several families to share the same privy, and in some of the oldest back-to-backs there was just one toilet for twenty houses. In a yard in Leeds, where thirty-two homes shared two privies, the yard was 'saturated with disgusting matter'.[22] A sanitary report of Deansgate in Manchester in the 1850s revealed that 114 people from Fogg's Place and Alpha Place shared six privies.[23] Queues on Sunday mornings were long.[24] Water supplies could also be shared. A Parliamentary report of 1848 described Little Colling-wood Street in Bethnal Green as:

> divided into two portions, one contains 20 houses, and the other 22 . . . four of the houses . . . are wholly without water, and their inhabitants have to beg it of their neighbours, who, in supplying it, subject themselves to a penalty of, I believe 5l. The first 10 houses are supplied by a stand-pipe, each householder having a key. This stand-pipe is the cause of much quarrelling for turns, and because it is frequently left running, and thereby annoys the person who lives in the house next it, frequently floating the floor, the other houses all have water laid on.[25]

Water companies would turn water on for part of the day and cisterns could be filled then. Some houses had no cistern and sharing families would need to ration water carefully and not let the tap run.[26] In 1887, Maud Snow of Southampton assaulted her young next-door neighbour Jennie Wheeler after the Wheelers had partly turned off the joint water supply. Finding no water, Snow assumed that Jennie was to blame and ran out calling her 'a dirty little cat', slapped her and pulled her down by her hair. In court, Alderman T.P. Payne declared that the water company had inflamed the situation by failing to provide each house with a separate supply of water.[27] The inhabitants of Fogg's Place and Alpha Place shared one tap. In the sanitary report it was noted that 'it is everybody's business to give notice to the authorities to cleanse the ash pits and therefore it is never done'.[28] It was everybody's business, but nobody's responsibility.

Mayhew described the narrow streets that branched off London's Drury Lane. Here, the people 'could not exactly shake hands' with those opposite through their open windows, 'but they could talk together very comfortably'. Along the way, Mayhew observed 'several women with their arms folded up like a cat's paw on the sill, and chatting with their friends over the way.'[29] These close domestic spaces could become an extension of the public realm. Shani D'Cruze has used witness statements to show how a Preston kitchen 'seems to have been very much open domestic space, a site of assembly and gossip for neighbours'. One neighbour popped in for a chat after eleven o'clock at night, finding the door ajar.[30]

This closeness fostered friendships, but it could also entrench enmities. Up before the Chester Police Court in 1882, Sarah Bellis found herself needing to explain her abusive words to her next-door neighbour, James Phillips. According to Phillips, at nine o'clock one September morning, while he stood with a brush in his hand speaking to his wife (who was shaking a mat against a pear tree), Bellis bustled past with a bucket of water, almost knocking the couple over. Argy-bargy and name-calling ensued. The court heard that the yard and a footpath were common to the neighbouring houses. Bad blood had developed over rights of way. Catherine Deal, a neighbour called by Bellis's solicitor, deposed that she had seen Mr Phillips push Bellis, grab her bucket, and tell her she was forbidden from coming that way again.[31]

Not all shared outdoor spaces were battlefields. Many were places of conversation and conviviality. Living amongst *The Great Unwashed* in 1868, Thomas Wright described his neighbours in London's Lock Court. They were a mixture of hawkers, whores and the unemployed, who had mutual reliance and support. Domestic equipment such as linens, washtubs and cooking pots was freely shared, and communal eating was common.[32] In the more crowded areas, a lack of space indoors forced life outside. Photographs taken before the clearances reveal fuzzy boundaries, and street space used for work and socialising. Windows were opened wide to ventilate homes, or were broken with panes missing, allowing neighbours to see and hear what was going on next door or across the yard. A housing historian has noted that the lives of people living in such conditions were 'more interdependent and more public'. This was in contrast with other Victorians, who lived in the terraced houses that fronted public streets, exposed to 'the general gaze and attention' (rather than the neighbourly gaze). The better-housed Victorians retreated into back rooms and back yards, allowing a new type of family life to develop, one that was less entwined with the neighbours.[33]

NOT SO GOOD TO BORROW AS TO BE ABLE TO LEND

Charles Bosanquet, a barrister, thought that one of the 'greatest evils of London' in 1868 was that the rich and poor lived apart, and therefore had 'very little knowledge of each other'. He advised his readers (whom he assumed to be 'young professional men') to visit poor families who lived nearby to give advice and support. Bosanquet thought that philanthropic endeavours that resembled 'the original neighbourliness' were most successful, and so advised his readers to describe themselves as neighbours, highlighting their differences from district visitors (who were generally female).[34]

For poorer families, with little state support to cope with old age, illness and unemployment, neighbours were the warp and weft of the Victorian welfare safety net. Small sums of money, like a penny for the gas, were passed back and forth. On Burdock Road, the bohemian Gerrard family, whose 'allowance arrived rather irregularly towards the end of the month', were helped out by the

Willises. This was often reciprocated; 'each family came to the rescue of the other at critical periods'.[35] Such networks of exchange and reciprocity were extensive and usually unsentimental. Within tight communities people arranged whip-rounds for the sick or for funerals. In 1875, a millworker from Preston called Dorothy Fiddler was murdered by her husband. Neighbours, led by Fiddler's land-lady, organised a subscription to pay for her funeral, and her body was wheeled through the neighbourhood past those who had helped restore dignity to her in death.[36]

Cooking, cleaning and mending paraphernalia were lent and borrowed. In 1844, Timothy Sheils, a mason's labourer, wanted to mend his boots and borrowed a hammer from a neighbour three doors away from his London house. In 1877 Sophia Cannett, living off London's Euston Road, borrowed a hobbling iron from the folks opposite.[37] The kindness of neighbours had limits, though. In his song 'Neibors belaw' ('Neighbours below'), the Tyneside song-writer James Weams warned that 'whativvor they get they nivvor retorn'.[38] In one newspaper, mock advice to avoid excessive borrowing suggested that each time the next-door neighbour asks to borrow the lawn mower, ask to borrow his bicycle.[39] Living too deeply in a neighbour's pocket seems to have been a subject that Victorians tackled obliquely, using humour and psychological chicanery. A quip in an *Almanac* of 1889 hints at it:

'Where is the island of Java situated?' asked a school teacher of a small, rather forlorn-looking boy. 'I dunno, sir.' 'Don't you know where coffee comes from?' 'Yes, sir; we borrows it from the next-door neighbour.'[40]

One ploy involved purposely lending too much because the borrower would then neither want to return a valuable item nor ask to borrow more for fear of being asked to give the first item back. In contrast, small loans were forgotten by neighbours and often not repaid. In the words of the late-nineteenth-century poet Rowland E. Egerton-Warburton:

My neighbour – an eternal ninny –
Is ever knocking at my door.
Lend him, when next he calls, a guinea,
He'll come, I warrant him, no more.[41]

It is unlikely that he had personal knowledge of regular visits from
neighbours wanting pennies, living as he did in stately detachment
amid the fecund acres of Arley Hall in Cheshire. However, the
richer Victorians did enjoy some exchanges with their neighbours.
They could give and receive company and possessions, and even
provide a cultural exchange. The Lutgens next door to the Farjeons
on Adelaide Street were not just a source of playmates; one member
also taught Italian to one of Eleanor's brothers.[42]

Not everything that came from neighbours was borrowed with
consent. Neighbours were often in an ideal position to notice
unsecured items and swipe them surreptitiously. In 1867, Mary Bath-
urst of Sheffield pawned a sheet she had stolen from the line next
door.[43] After Mrs Trusswell of Hartwell Street, Nottingham, hung
her bedtick insecurely in her yard in 1870, the wind blew it over
the wall into the yard of Mary Jessop, who passed it on to her
mother.[44] Mary Alleard, living in a court in Sheffield in 1884, stole
clothing and fabric from her neighbour. When the theft was discovered, Alleard had the chutzpah to arrange a whip-round amongst
the neighbours to cover the loss, whilst knowing she had pawned
them (she had hoped to redeem the items before they were
missed).[45] It was Ellen Batty of Leicester whose offence was most
audacious. She pinched a neighbour's washing stool and then
borrowed a gorsehook from the same neighbour in order to chop
the stool into pieces and burn it on a winter's day in 1846.[46]

THE KINDNESS OF NEIGHBOURS

Many families helped each other with childcare without opportun-
istically robbing them. George Sims thought it 'not uncommon for
lactating mothers to wet nurse babies of dead or ailing' neighbours,

even if it meant that they could earn less money at their work. According to Sims, slum-dwelling neighbours often fostered or adopted children. When the recidivist Barkers were simultaneously imprisoned, their neighbours looked after their children until one parent was released. Such altruism was thought to be most pronounced amongst the poor. 'No where', Sims declared, 'are the bonds of human sympathy so strong as down the courts and alleys . . . The poor help the poor.' Likewise, orphaned children were 'almost always' adopted by fellow slum-dwellers.[47] Arrangements could be complicated. Before Charles Sabin died in 1877, he had asked his lodger, Thomas Crask, to take care of his three children, including one in the womb. When Sabin died, Crask 'arranged to live with Mrs [Emma] Sabin as her husband'. The new couple quarrelled, and when Crask became violent, Emma left to stay with another neighbour.[48]

A journalist criticised plans drawn up by the President of the Local Government Board to look after pauper children, on the grounds that state provision interfered with the kindness of neighbours. 'Hitherto', he remarked, 'our rural poor have had, most deservedly, a high reputation for what they call neighbourliness, and in nearly every parish are to be found several instances where the orphan children of a labourer dying in his prime have been at once adopted by some fellow-labourer.' Although he hoped that this kind spirit would prevail, the commentator worried that orphans would henceforth be left to the mercies of the state, amidst a rising tide of self-interest.[49] In an 1873 Parliamentary Report concerning imprisonment for debt, a similar degree of neighbourly compassion was noted. Hugh Carmichael, a Liverpool accountant and 'Trustee in Bankruptcy', observed that 'the working classes, in cases of sickness, far exceeded the higher classes in neighbourly kindness'.[50] In the early 1870s, a report on the Poor Law administration considered neighbours' collections to widows, concluding that 'what amounts to interchange of charitable assistance among the poor in London is not uncommon . . . they assist each other to an extent which is little understood, and for which they receive little credit'.[51] Sims thought that the pronounced lack of privacy in the slums meant that the poor knew well the plight of their neighbours, and so could offer help. 'They live their lives before each other's eyes, and their joys and sorrows are the common property of the entire community.' Each neighbour 'sees every link in the chain of circumstances that brought his trouble about. What is the fate of one to-day may be the fate of another to-morrow'.[52]

Neighbours alerted others on the street to the arrival of bailiffs and debt-collectors. In 'The Barnsley Anthem', a husband sings about hiding from the bailiffs in the cellar hole with his family, while his wife gossips with neighbours:

> T'waaf she's art callin' wi' t' neebur next dooer
> 'Cos we're all dahn in t' cellar 'oil
> Wheer t' muck slaghts on t' winders.[53]

Thomas Wright recalled how the tenants of Lock Court would club together to confound the tally-man coming to collect his dues. His presence was signalled, doors were shut, scouts positioned at windows and as a last, desperate, resort, neighbours would also help to form barricades.[54] In 1845, a man living at 5 Little Collingwood Street was illegally distilling. Believing the still had been moved to number 7, excise officers tried to gain access to it, but were forced to retreat by a mob of neighbours.[55] In Liverpool, an unlicensed beer seller called Moss persuaded his next-door neighbour to keep a barrel of his beer, into which a gutta-percha tube was fitted. Beer would be siphoned off and sold from Moss's house.[56]

People also helped neighbours in mortal peril.[57] In November 1859, Sarah Steele of Huddersfield became the latest victim of an increasing hazard – flammable crinoline clothing. She ignited while combing her hair by the fire. Her next-door neighbour, hearing her screams, 'came in and told her to lie down'. The crinoline wires prevented extinguishment. She had narrowly escaped immolation by crinoline once before, but this time 'she blazed like turpentine' and died.[58]

Fig. 7 The aftermath of a fire in Littlehampton's Western Road, *c.*1895. One of the young girls could be Edith Swann (b.1891), who went on to write 'indescribably filthy' letters to her neighbours in the 1920s (see Chapter 5).

IT IS AN ILL DWELLING BY BAD NEIGHBOURS

Gas-fuelled lighting became increasingly common from the mid-nineteenth century and was a new threat to the neighbours. A damaged or defective supply could maim or kill. Unrestricted competition meant that up to eight sets of mains could be installed along one street, increasing the opportunities for explosion.[59] One evening in November 1859, an explosion damaged back-to-back properties belonging to a landlord, Joseph Pickles, on Kensington Street in Girlington near Bradford. A fitter had left one end ready for connection in Uriah Bottomley's house, which was occupied at the time by three unattended children: two little Bottomleys and a Pickles boy. Perhaps the fitter was unaware of the power of negative suggestion on children; when he left, he 'charged the children in the house not to touch the stop-cock, which was under the sinkstone and quite accessible'. All three children were injured half an hour later, when a 'terrific explosion' wrecked the

Bottomley residence and shook the adjacent buildings. It was noted that a 'partition wall, dividing the cottage from the one at the back, was blown down, so that there was an uninterrupted passage to the next dwelling'. Suspicion fell on little fingers.[60] A broken gas main in 1884 along Little Collingwood Street caused neighbouring houses to be filled with gas.[61] October 1884 saw further gas fatalities in London with a blast at 28 Edward Street, Star Corner, Bermondsey. This house, 'one of a number of four room tenements which abound in this thickly-populated neighbourhood', contained three families. The Jones family, with three children, had the ground floor. The Watkinses, an elderly couple, occupied the first-floor front room, with the Skinners to the rear. Mrs Jones, on smelling gas, asked a neighbour at number 27 to help her to move the children's beds to the back room, which she thought would be safer, and then she went to the gas company office. An employee, Thomas Honey, returned with her and sought the source of the leak using a 'piece of lighted tow'. He found the leak quickly, or rather, it found him. The ensuing explosion blew out walls, floors and roofing. The Joneses, the Watkinses and Honey were all buried under debris, and numbers 27 and 29 were also badly damaged. Neighbours raced to the scene. The youngest Jones child lay dead. With some poignancy, it was reported that 'a portion of a red Holland blind of the upstairs window of the ill-fated house was blown across to the opposite row of houses, where it caught on a nail and remained as a sign . . . of the havoc and force of the explosion'.[62]

Gas was not the only silent killer in the period. Far more deadly and feared was cholera, a water-borne disease that was transmitted differently to plague and smallpox, the big killers in earlier times. The arrival of cholera in 1831 had jerked the authorities into action and created the impetus behind the Public Health Acts. Statistics in sanitary reports of the 1840s revealed the role of human waste in the spread of disease, and 'the poor became unacceptable as near neighbours'.[63] Neighbours often shared the same water source and were therefore communally afflicted. Dr John Wright, a general practitioner, noted the prevalence of cholera in crowded 'low lodging-houses' in the poorer parts of Westminster, where overcrowding had been worsened by clearances for improvements. 'Whenever there is an epidemic', explained Wright, 'we have it on a large scale.' Members of the Metropolitan Sanitary Commission asked Wright if he thought that 'instances of the abandonment of cholera patients by friends and neighbours was a common occurrence'. Wright confirmed that desertion of the sick was common, that friends and neighbours 'were afraid to go into the sick room and this fear, and the consequent neglect of the sick by neighbours, and even occasionally by relatives, is no uncommon occurrence even in fever, especially amongst the Irish.'[64]

The menace of cholera and the cracking of the riddle of its causation by John Snow in 1854 spurred neighbourhood clean-ups and further medicalised the notion of nuisance. Privies, cesspools and pigs were all targeted by health inspectors. Engels described how Allen's Court in Manchester was cleaned up by sanitary inspectors who ordered it to be evacuated, 'swept and fumigated with chlorine'.[65] A journalist described the process of inspection following the discovery of an outbreak of cholera, smallpox or fever. Many cases were concealed, to avoid the expense and upheaval of disinfection – which involved the removal and burning of wallpaper. If told at the door that there was no infectious disease, a suspicious inspector might question the neighbours.[66]

Public Health Acts brought improvements to sewage, street widths, and enlarged spaces between new properties. The Nuisance Removal Act (1855) required the complaints of two householders for an inspector to follow up a report of filth, although only one was needed if it might be injurious to health. The Local Government Board, established in 1871, gave some central organisation to sanitary administration. Various existing authorities were adapted to fit new frameworks. All of these developments meant that neighbourhoods could be monitored and cleaned up more easily than before. In 1866, the Gloucester Inspector of Nuisances reported various slaughterhouses along

Commercial Road and identified them as the source of illness in
the vicinity.[67] Neighbours could report piles of filth and other
dangers to health. In theory, this meant that dirty neighbours
would be required to clean up. Christopher Hamlin, a historian
working on public health, has suggested that many nuisance
inspectors would have enforced 'the bourgeois standards of the
Victorian suburb', and uses details from a handbook that guided
inspectors in how to avoid being 'the dupe of ill-will or idle
rumour'. Notebooks reveal concern not just about health issues,
but about petty matters like overhanging vegetation and unfilled
potholes. Hamlin describes one inspector as being 'led in his
inquiries, at least partly, by the complaints of neighbours'. A *Handbook for Inspectors of Nuisances* (1873) instructed inspectors to obtain
their knowledge by observation, 'without ostentation or obtru-
siveness and without making more verbal enquiries of the
neighbours than the necessity demands'. Inspectors should not
be sucked into neighbour wrangles; they should resist being 'led
into gossiping'; they should not act on information without
checking it out themselves.[68]

MY LOVELY NEIGHBOUR, OFT WE MEET

It is unsurprising that relationships formed in sweaty adversity could
turn amorous. In Somerset, William Penry Williams, an organist
and music teacher, and his wife Mary lived opposite a farmer called
George Padfield, who, like Mary, was in his twenties. William was
ten years older. It was reported that 'an intimacy subsisted between
the two families' prior to Padfield's mother suspecting that her son
'was carrying on an adulterous intercourse' with Mary. When she
confronted him, 'he did not deny it'. Mary confessed to adultery
and fled, seeking refuge with her mother in Southampton. Her
marriage was dissolved two years later.[69] In October 1840, Henry
Loughead of Upperley near Carlisle publicly auctioned his wife,
who had been 'openly living with another man next door to him'.
He wanted to humiliate them. A throng enjoyed the spectacle –

except the hapless neighbour, 'who wept and wailed, and had not the hardihood to go and offer a bid for her'. Bidders were scarce – she was 'not very handsome either in person or conduct'.[70]

Trouble could develop if loving relations between neighbours turned sour. In 1857, Miss A sat before a court in Darlington, up against a charge that when she met her next-door neighbour Mr B in the street, she 'spat in his face and over his dress', calling him a liar and a coward. Miss A admitted this, and revealed the reason for the attack. Miss A (probably Isabella Atkinson at number 6 Harewood Grove) had believed she was to be betrothed to Mr B (likely one of the Bowes brothers at number 5), following an attachment of the last decade. However, she had lately heard from her grocer (Mr R) that 'it was only for a past time' and Mr B had no honest intentions towards Miss A. To compound the injury, Mr B had pushed a 'disgusting and blackguard letter' under her door. Miss A was fined.[71]

In 'My Neighbour', the poet Gerald Massey lyricises about his obsessive love for a neighbour who is innocent of his desires and doesn't seem to notice him.

> My lovely neighbour; oft we meet
> In lonely lane, or crowded street;
> I know the music of her feet.

Massey hangs on to the rustle of her dress and her passing song. Switching his audience at the end of his poem from the reader to the neighbour, who is destined never to read the words, Massey says:

> You know not, dear, how dear you be;
> All dearer for the secrecy

He will not act on his infatuation. He ends with the enigmatic statement, 'There are reasons why.'[72]

There were happy outcomes to some neighbour affections. Julia

Duckworth (later to become Virginia Woolf's mother) was expecting her third child when her husband died. In 1875, the bereaved family moved to 13 Hyde Park Gate South, a respectable Kensington cul-de-sac. Shortly afterwards she helped her newly widowed friend Leslie Stephen to move in next door. 'Proximity and bereavement soon turned Stephen's shy neighbourly friendship into affection', and in 1878 the couple married and he moved into Julia's house.[73]

THE POSSESSION OF AN ENTIRE
HOUSE IS STRONGLY DESIRED

Foreign visitors had long remarked on the preference for single family homes, high walls and heavy locks among the wealthy English. 'High stone fences, and padlocked garden-gates announce the absolute will of the owner to be alone', remarked American Ralph Waldo Emerson.[74] In his introduction to the 1851 census, the Registrar General, Major Graham, noted that 'The possession of an entire house is strongly desired by every Englishman; for it throws a sharp well-defined circle round his family and hearth.'[75] His enumerators found few castles and very many houses in multiple occupation.

Sometimes people had to walk through their neighbour's space to get to their own lodgings. Frederick Willis described his aunt and uncle's 'shabby house' on London's Goswell Road at the end of the century. To access the first floor (where his relatives lived), Frederick needed to go through a glass door leading to a studio of a maker of naked wax mannequins.[76] Spaces were not always neatly divided. William Bernhardt, a German barber living in Chester in 1869, had a cupboard that 'projected into' the neighbour's house, and Mrs Williams next door habitually knocked on it to annoy the barber. When he went round to challenge this, Mr Williams pushed Bernhardt and Mrs Williams called him a 'd—— German'. A crowd gathered and Mrs Williams was summoned to the police court.[77]

Arguments in slum courtyards caused a spectacle. Henry

Mayhew describes a public slanging match about a sweep who beat his wife. A woman with bird's-nest hair was 'haranguing a crowd' from her first-floor window and calling the sweep's wife 'an old wagabones as she wouldn't dirty her hands to fight with'. The commotion drew all the tenants and lodgers to their windows, 'their heads popping out as suddenly as dogs from their kennels in a fancier's yard'.[78] Thomas Wright, over in Lock Court, describes a similar public kerfuffle. One woman boasted that 'if her (the speaker's) husband had thumped her on the previous night, it had not been for getting drunk'. Her opponent, 'also speaking to the spectators', retorted that she would 'rather be hammered half-a-dozen times for having a drop too much, than once for going with other men'.[79]

Jerome K. Jerome found himself in a selection of lodgings during the last quarter of the nineteenth century. In his autobiography he recalled a house in Camden town:

> There were other lodgers on the floors below. I could hear their muffled voices as I climbed the stairs. A man hanged himself in one of the back rooms. His body was not discovered until the Saturday morning, when the landlady came round for her rents. I had heard a sound one evening, when passing the door, as of a man hammering on the wall with his hands – maybe it was his stockinged feet. But it was not etiquette to be inquisitive about one's neighbours.[80]

We have already considered legal options for dealing with over-looking properties in the pre-modern period. According to the historian of law David Seipp, 'by the 1860s the courts' attitude had hardened against all . . . claims by neighbour versus neighbour' (these included the blocking of windows, nuisance, and issues to do with privacy). Sitting in judgement in 1865, Baron Bramwell said, 'it is to be remembered that privacy is not a right. Intrusion on it is no wrong or cause of action.' One judge remarked that 'no doubt the house would prefer that a neighbour should not have right of looking into his window', but declared it not to be an invasion of privacy. Another judge allowed a neighbour to build a twenty-three-foot-high wall, cutting off a neighbour's vantage. Seipp concludes that 'the English householder at the close of the nineteenth century was at the mercy of curious and resourceful neighbours'. People could more easily prevent invasions of privacy by members of the public or strangers than they could invasions from their neighbour.[81]

People who did not want to be overheard or overseen by neighbours usually had to be careful. Other people were lucky. A pair of anarchists who set up an illicit printing press in London's Boundary Street in 1885 were blessed that the room next to them was shared by two deaf-mutes; both unable to either detect or report on the activities under way next door.[82]

THE NON-SOUNDPROOFED SOUNDPROOF STUDY

Jane, the long-suffering wife of Thomas Carlyle, described the neighbourly irritations her husband experienced over many decades. His reactions were extreme, and seemed to heighten Jane's. Eventually the Carlyles created a soundproof study with double walls at the top of 5 Cheyne Row, Chelsea, for Thomas to work in. It was a white elephant, because the job was badly done, and 'proved in fact the apartment most accessible to sound in the whole house'. Through the skylight Thomas heard river hooters and church bells, and he became 'morbidly devoted to . . . railway whistles'.[83] However, most of the Carlyles' troubles came from number 6, next door. Jane took the lead in smoothing relations and managing the noise, getting the Lamberts to quieten their piano in 1839, and silencing the cocks and macaw belonging to later tenants, the 'rumbustious' Roncas, by paying £5 to get rid of the birds and binding them to not keep any more.[84] Jane's curiosity was pricked in 1865 when a new tenant, 'a very mysterious dressmaker', and her lodgers settled in. When poultry (including 'a magnificent cock') appeared again in the backyard, Jane struck another deal, and gave reading lessons to 'a small Irish boy' who was 'too excitable for school' in exchange for the birds being kept in a cellar during their noisiest hours.[85]

Ownership of musical instruments increased during the Victorian era. Henry Lunn had a lot to say about this. He and his wife formed the consummate musical pairing: he was the editor of the *Musical Times* and Professor of Harmony at the Royal College of Music, and his wife Ann was a singing teacher. Using his journal, Lunn 'strenuously' advised musicians to live in detached villas (he still lived in a terrace) 'with a sufficient amount of private garden-ground on each side to prevent the possibility of any human habitation being afterwards built in too close proximity'. If this was unaffordable, the next best option would be a semi-detached house, 'providing that the rooms for musical study and practice can be on the "detached" side. It is true that this may appear somewhat unsociable, but then musical men *are* unsociable.' Lunn also wonders if it could be possible to establish a music ghetto, whereby streets were 'kept strictly for a specific style of music'.[86] One can imagine the freakish results of this social experiment. Taking a stroll around town you would turn the corner into Comic-Opera Street to be buffeted by the bumptious strains of *HMS Pinafore*; turn another corner and the blood might be stirred by the earnest maestros of Wagner Villas.

In the 1840s, the Lamberts' piano was positioned the other side of the panelled wall from Thomas Carlyle's study (not the 'soundproof' one), and was played mostly during the morning, when he wrote. Jabbing the wall with a poker bought him twelve hours of peace. The following day, a resumption of scales and snatches saw Thomas pen a letter to Miss Lambert, asking her to resist the temptation to play until after two o'clock in the afternoon. Eventually the offending piano was moved and things were quiet for a while. Building work carried out by the Carlyles, for which Jane wrote to apologise, seemed to bring the piano sounds back. Thomas tried a charm offensive, writing to Miss Lambert enclosing a copy of his latest book, and thanking her for trying to observe the morning quiet. It worked.[87]

In the second half of the nineteenth century, the piano became
the pre-eminent piece of sonorous furniture possessed by all households with pretentions to respectability.[88] *The Child's Guide to
Knowledge* (*c*.1870) included this question:

> Q. What musical instrument is now seen in almost every household?
> A. The pianoforte.[89]

The piano came to symbolise status and progress. By the 1860s,
many families obtained a piano through hire-purchase schemes,
which put ownership within the reach of the working class. A
Lambeth rag seller explained how she rescued her piano ('what I
prize most, next to my daughter who plays it') from floods in the
1870s, and how she paid for it 'in a few shillings or a few pence at
a time'.[90] John Normansell, a South Yorkshire miners' representa-
tive, giving evidence to the 1873 Select Committee on Coal, stated
that 'we have got more harmoniums, and more pianos and more
perambulators than ever we had before'.[91] Martin Daunton has
described the piano and the lessons thumped upon it as aural indi-
cators to those around of 'spare resources'.[92]

Henry Lunn was irked that his 'opinion is not the opinion of
the world' and disapproved of instruments kept merely for show.
In *Musings of a Musician*, Lunn had sneered at the 'certain class of
persons' who sought to impress 'their more prudent, but equally
shallow, neighbours, by assuming an air of profound wisdom'. He
berated people who shunned the 'inclination to devote their time
to *being* musical', whilst directing their energies to '*appearing* so'.
In a sketch entitled 'The Piano "Going"', he complained that a
pianoforte was no mere item of furniture. In his scathing account,
he suggests that some ladies go at their pianos merely to appear
musical to the folks next door. 'Mrs Jones's piano next door', our
harmonic professor railed,

> . . . is always 'going' between twelve and two o'clock in the afternoon.
> It can be heard distinctly through the wall. Mrs Robinson's piano, over

the way, is always 'going' when the morning-calls arrive. And as for the Grahams' piano, it's really 'going' all day. But then the Grahams rather overdo the thing, because, being 'genteel', they are innately vulgar.[93]

Other sounds could also disturb neighbours. A fellow lodger in a Nelson Square house occupied by Jerome K. Jerome was a 'law-writer' in the front attic: 'Often he would work all night, coughing incessantly. I got used to it after a time. It was so incessant that it seemed to be part of the night.'[94]

A NUISANCE IN BELGRAVE SQUARE WOULD NOT NECESSARILY BE SO IN BERMONDSEY

Towns continued to secure Local Acts, creating bodies that would have given neighbours affected by nuisances an outlet for their complaints. Sanitary legislation of the mid century was enforced by a variety of local bodies. These gave people more straightforward means to fight nuisances without legal action. Inspectors of nuisances could order that drains, cesspits, overflowing privies and dunghills be cleaned up, and filthy houses be improved to prevent infection, which endangered the occupants and their neighbours.[95] In 1856, a local medical officer of health reported the nuisance of piggeries near Sloane Square to the Committee of Works, who referred it to the Vestry of St Luke's Chelsea, and eventually the nuisance was abated. By the mid nineteenth century, neighbours had more official help (albeit often chaotically organised) than they had had a century before.[96]

Officials were not diligent enough for some people, however, and direct vengeance or court actions were still used to deal with some nuisances. In 1851, an artificial-flower maker called William Carey, on London's Berwick Street, took a neighbour to court, 'in conjunction with the neighbours of him', after the Committee of Sewers and Paving had failed to act on his behalf. Carey was annoyed by the activities of Joseph Barnett, a butcher, who had apparently slaughtered a hundred sheep on his premises.[97] In 1869, a Sheffield man, annoyed by smells from sugar boiling next door, took matters into his own hands. He bashed a hole through the party wall and directed a jet of water on the fire, spoiling some spices.[98]

The ability to report neighbours to the inspectors caused some local difficulties. Lucy Keeling from Leicester got back at a busy-body neighbour in 1854, after he had informed the authorities about her dungheap. In criticism of his 'unwarrantable officiousness' she assembled various neighbours to play a concert in his garden upon an old tin kettle, a tea tray and a cracked horn. This charivari-like performance saw Keeling in court, where she was told to live more peaceably in future, and 'to leave the getting up of popular concerts to the professional gentlemen who are so much better to manage musical matters'.[99]

By the mid nineteenth century, neighbours in mixed areas could find themselves bang up against factories, big and small, or polluting backyard enterprises. Lawsuits were costly and time-consuming.[100] A district of Leeds saw a proliferation of noxious trades, and people in the neighbourhood surrounding a Russian tallow-boiler's establishment suffered from sore throats and lost their appetites.[101] In Manchester in the 1880s, neighbours reported cases that included a steam-boiler at a slaughterhouse, fried fish shops on Deansgate and Great Ancoats Street, steam from a tripe-dressing works, odours from the Castle Rubber Works, making barrels in the street, and a 'strong offensive smell' from a blood-drying works. A sausage-skin factory was permitted to remain in operation on Mount Street on account of 'there being no dwelling houses within a considerable distance of the premises'.[102] A complaint was made about Henry Woodford's pickle works in Vernon Street by a person living next-door-but-one. It was kept open because the person living next to the establishment saw no reason for complaint.[103]

The Bridgman confectioners on Wigmore Street, in London, had been pounding mortars in their kitchens for decades to create sweets for the family business. Neighbours did not complain until 1879, when a physician built a consulting room in his garden next door. Finding pestle sounds to be a nuisance, the physician sought an injunction. The resulting case was significant: although he had 'come to the nuisance', the physician was granted an injunction. The ruling dismissed fears that a person might move next to a Bermondsey tannery and ask for an abatement of the trade, because context was all. On appeal, it was noted that 'what would be a nuisance in Belgrave Square would not necessarily be so in Bermondsey'.[104] The *Graphic*, recording the outcome of the case, noted that 'Unfortunately, it is only the rich who can resort to such methods of obtaining relief; the poor must put up with noises and evil odours, unless the nuisance reaches such a pitch as to warrant the interference of some official authority.'[105] Nuisance-makers located in poor areas such as Bermondsey were effectively immune from prosecution.[106] Mr Salmon ran an artificial manure factory there. He was one of several manure-makers accused of creating a public nuisance in the late nineteenth century. They had originally been at the edge of the city, but housing was built around them. The occupants of the dense collections of humble cottages found their gardens and streets pervaded with the stench of slaughter waste, fish heads, 'putrid animal matter' and garbage. This heady mix was boiled up with pig hair and sulphuric acid. A court heard that the 'neighbourhood has never been very nice' and the manufacturers had previously seen off nuisance challenges on account that the works were deemed to be for the social good, using up refuse. However, a biscuit factory had recently set up nearby and the owners were becoming increasingly worried about the effect of the stench on their baking. The court decided that the manufacture itself was not a nuisance, but ordered Salmon to clean up his storage facilities.[107]

Cow-keepers who had been located near Belgrave Square for decades while the area built up around them found themselves increasingly scrutinised by the inspector of nuisance, and residents complained of the smells.[108] In some parts of some cities pig-keeping was still common. In part of Kensington called 'The Potteries', most families kept pigs, and the creatures 'usually outnumbered people three to one, and had their styes mixed up with the dwelling

Fig. 8 'An artful monkey, my next door neighbour',
Illustrated Police News, 24 August 1872.

houses'.[109] The Manchester Nuisance Committee took no action in
a case they inspected of a nuisance arising from pig-keeping in 1882,
as the subcommittee opined that 'the complaints have arisen
through ill-feeling' and not genuine porcine annoyance.[110] One
couple were forced to endure a rather peculiar nuisance. The person
who lived in the adjoining house owned 'a large-sized, old, and
artful monkey', which had been won as a prize (**Fig. 8**). Although
kept on a chain, the monkey could escape and on occasion had
pursued the man's wife, 'who had to jump over a fence to avoid
it'. The couple requested that the Greenwich Police Court ensure
that the monkey be secured. They were informed that they would
need to make a civil case because the law covered dogs, not
monkeys.[111] Dogs remained ubiquitous sources of neighbourly noise
(and friction).[112] In Eaton Square, just south of Belgrave Square,
dogs belonging to Gerald Fitzgerald, son of the 4th Duke of Lein-
ster, annoyed 'a wakeful neighbour' in 1871 and legal action was

threatened.[113] A Yorkshire woman literally put the cat amongst the pigeons in 1876 and was fined for the death of her neighbour's birds.[114]

A SLIGHT PARTING BETWEEN TWO DWELLINGS

In 1862, a young Irish couple – a pitman and his wife – living near Chester-le-Street were convicted of the wilful murder of Ann Halliday, their elderly next-door neighbour. Halliday lived at Hobbletrot, a small cottage separated from that occupied by her killers 'by a thin party wall'. These properties were barely separate – it was stated that there was 'a doorway between the two compartments, which had been bricked up, but not so effectively as to prevent the slightest noise made by the deceased being heard by the prisoners'. Their cottages, which had once been one house, were distant from other properties, 'near a lonely quarry'. Newspaper accounts revealed that the 'parting between the two dwellings was so slight that the tenants in the one house could distinctly hear those in the other moving about while performing any trivial act of household duty'. At four o'clock in the morning, Mary Cox, one of the accused, claiming she had been aroused by shouting and moaning, alerted the people in the nearest house, and various neighbours and a policeman attended. The old lady was found bloodied though alive, but later died. Mary Cox maintained that her neighbour must have fallen from her bed in a 'duzzy fit'. During the trial, a witness, John Dawson, an erstwhile occupant of the Coxes' portion of the cottage, gave evidence of his neighbour's activities, all detected through hearing and watching. Dawson knew when Halliday went to bed (between midnight and one), and that she read first. He knew that she would fasten her 'outer door by putting something above the sneck'. Dawson's wife, Jane, added that she had talked to Halliday during the week before her death, and that Halliday had asked her the name of 'that man next door', indicating a lack of personal intimacy between the old lady and her young neighbours. Conversely, the Coxes, who never admitted the murder, seemed to falsely suggest a familiarity with the neighbour – referring to her as 'Old Nancy'.[115]

Halliday was described as 'respected by the neighbours as a model of cleanliness and thriftiness'. The Coxes were newcomers. The case against the couple hinged on the fact that they were the only people near enough to Halliday to overhear the murder, and yet they only seemed to have heard the moaning in the aftermath, not the attack itself (Halliday's injuries were assessed to be too severe to have been caused by a fit).[116] We will never know why (or even if) the Coxes killed their neighbour.

In this period, as in earlier times, neighbours could find themselves as witnesses to crimes and misdemeanours, often overheard through party walls or observed from the street. As we have seen at Hobbletrot, neighbours often mentioned the ease with which they could hear the goings-on next door. Cases of child or domestic cruelty made neighbours feel especially conflicted and uncomfortable.[117] This is evidenced by a Stepney couple, William and Harriet Humphreys, who quarrelled so frequently in 1881 that the neighbours stopped taking any notice. The arguments became more violent and Harriet asked her neighbours if she could sleep in their house.[118]

In the summer of 1866, Joseph Williams of Kidsgrove in Staffordshire found his wife Mary seeking sanctuary next door. The neighbour refused to exclude Joseph, who battered his wife's head against the neighbour's chest of drawers and then pushed her on to the sofa. The 'neighbour witnessed all this thrashing, but interfered not beyond a mild appeal to the defendant to "give over"'. He was described as 'a cautious man who had perhaps had previous experience of matrimonia[l] quarrels'.[119] As before, many neighbours kept shtum when domestic incidents played out nearby.[120]

Sounds of children in distress were not necessarily noted by neighbours. It took a comment from another neighbour for Frances Blott, of Mint Street in London, to pay heed to the sounds made by a toddler who lived in the room above her. Giving evidence after the child died in 1860, Blott recalled hearing 'the mother slap the child repeatedly, and scold it for being dirty . . . the child cried very much . . . very violently'. Blott had approached the child's mother, but was accused of interfering. Blott felt that she had offended the family, who stopped being friendly towards her.[121]

Some neighbours seem to have used the idea that crimes could be overheard to make false accusations against their neighbours. In 1863, in the outskirts of Bath, a young newly-wed couple, Alfred and Lucy Wensley of 11 Hampton Row, were charged with the manslaughter of their servant, Jane Reynolds. It was claimed that threats and blows were overheard by a next-door neighbour, Jane Fackrell (at number 12), through 'a very thin wall'. Another neighbour claimed to have seen a pattern of injuries on the servant, and in court said that she had 'told the neighbours what I had seen; probably every neighbour in the row. I may have told all the neighbours.' As part of the investigation following the death of Reynolds, Mr Aust, a builder, was called upon to assess the party wall between the Wensleys and their immediate neighbours. His report was surprising – the walls of the 'best first-class houses in Bath' could not have had a 'greater thickness in the party walls'. The houses still stand and the walls are thick stone. Aust judged that 'words could not be heard from house to house, nor could the sound of blows. It is impossible. Articulate words could not possibly be heard. There were no cracks in the wall.' This despite rumoured attempts to make sounds more penetrating on his visit by throwing open a cupboard door in number 12. An architect corroborated this evidence, and the Wensleys were found to be not guilty. There was a status clash between the Wensleys and the Fackrells. The Wensleys were a notch above their neighbours, and had prospects and a servant.[122]

The way many people lived at this time meant that contact with their neighbours would be regular and inevitable. Spaces and resources were often shared, and this sometimes caused conflict; 'tension within neighbourhoods, even those with a strong communal feeling, was a fact of daily life'.[123] Neighbours could get along – they were expected to – but their environments could make friendship difficult to maintain. Tensions did not mean that people did not value their neighbours. Sharing, caring and supporting networks were evident in pre-war London.[124] In small houses and back-to-backs, domestic spaces were surrounded by neighbourhood spaces; streets, backyards and alleyways. Each area provided space for activities, but also for support networks and for surveillance.

By the end of the nineteenth century, neighbourhood spaces were changing. Model by-laws created to guide municipalities were adopted in the 1880s. These provided more space at the rear of properties, established certain distances between buildings and ensured access to drainage and privies.[125] As fewer households shared communal space and resources, demarcations between the private and the public became clearer. Many new properties were more enclosed than the old back-to-backs had been, and families could be better contained within four walls. There were fewer 'liminal' spaces – back alleys and areas that needed to be criss-crossed en route to the shared toilet, coal house, pump and tap. In many Victorian streets, the boundaries between communal areas in court-yards and on the pavement and the domestic space inside homes had been 'weak and easily crossed'.[126] The historian Martin Daunton shows how, during the nineteenth century, housing developed 'from a *promiscuous* sharing of facilities to an *encapsulated* or self-contained residential style'. The introduction of the pail closet in the 1860s, and then the increasing availability of the water closet from the 1880s, meant that a shrinking proportion of households would share toilet facilities with neighbours. As more homes became connected to water supplies, opportunities to meet at the shared tap were also curtailed.[127]

For many people, sharing was still their daily routine, but houses were becoming more privatised, a trend that was to continue in the next period. The spaces around these self-contained properties were not shared, as the yards and streets around the back-to-backs had been. For both working-class and middle-class families, 'outdoor life was ceasing to be a social life and disappearing from view behind the garden hedge or yard walls'.[128] Over the course of the nineteenth century, the 'respectable' working class had increasingly separated themselves from the 'rough' working class into different areas of expanding cities. Despite some movement out to the more salubrious suburbs, in the old city centres there was still often a rich mix. In villages people also lived hugger-mugger, with rich and poor on the same street.

4

Suburbia Grows Up (1890–1918)

The Joneses became the family to make Mr and Mrs So-and-So jealous thanks to an American cartoonist who coined the term 'keeping up with the Joneses'. In 1913, Arthur R. 'Pop' Momand's comic strip appeared in the *New York Globe* and the Joneses, neighbours of the main characters, were spoken about but never drawn. Momand decided against 'keeping up with the Smiths', settling on the Joneses 'as being more euphonious'.[1] Even by then, the Joneses (along with the Robinsons) had been archetypal neighbours or social equals for some time.[2] Snobbery and status envy is evident in this H.M. Bateman drawing, also from 1913 (**Fig. 9**). A respectable Tiddlington family, the Smythe-Robinsons, take tea with their backs hunched against the neighbours. With tongue in cheek, the caption refers to the cool and shady dining spot. It is in fact completely overlooked by their coarse neighbours, who lean out of windows to gawp at the al fresco tableau.

Thorstein Veblen linked conspicuous consumption to status in *The Theory of the Leisure Class*. Noting that neighbours are often not friends, but that their 'good opinion has a high degree of utility', Veblen decided that the 'only practicable means of impressing one's pecuniary ability on these unsympathetic observers of one's everyday life is an unremitting demonstration of ability to pay'.[3] A century earlier, William Godwin had argued that people liked to show off and gained satisfaction from making poorer neighbours feel envious. A rich neighbour 'could never be satisfied with his possessions unless he could make the spectacle of them grating to others'.[4]

Fig. 9. H.M. Bateman, 'During the hot weather the Smythe-Robinsons of Tiddlington take their meals in a cool and shady spot of the garden', 1913.

NOBODY'S ANCESTORS EVER LIVED
IN A SEMI-DETACHED VILLA

Suburbia, the ideal place for keeping up with neighbours, was already burgeoning when Edward VII ascended the throne in 1901. That year, an essayist advised city workers to move to more spacious and healthy homes in the suburbs, where 'his neighbours will be of his own class, a matter of chiefest importance to his wife and children, the greater part of whose lives will be spent in these surroundings'.[5] The extension of railways, trams and trolley buses into the countryside around English cities, coupled with agricultural depression, had made houses a more lucrative crop than corn. However, Edwardian working-class families did not move to the suburbs in great numbers, even though the 1883 Cheap Trains Act had made commuting more affordable.[6] The vast majority still paid rent to private landlords. In 1914, only about 10 per cent of prop-

erties were owner-occupied, and less than 1 per cent were let by
local authorities.[7] Giving evidence towards the Housing for Working
Classes Act of 1890, Thomas Fatkin, the secretary and manager of
the Leeds Permanent Building Society, revealed that over a thousand
of the society's members each owned two adjoining pairs of back-
to-back houses. The member lived in one of the four, renting out
the other three. This meant that a neighbour was also the landlord,
potentially complicating these relationships.[8]

Greater numbers from the middle classes relocated to semis in
the suburbs, leaving behind the stench, noise, dirt and chaos of the
mixed areas in the centre. The novelty of these houses is captured
by a character in George Gissing's *The Whirlpool*, who mused, 'Oh
what a pleasant thing it must be . . . to have ancestors. Nobody's
ancestors ever lived in a semi-detached villa.'[9] Some pundits worried
that the suburban migration was fracturing neighbourhood identity.
The German philosopher Georg Simmel saw a change in interper-
sonal relations caused by the commute from the suburbs: 'people
were never put in a position of having to stare at one another for
minutes or hours on end without exchanging a word'.[10] Extra
domestic intimacy was sought to make up for this anomie and
discomfort.

It is fallacious to think of Edwardian building as a monotonous
tract of semi-detachment. More terraced houses were still being
built than any other type; it remained the predominant form of
housing for the working classes. There was a range of houses, with
the humblest built to comply with the minimum standards laid out
in the 1875 Public Health Act. Narrow terraces had an L-shaped
plan, with the back part housing the kitchen and often a bedroom
above. They were gloomy because windows in the back would look
out into the narrow space between the neighbouring houses. The
layout also meant that these rooms often intrusively faced the neighbours' equivalent rooms, or were shielded by fences that reduced
light indoors.[11] When the middle classes moved to the suburbs, they
left large terraced houses that the working classes colonised more
densely than the builders of the houses had intended. By the end

of the nineteenth century, many houses designed for one family were home to several. Charles Booth, the social reformer and author of the massive *Life and Labour of the People of London*, observed that only 'slight alterations' were made to the houses, perhaps water installed in each floor, and noted their preponderance in Wapping and Deptford.[12] Booth's enterprise to create a 'Poverty Map' ranked the character of entire streets, masking subtle stratification within them. The mixing of different types of household on the same street did not fit neatly into his system, leading him to categorise many streets as 'purple': home to all types and classes.[13]

NOT ROOM TO SWING A CAT

One housing innovation was the 'half-house' (a purpose-built version of the early-modern 'divided house'), with a shared lobby behind the front door or front doors side by side, often in a porch (**Fig. 10**). They each contained two flats disguised to look like houses, accommodating one family upstairs and another downstairs.[14] Some half-houses were further divided, with each flat occupied by more than one family. Houses on the south side of Whateley Road in East Dulwich were surveyed by Booth and appeared from the outside to be occupied by a single family, but were actually in multiple occupation, mainly by itinerant costers and 'a very rough set of others'. The 1901 census enumerators could not work out who belonged where in the divided interiors.[15] Families migrated here from various places across the country and abroad. Trouble brewed.

Drink was a likely factor behind an altercation between a fifty-seven-year-old watchmaker and his younger neighbour in 1900. On the night of the August Bank Holiday, Richard Adkins attacked his neighbour Henry Pybus after the two men returned home from a nearby pub. Adkins claimed to have been provoked by an initial attack from Pybus, involving a poker and a dog. Pybus, at number 51 Whateley Road, was said to be unhappy about the 'number of children next door'.[16] There were at least eighteen children amongst

Fig. 10 Half-houses in East Dulwich, 2011.
The forecourts struggle to contain waste receptacles.

the residents at number 53, spread between the five families who
lived there (**Fig. 11**). Indeed, Henry and Rosalie Pybus were flanked
by houses containing numerous children; there were at least eight
children at number 49. A further dozen children lived in the same
house as Pybus – including three babies. Pybus was destined to
have even more small neighbours the following year, including
twins Bertram and Charles Dolding. Misidentification added a
further twist to this tale – the Sowdens were a German couple who
had recently settled in number 53, and whilst in the pub, Pybus
seems to have mistaken Adkins for Mr Sowden.[17]

The Fabian Women's Group made visits to several Lambeth
families between 1909 and 1913 to record how they survived on
twenty shillings each week. *Round About a Pound a Week* by Maud
Pember Reeves describes how most of the families lived in
cramped and insanitary conditions, usually sharing their house
with a subletting tenant. Pember Reeves worried that a casual

Fig. 11 49–53 Whateley Road in 2011.

visitor might see uniformity in the slums, and highlighted the individual characters of the women she met. She asserted that her subjects and their homes had as much individuality as the residents of Belgrave Square. Some of the properties contained an internal passageway from front to back, which gave access to the stairs, front room and back room. These houses suited subletting, with the subtenant enjoying some privacy in the separate front room. Many other four-roomed Lambeth houses had no passage and the front door opened directly on to the front room, which led to the back room. In this arrangement, upstairs tenants had to pass through the ground-floor rooms to get to and from their space (see **Fig. 12**). 'The inconvenience and annoyance of this is intense', notes Pember Reeves. 'Both exasperated families live on the edge of a bitter feud.'[18]

Overcrowding was still a problem in the first decade of the twentieth century. By 1911, nearly 44 per cent of single-room tenements

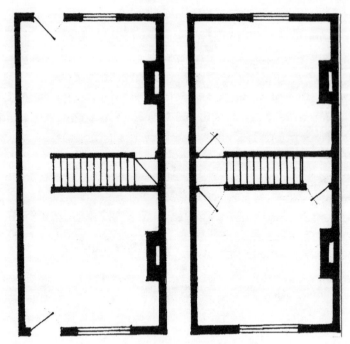

Fig. 12 Lambeth house plans, from Maud Pember Reeves' description.

were overcrowded.[19] Booth noted that when slums were demolished, 'the fairly comfortable are the first to move, the poor refuse to and have not the money to go far'.[20] The overcrowding merely shifted to nearby areas.

Neighbours stood together for the photograph in **Fig. 13**, taken of Little Collingwood Street in Bethnal Green by the missionary John Galt in the early twentieth century. The 1901 census may reveal the names of some of the people pictured, but we cannot put them to faces. The Feeneys at number 2 were a family of seven, headed by bill-poster Charles. Occupying number 3 was a middle-aged couple, James and Mary Hutchings. Mary jumped from her first-floor window to escape a fire in 1902. Three lodgers who were not counted by census enumerators were rescued from the property.[21] On average, six people were living in each house. Two widows and their children (five between them) lived at 15, and two families also lived at 16. At 18, Henry and Alice Applin lived with Alice's son, and they had the Trotts next door – a blacksmith, his wife and their two children.[22] Conditions were better in 1901 than they had been in 1847, when a local doctor reported that there would typically be eight, nine or ten people sleeping in each bedroom.[23]

The number of families occupying just one room declined during the twentieth century, but in the first half of the century lodging was still common. Lodging could try the patience of lodger and landlord alike; the novelist George Gissing thought that 'to occupy furnished lodgings, is . . . the least tolerable status known to civilisation'.[24] A landlady also sacrificed freedom and privacy by taking in lodgers. She had to provide the 'material comforts of home' and also 'to keep the emotional atmosphere on an even keel, to apportion scarce resources of time as well as things, to soothe ruffled feelings and to arbitrate between lodgers, servants, and her own family'.[25] The memoir-writing hatter Frederick Willis thought that

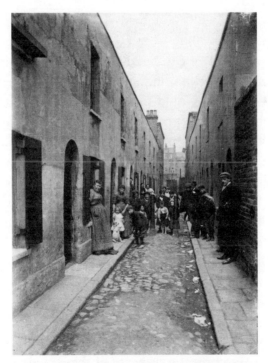

Fig. 13 Little Collingwood Street, photograph
taken by John Galt, between 1900 and 1907.

those with lodgers never wholly occupied their own homes, and endured a 'fly in the ointment'.[26]

ROUGH WOMEN WITH HAIR IN METAL CURLERS

In the late nineteenth century, tenement blocks were being built by philanthropic organisations like the Peabody Trust. Facilities were good but the rules were strict. It was not easy to keep a coster's barrow, a knife grinder's wheel and other vending or mending paraphernalia in the grounds, and it would be impossible to hide a donkey. Tenants took turns on Saturdays to clean communal areas, including passages, steps, closets and lavatory windows. The 600 children living in the East End Rothschild Buildings were not allowed to make a noise on the stairs or in the passages (Rule 7), and these areas had to be washed and whitened each weekend by tenants in rotation (Rule 5).[27] Inveterate do-gooder Octavia Hill thought these rules and regulations put the poor off flat-dwelling – they preferred 'the most wretched tenement house to living in buildings'; they liked to have a yard, even if it was shared with numerous other families. Hill pointed out that block-living would inhibit individualism amongst the residents, who could not grow 'creepers in the back yard' or keep rabbits, build sheds for tools, or make 'washing arrangements to their own taste'. Prams were hard to accommodate and pets were usually prohibited. Instead, she thought that the poor should be 'trained' to be respectable neighbours, though she was cautious about which types of resident were best placed to make good neighbours in the new flats in the model dwellings. Hill worried that some hard-working families could be easily disturbed by rough elements. These bad apples might cause good, 'tidy' tenants to leave, whilst 'the rampant remain and prevail', leaving the whole block to slide into 'a sort of pandemonium'. She advocated refusing rooms in blocks to 'the noisy drunkard'. Some households needed 'the comparative peace of the whole separate home' more than the better sanitation afforded by the new flats. Hill thought that isolation 'made family life and neighbourly kindness more possible'. If they were allowed to 'herd on staircases', the working classes might 'corrupt one another'. Better, therefore, to tuck them up in 'their own little house or as lodgers in a small house'. Here they can be taught in the art of 'considering his neighbour'.[28] Rules for Peabody Dwelling residents dictated where laundry was done and that only the tenant's clothing could be washed (thus preventing occupation by washerwomen). They also forbade various home workers, including rabbit pullers, fur-dressers and people using glue.[29]

A 'Lady Resident', writing for Charles Booth, was more positive about model dwellings, suggesting that, with co-operation and a good caretaker, life could be comfortable. One advantage was the ease with which 'neighbourly intercourse both between children and between the grown up people' could occur. The elderly were not neglected, because they lived in the heart of a community. However, her detailed account of the lives of her own neighbours suggests a rather limited ability to maintain privacy in such surroundings. She was able to work out that a neighbour above rose at five, his wife snoozing until after the children had left for school because she laboured late at her sewing machine. The neighbour to one side ('Mrs B') got up at eight (when she raked and cleaned out her stove). Various other domestic comings and goings are recorded. She sums up her experience positively, but does note that the 'chief disadvantage' is the 'absence of privacy'. This 'Lady Resident' felt that the sense of 'neighbourly responsibility' was impossible to maintain in a larger block. Very many people sharing communal spaces made 'domestic disputes and crying children more disagreeably prominent'.[30]

Robert Roberts, author of Classic Slum, explained how, in his Salford community 'as in every other of its kind, each street had the usual social rating; one side or one end of that street might be classed higher than another'. Roberts argued that social position was judged in his part of Salford not just on what items were owned, but which of these were pawned: 'The neighbours . . .

noted everything, with pleasure or envy.' The material hung in
windows signified nuances of status. Drapery and lace were posh,
but newspaper showed the household had been 'forced to hoist
the grey flag of poverty'.[31] As a boy, Robert Hyde, who was to
become a campaigner for improved industrial working conditions,
had no 'presentable shoes' to wear at a neighbour's party. Instead,
he wore his sister's, with laces improvised from string dipped in
ink, and spent the party feeling ashamed and 'tucking my feet
underneath me'.[32] In his memoirs, Frederick Willis described his
own street, Burdock Road, as designed to 'fill a long-felt want',
that of housing for the 'class in between', the managing clerks
and their families. His neighbours in this early commuter belt
were mostly 'something in the city'.[33] According to Charles Booth,
writing shortly afterwards, Burdock Road had experienced a swift
decline, perhaps because a more distant ring of suburbs had drawn
the money further out.

> At first there was a fairly good class of tenants . . . But after a year,
> two or three bad lots got in on the odd number side, and then the
> street changed as by magic. The better folk left and people came who
> had hardly any furniture – the rejections of other districts.[34]

Nellie Benson was the daughter of an archbishop who died young
while she was forging a career as a social worker. She had been a
member of the Women's University Settlement in Southwark. Her
memoirs reveal distaste for the idea that a rough/respectable division was lifelong. She believed that people could learn to be
respectable by example, and that neighbours played a role. Respectable people living amongst social inferiors who say 'I don't associate
with my neighbours; I keep myself to myself' were missing an
opportunity. Integration was key to Benson, and the severance of
the respectable from the rough was the 'most serious barrier' to
social mobility. 'Nothing', she said, 'can improve either a family or
the individual so much as friendly intercourse on an equal footing'
with socially superior neighbours. Keeping oneself to oneself was

no mark of superiority to Benson. Exclusivity was the route to social ruin.[35]

A division between the 'rough' and the 'respectable' poor was evident in pre-war London, with the latter being 'not the sort that would sit on the doorstep'. These were shifting categories, and judgements were made on the basis of cleanliness, creditworthiness and dependence on charity (suggesting many similarities with the early-modern neighbours from Chapter 1). Working-class women cleaned to impress each other, and accusations of bad housekeeping were feared. On moving to Chelsea in 1913, one woman fretted that the behaviour of her drunken husband might 'disgrace us before our very respectable neighbours'.[36] Booth's researchers had adopted this rough/respectable dichotomy. In a Southwark court in 1899, the site of 'rows on Saturday nights', we meet 'rough women with hair in metal curlers'.[37] The inhabitants of Little Collingwood Street were described as 'very poor & very rough'. The houses along this narrow street (it was only about nine feet house-to-house) had many 'windows broken & stuffed with rags, some not stopped at all'.[38] The narrowness of the streets and the lack of sound-tight windows had implications for levels of privacy.

A photograph of a court off Manchester's Corporation Street (**Fig. 14**) shows a tap, barrels, buckets and various other items of domestic clutter in the shared spaces in front of the houses. Washing hangs to the right, and lines cross the centre of the court. In his study of poverty in York in 1899, Seebohm Rowntree counted the number of families sharing various facilities. One water tap and one water closet served fourteen tenements. One family lived in a 'house lost in dirt' whose shared toilet facilities were choked with refuse in a partially flooded yard.[39] A Lancaster woman born in 1896 spent her childhood sharing a toilet with her large family and four other families. She remembered the old man from next door, who 'used to go to sleep in it sometimes and then of course if you were destined to go, it was a bit awkward'. A fellow citizen recalled the embarrassment of walking in on a toilet-sharer.[40] Residents of Thanksgiving Place had little to be thankful for. Between them,

Fig. 14 Housing off Corporation Street, Manchester, 1908.

they shared five water closets, but one was used as a dustbin, which overflowed into the narrow court, 'just wide enough to accommodate a barrow'.[41] Neighbours peep from their doorways in this photograph of a Manchester court taken in 1908 (**Fig. 15**). A buttressed wall separates them from the houses opposite, and a shared privy sits in a lean-to structure.

The women sorting piles of clothes in Ruston's Place, off Nottingham's Bellar Gate, in 1919 (**Fig. 16**) are rag-pickers. Chairs have been brought outside in an informal way that suggests regular habit, rather than showily for the photographer (**Fig. 17**). Work and socialising clearly took place in this space. Most windows are wide open (there was no through-ventilation in these backed houses), putting the occupants' activities on show. Window shutters have been retained for warmth and privacy. The sharing of facilities could lead to arguments, but it could also foster a sense of open-

Fig. 15 Pearson Court, Corporation Street, Manchester, 1908.

ness, in contrast to the self-containment of less entwined dwellings. In such circumstances, some rooms in the house, especially the kitchen, seemed to have been easily accessible to neighbours.

As a young and struggling writer, George Gissing moved between squalid lodgings every six months or so. He had many neighbours during his life. In a period of eighteen years he moved more than eighteen times. A novelist, working mostly from home, Gissing was well placed to observe the comings and goings of the people around him – the people who inspired his writing, and the people who hampered it. Most of his early moves edged him slightly higher up the social ladder, until he gradually climbed into a bachelor tenement and then to a suburban villa (although only a share of one) in Exeter. These moves reveal the variety of Victorian housing. Gissing was twice married and was embarrassed by both wives and by the impecunious state in which he often found

Fig. 16 and **Fig. 17** Ruston's Place, off Nottingham's Bellar Gate, 1919.

himself.[42] He sought to exclude friends and neighbours from his home, but he did not work well in seclusion and needed urban hubbub to keep his pen moving. He was especially settled in his bachelor pad, 7K Cornwall Residences, Clarence Gate, Regent's Park, which he occupied between 1884 and 1890. The neighbours were well behaved and respectable. In a letter to his brother, he described the 'seclusion of the place' as 'amazing', and boasted, 'by the bye, just under lives [Procida] Bucalossi, the composer'. It was the lack of inquisitiveness that most impressed the writer – he found his privacy to be 'absolute. I have not yet passed two people in going in & out . . .'[43]

A POUND OF CARE WILL NOT PAY AN OUNCE OF DEBT

In September 1894, Accrington in Lancashire was the scene of a blood-bath that was overheard by those nearby. Between six and seven o'clock in the morning, a neighbour heard screams at 43 Hyndburn Road. She knocked at the bedroom wall and a loud knock was returned, which reassured her. Sensitised by these sounds, she noticed later that day that the blinds were still drawn, which made her suspicious. This is an example of subtle surveillance, where people observe, often without effort, their neighbours' patterns of activity, allowing them to detect when things are awry. She shared her concern and word reached a relative who lived nearby in Steiner Street. The relative broke in and 'beheld a horrible spectacle'. Young Hannah Farrar lay dead on the bed, her throat cut from ear to ear. Her two younger sisters, Elizabeth and Isabella, lay alive nearby but with wounded throats. They were taken next door to have their wounds dressed. Alice Farrar, the girls' mother, 'presented a pitiable sight. Manifestly she did not know what she had done.' Her mental balance had been affected by the death of her infant son in May and the problems her husband Richard was experiencing at work. Richard had two sisters living in Steiner Street, and he was taken to one of their houses after returning from work. Meanwhile, Alice was taken to Accrington police station. Another neighbour, Mrs Heaton, of 82 Steiner Street, visited her in the cells and agreed to bring her some clothes to replace the ones she was wearing, which were soaked in blood. In October, the Home Secretary consigned Alice to the Lancashire County Lunatic Asylum in Prestwich, where she remained until her death in 1915. Richard continued living in the neighbourhood with his daughters. They moved to 58 Steiner Street sometime before 1901, even nearer to his sister who had discovered the grisly scene and still lived at number 47. In 1911, with all three members of the family now working in the cotton industry, they moved a few doors up, to 50 Steiner Street.[44] Presumably Richard found the neighbourhood (which was also home to kinfolk) comforting enough to remain so near to the scene of personal tragedy.

Maud Pember Reeves saw that even 'the most stand-off neighbours' would show 'extraordinary kindness' and 'unite instinctively' if a family fell on hard times. However, when a family moved away, the neighbours swiftly forgot about them, leading Pember Reeves to speculate that 'it was not mere personal liking which united them; it was a kind of mutual respect in the face of trouble'.[45] Looking at life in an East End tenement, the historian Jerry White found evidence of a 'complex support system of mutual aid' amongst the residents. They would lend each other money to pay the rent, thwart evictions and mount collective actions against the rent collectors.[46] Exploring 'survival networks' in London before the First World War, Ellen Ross revealed the lengths to which women would go to save each other from destitution. Outside charity was ad hoc and insubstantial and the providers could be interfering. Neighbourly help included loans and gifts of things and money, offers to provide childcare or help with repairs, or emotional support, advice and watchful concern. It could be given when needed, because people nearby could easily see when it was required.[47] There was a tendency for tenants to 'shoot the moon' and do a flit from the landlord, often with the complicity of neighbours. The *Manchester Courier* reported in 1910 that the 'difficulty of tracing these removals is enhanced by the disinclination of neighbours to assist in giving information – for reasons of delicacy maybe'. Edwardian policemen shuddered when asked to attend evictions, due to the likelihood of intimidation or attack by neighbours.[48]

Support extended to safeguarding employment. Giving evidence to a Parliamentary Committee on 'Physical Deterioration' in 1904, Hilda Martindale, a lady inspector of factories, noted the 'neighbourly kindness' common in the Potteries, which meant that when they were unable to work shifts, 'women have no difficulty in procuring a neighbour to "locum" for them'.[49] Help came during confinements too. The Women's Cooperative Guild expressed concern, in April 1911, that poor women could not afford to employ a trained midwife, and that many still relied on neighbours to help out at a birth.[50] The Maternity and Child Welfare Act (1918) gave local authorities the power to appoint health visitors. Help was given at the other end of life too. In Shelton Street, one of the poorest streets surveyed by Charles Booth, the neighbours showed respect at the wake of one from their street 'by covering the coffin and almost filling the one room in which these women lived with costly wreaths and quantities of beautiful flowers'.[51]

Neighbours nationwide minded each other's children. Anna Davin describes poor childhoods in London where the 'boundaries of the household were relatively permeable . . . A child . . . might sleep in one house and eat in another.' Children were watched as they played on the streets. 'Adult supervision had an informal, collective quality.'[52] In a piece weighing up the pros and cons of 'blocks of model dwellings', Octavia Hill thought that young widows with children should be barred from flats in such blocks, and advised that these women be encouraged to find a place in 'a small house where the resident landlady would see a little to the children'.[53] Gissing was alert to this potential perk of room-tenancy; Nancy Tarrant, a character from *In the Year of Jubilee*, rented rooms from Mary Woodruff, who looked after Nancy's child while she wrote.[54] Neighbours took turns to care for the seven children of a resident of the East End Rothschild Buildings after she broke her leg.[55] Evidently such occurrences were common. Discussing care arrangements at a select committee in 1908, Miss E.H. de K. Curtis, the Superintendent of the District Nursing Association of Hammersmith and Fulham, revealed that

> . . . it is our custom to keep a list of respectable women who will at short notice, and for what money is forthcoming, undertake the charge of an infant . . . The majority of these women take these children for sheer love and for neighbourly kindness, provided they can receive sufficient money for out-of-pocket expenses.[56]

For his study of *Poverty*, Rowntree interviewed York folk who provided domestic help for their infirm neighbours such as a seventy-year-old woman described as a 'harmless imbecile' whose neighbours cleaned for her. Rowntree noted: '[t]here is much of this mutual helpfulness among the very poor. In cases of illness neighbours will almost always come in and render assistance, by cleaning the house, nursing . . .'[57] Indeed, care might even be offered when the sick had communicable diseases like tuberculosis.[58]

Neighbours left keys with each other. In 1894, Charles Appleton

of Swanage Road, Wandsworth, went on his holiday, leaving the
key to the garden entrance with his neighbour, Mr Hobbs. The
house was burgled but there was no suspicion that Hobbs was
involved, because the door was forced and Hobbs helped to catch
the burglar after hearing noises next door.[59] However, some did
help themselves to their neighbours' things.[60] In 1891, Ruth Greasley
of Bridge Street in Loughborough stole clothing from Mrs Glue
next door. The women 'had been in the habit of visiting each
other's house' and Glue had lent Greasley some items to pawn. On
two occasions, another neighbour saw Greasley coming out of the
Glue house 'with a bundle' that she took out of the yard while
Glue was in Greasley's house, minding her baby.[61] An inebriated
architect's clerk, Herbert Tatton, died in 1894 after being arrested
for taking a clock from his landlady's dining room.[62] Automatic
'penny in the slot' gas meters provided a new quarry for thieves at
the end of the nineteenth century. Booth's researcher notes: 'These
have already given employment to the police – when people move
out, as is frequently the case, the neighbours will rifle the gas meter
for the coppers deposited.'[63]

NOBODIES AT HOME

Again, in the early twentieth century, neighbours fell in love and
married each other. These included physicist Norman Campbell,
who fell in love with a near neighbour in Leeds, Edith Utley Sower-
butts.[64] Friendships between neighbours are a more typical yet less
recorded experience than the accounts of conflict that muscle out
of police court records. So common were little kindnesses and fond
words that most people would never have thought to comment on
them or record them for posterity. Gissing is one exception. His live-in
landlords at 17 Oakley Crescent, Chelsea, proved so beguiling that
he moved out 'solely because I had grown too friendly with the
people in the house, & found it increasingly difficult to force myself
to solitary work'. Gissing also maintained a relationship with Charles
Tinckam, another landlord with whom he had a good rapport. They

dined together long after Gissing had moved out of Tinckam's house.[65]

Gossip lubricates relationships between neighbours, but male hacks tut-tutted at mothers who they thought were shirking domestic duties when they chatted. Booth's researcher saw 'many gossiping women and ill-clad children' along Tiverton Street, Borough, in 1899.[66] This attitude to parenting was considered to be not merely idle, but at times homicidally negligent. A 1905 exposé in the *Manchester Guardian* probed 'Is Flannelette Dangerous?' This was superficially a chemical analysis of flammability, but the real target was mothers who blithely gossiped while their kids played by unguarded fires and burned in their flannelette. 'From careful observation', observed the concerned author,

> I have come to the conclusion that in nine cases out of ten where children are burnt to death it is the result of gross carelessness or indifference on the part of the parents. In the poorer districts of any of our large towns children may be seen playing about in their nightgowns at all hours of the morning, while their mothers are gossiping with their neighbours.[67]

What the critics miss is the precious camaraderie and the flow of useful information that women circulated through gossip. Looking back at his childhood community, Robert Roberts could remember 'matrons in converse' who were 'both storing and redistributing information that could be important economically to themselves and their neighbours'. This network of tattle could be unforgiving. A former prostitute now ten years 'clean' was still not accepted in Roberts's Salford community and was cold-shouldered by her neighbours. Drunken and aggressive behaviour could also leave a lasting stigma, often on an entire family. Roberts thought rose-coloured spectacles should be taken off when viewing slum communities, because it is clear that 'close propinquity, together with cultural poverty led as much to enmity as it did to friendship'.[68]

By the time they found themselves in the police courts, neigh-

bours had often been at loggerheads for some time. Balls thrown
into the garden next door were the start of upset between two
Southampton neighbours in 1895. Ernest Churcher had leant over
the garden wall and threatened to punch Emily Jeffery in the head.
Churcher's defence argued that it was a 'storm in a teacup', and
that the Churchers had long endured annoyance from their 'troublesome' neighbour.[69] A 'respectable lady' from Wandsworth called
Ellen Twigg was accused of threatening behaviour and throwing
a brick at her neighbour, Elizabeth Finch, in 1896. Their squabble
had its basis in ill-feelings about garden produce grown in the Twigg
garden; Twigg accused Finch of touching her tomatoes and ruining
her roses. When told to go inside, Finch told Twigg to 'Go in
yourself and mind your rags.' There is clearly a backstory to a fight
in Leicester in 1899. Emma Burley invited her next-door neighbour,
Emma Chambers, round to challenge her about some gossip she
had heard. When Chambers refused, Burley hit her with a poker
and other neighbours overpowered her, stopping her dragging
Chambers by the hair.[70]

    Not all of Gissing's living arrangements were as cordial as those
he enjoyed with the Tinckams in Brixton. On moving to Exeter
back in 1891, he had found unfurnished rooms for himself and his
new wife, Edith, in Prospect Park. The landlord's sister, Susan, was
due to move in to the house with her fiancé, Charles Rockett. The
two couples unwisely arranged to share the kitchen.[71] When he
and Rockett were alone preparing the rooms for Edith, Gissing
started to endure 'much misery of solitude', and noted in his diary
that 'I rarely speak a word with Rockett.'[72] Sharing with the Rocketts was not a good start to married life. In a letter to a friend,
Gissing complained that 'there had been no possibility of associ-
ating with the people downstairs, who are extremely selfish & vulgar
beyond belief'.[73] Ruminating further in his commonplace book, he
added the following comment in the category of 'Lower Classes':
'People in the position of the Rocketts – how is one to class them?
– are incredibly ignorant of everything relating to books.'[74] In August
1891, Gissing recorded in his diary:

Fine days, but rendered utterly miserable by vile squabbles here in the house. The Rockett people behaving with every kind of vulgar malice. It makes me ill; I pass the time in sick, trembling rage unable either to read or think – Yet I do think in a way; there has come across me, out of these miseries an idea for a volume of short stories, to illustrate the wretchedness of life in lodgings, to be called 'At a Week's Notice'.

Only a few days later, he left with 'not a word to the people of the house, who had proved intolerable'.[75] Gissing's 'Nobodies at Home' series, written for Jerome K. Jerome's *To-Day* magazine in 1895, was partly inspired by his own sour relations with the Rocketts.[76] Gissing moved 'with profound thanksgiving' across Exeter to a more spacious abode in St Leonard's Terrace. His new landlord, Charles Bryan, a schoolmaster, lived on the same terrace.[77] We will leave Gissing here for the while, happily gathering marigolds from his new front garden.

INTIMACY CLOSED THROUGH DISPUTES

While Gissing had fought with his pen and his tongue, fists were the weapon of choice in many working-class neighbourhoods. Disagreements were often sorted in the street. Robert Roberts told of frequent Saturday-night drink-fuelled fights in his part of Salford. Tussles were often triggered by arguments about children, and 'before the fighting proper began between the males, housewives shrieked abuse'. Roberts viewed these skirmishes as a way of placing each family socially, and in their aftermath (through gossip) the community 'made grim readjustments on the social ladder'.[78]

In 1909, working-class Constance Waller, her elderly mother, her husband William and their children lived in a ground-floor flat in Lambeth beneath joiner Frederick Sibbe, his wife Julia and their children. After Constance was stabbed with a chisel by Frederick, she told the court that they had 'not lived on neighbourly terms; his wife would not let me. Everytime she got drunk she slapped me.' By the time of the assault, both families had lived on the street for about two years. The Sibbe family moved out shortly after the incident. The Wallers were no longer living in Townsend Street by 1911; they had moved to Bermondsey. When the case was heard in the Old Bailey, Frederick accounted for his behaviour by saying that Constance had insulted and ill-treated his wife 'by throwing her to the bottom of the stair, calling her bad names'. He was found guilty of 'unlawful wounding, under great provocation.'[79]

A case from Ipswich in September 1892 showed what happened when neighbouring turned poisonous. John McCabe, a young leather-dresser living at 14 Beaconsfield Road, and William Francis, a plate-layer who lived at number 12, had been thick as thieves. The two had been employed by the Great Eastern Railway Company until McCabe had to leave as a result of their plot to embezzle two shillings in a dodgy salt deal. McCabe was bitter because only he was sacked, and a feud began. Their wives argued but the taciturn men would pass each other without speaking, until, one month before the episode that led to McCabe's trial, McCabe was heard threatening to 'corpse' Francis.[80] He was true to his word. The *Manchester Times* reported that 'McCabe went into Francis's house and deliberately struck him on the head, fracturing the frontal bone, death ensuing soon afterwards.'[81] The judge, with the black cap on his head, sentenced McCabe to death.[82]

It is clear that conflict was also a feature of life in genteel households. Even neighbours in fine villas could nurture mutual loathing. The Police Court of West London heard about the antics of the wives of stockbroker Ernest Roth and solicitor Frank Tatton. The Tatton children at 25 Prebend Gardens had thrown their ball into the Roths' garden next door. (We met their uncle earlier – he was Herbert, the inebriated clerk who died after stealing from his landlady.) Evelyn Roth, at number 27, was irritated by having to repeatedly return the Tattons' balls. On 11 August 1898, she had been bathing her baby, and was reluctant to send the ball back until little Ernest was dry. An impatient Helen Tatton threatened to smash up Roth's dining room, damaged the curtains and took several items after being provoked by Roth's servant, who had stuck her tongue out. Eventually, the two women fought. During the subsequent court case, Tatton remarked that they had initially enjoyed friendly relations, but that 'intimacy closed through disputes about the children'. The courtroom found the case entertaining and it was dismissed.[83] The Tattons had lived on Prebend Gardens for longer than the Roths; the two families were still neighbours in 1899, but the Tattons had moved a few houses down the street by 1901. By 1911, the Roths had moved to Thorney Hedge Road, possibly attracted by the prickly-sounding barrier between them and their new neighbour.[84]

PLANNING TO SPITE ME

Silverdale, near Carnforth in Lancashire, is the location of an extraordinary 'spite wall', and there are also remnants of other spite walls in the village. In 1875, two large houses were built along Stankelt Road a good distance apart. In 1880, one neighbour built a house (The Limes) between them, but positioned it as far from his own existing house as possible, right on the border of the neighbouring property. As the house was erected, the neighbour matched it, brick for brick, with a wall twenty-four inches from the building (**Fig. 18**). This obscured the windows and formed a massive barrier between the properties. A squabble between two past neighbours can spell darkness for future ones. Often these spite walls are removed once the original neighbours have moved on. Another spite wall in Silverdale, along Wallings Lane, was partially removed in the 1960s by a descendant of the original builder. A surviving example on the forecourt of Manor House in Leg Square, Shepton Mallet, is protected by being listed.[85]

Even the activities of the most erudite members of the Victorian literary world were capable of causing annoyance. In 1885, Dr James Murray, the editor of the *Oxford English Dictionary*, moved to Sunnyside on Banbury Road in north Oxford. He needed a scriptorium to hold masses of notes on paper, used to compile the dictionary. The Bursar of St John's was keen to accommodate Dr Murray's

Fig. 18 Spite wall, Silverdale.

wishes and wrote to Albert Dicey, the Vinerian Professor of English Law who lived next door, at number 80, 'You are the only neighbour whom it could annoy, and I should be glad to know if you think it likely to be productive of any annoyance.' The iron structure, covering 15 x 50 feet, was to be situated opposite Professor Dicey's drawing room window, and was therefore deemed to be too great an annoyance to bear, as it would 'prejudice his outlook'. Dicey besieged Murray with complaints. The solution was to lower the structure three feet into the ground and top it with a glass roof. Murray and his lexicographers endured over a decade of extreme heat and cold. The neighbours were still upset about the piled-up bank of earth dug out to sink the corrugated den. However, bushes were planted and, contrary to the trajectory of most other neighbour disputes, the Murrays and the Diceys gradually became friends.[86]

Until 1909, there was no central control or consistency in town planning. Just because there was no overarching planning control, though, it did not mean that development was a free-for-all. Local planning regulations were codified in a variety of by-laws. In many of those towns that had passed private Local Acts for improvement, householders wishing to make structural changes would need to gain permission from the improvement commissioners. Some letters survive. In Hastings, householders sought permission to extend, build coal cellars, move entrances, and even erect scaf-folding. Neighbours would be consulted, or taken into account, when reaching decisions.[87] In London, building regulations had been in place since the aftermath of the Great Fire in 1666, and regula-tions in other towns also developed from fire safety measures. Action could be taken against people who made structural changes or additions without local planning permission. In 1864, two neigh-bouring photographers on London's Euston Road were found to have infringed the regulations by constructing buildings of glass and wood at the back of their houses. The district surveyor took the case to the Clerkenwell Police Court and the photographers were instructed to remove them. The 1909 Planning Act saw the Local Government Board (LGB) established as the central planning authority. Before a local authority could make a formal application to the LGB, they needed to consider objections to proposed alter-ations. The majority of these objections would come from neighbours.[88]

TROMBONES OF CONTENTION

Musical instruments were still causing problems between some neigh-bours, especially when practised by children on Sundays.[89] A columnist in the *Manchester Times* worried about the neighbours of any person obtaining a newly invented piano designed to be played in bed 'to cheer the loneliness of convalescence or the dreariness of chronic sickness'. He asks: 'one can claim protection from the street-grinder, but who's going to interfere with the man next door suffering from jim-jams . . . and [who] insists on working off

"The Rowdy-Dowdy Boys"?'[90] In 1891, a philanthropist based in Liverpool called Lee Jones wrote to his neighbour asking for a piano to be moved to the other side of their dining room. The neighbour, Mr Moores at 'Westleigh', obliged, remarking that 'the walls are not very substantial that is certain'. He assured Jones that he 'may rely on our care in the matter and trust that as long as we are neighbours our relations will always be kindly & neighbourly'.[91] In a letter to his sister, sent from 17 Oakley Crescent in Chelsea, Gissing growled: 'O Dear, O Dear; the wall between our house & the next is terribly thin, and there is some individual next door who practises hymns on the piano all Sunday *with one finger*. I am fond of music, but . . .'[92]

In 1919, *The Times* outlined the types of neighbour noise – 'piano playing, dog barking, and cock-crowing, with motor crank groaning and gramophone grinding thrown in'.[93] These years saw a peak in the production of pianos; an estimated 75,000 in 1910.[94] *The Times* complained that the notion 'every man's house is his castle' was more likely to safeguard the right to *make* noise than to be protected from it. Thus:

> a man maddened by noise goes to his solicitor, and is told:- 'What! The people in the semi-detached house next to you play musical instruments and sing until they are tired, and then the dog takes up the refrain and barks until the cockrel – kept in a coop in the back kitchen – is ready to relieve him. Dear me! But an Englishman's House is his Castle . . .'

Henry Lunn's proposition to establish music ghettos is pertinent in the 1893 case of *Christie v Davey*. The Christies, who had lived at 68 Angell Road, Brixton, since 1889, were a suburban musical family whose sounds annoyed the Davey family next door. James Christie was described in court as being very deaf, 'perhaps fortunately for himself', as he was surrounded by pianists for more than eighteen hours a week. His wife and daughter were accomplished musicians who both played and taught at home. It was stated about Christie's son that 'it seems to be his habit to go down into the kitchen and there practise the violincello from ten o'clock to eleven at night'. The Daveys became increasingly irritated by the sounds coming from next door. On 30 September 1892, Mr Davey wrote to his neighbours in a 'tone calculated to set up the backs of the Plaintiff's family', complaining about their music-making. Soon afterwards he began banging tin trays and hammering on the party wall between the two semis, 'which interfered with the comfort' of the Christies, and affected the lessons. The Christies requested, and were granted, an injunction to prevent this. Judge North, summing up, said, 'I think the party-wall cannot be very substantial' and ruled that noises were 'made deliberately and maliciously for the purpose of annoying' the Christies. The judge also suggested that Master Christie should not start a new piece of music on his violin after eleven o'clock at night. Twenty-six years later, *The Times* used the case to detail the difficulty of resolving neighbour nuisance issues through the courts.[95]

In 1894, one provincial paper included a spoof story about 'a public spirited' doctor, who is questioned about attending his neighbour free of charge. The doctor quips: 'Yes, and glad to do it, He's been practising on the trombone for the last six months and now I have got the chance to put an end to the nuisance.'[96] An advert for the calming tonic 'Mother Seigel's Syrup', sipped by the nervy, alluded to newspaper reports of

the man next door, who will persist in blowing a trombone after 10pm. A trombone is not a sweet-toned instrument assuredly, and a man need not have nervous dyspepsia very badly before it will set his nerves on edge, and destroy his sleep.[97]

At this time, class-consciousness combined with proliferating pianos to create a combative cocktail in which neighbours used their instruments for aural boasting, proving their cultural prowess. Much learning was done at home and many people would have endured the faltering first arpeggios and precocious pizzicato of their neighbours' children. The voice was also an instrument that could annoy as much as delight. The journal *Pick-Me-Up* included this little rhyme in an edition from 1900 (note how one of the Joneses plays a cameo role here):

> SIGNOR JONES has a beautiful voice,
> And his singing is certainly choice,
> And he goes up quite high,
> But we cannot think why,
> When he stops all the neighbours rejoice![98]

Gissing was riled by noises from inside his home as well as those that came from outside. Mostly these bothersome noises were made by his squalling sons and his wife's arguments with the servants. Writing to his friend Clara Collet in June 1896, Gissing revealed that his wife was apt to fight with the servants, and had recently caused such an uproar that the 'neighbours on both sides must certainly have heard the yelling & reviling – which went on for half an hour or more'. In August 1897, his diary included the entry: 'I believe, of all our lodging-houses, there was not one where she [Edith] did not openly quarrel before leaving.'[99]

Gissing was also bothered by one source of external neighbour-hood noise over a protracted period when he lived on Worple Road in Epsom: the sound of a blackguard drum and fife band. He seems to have attracted the attention of the band as early as October 1894, not long after he moved into the house. In a letter to his brother in July 1895, he moaned that the band had been encouraged 'by some people who live in the house opposite ours'. Annoyed that the noise woke his son, he complained to the police. This led to the band being forbidden to play on the street. It did not, however, put an end to Gissing's misery. The hapless author complained to his brother that 'the people opposite now take them *into their garden*, just to spite me'. This noise was occurring 'about once a week'. He asks Algernon if he can think of any legal steps he could take to prevent the noise, but his brother had no suggestions. In a letter written in October 1896, Gissing asks his young son Walter (who

was then living with Gissing's mother) if there were any barking
dogs nearby.

> Here we are plagued with them dreadfully. All through the evening
> they keep rushing out from one house to another, & waking Alfred
> out of his sleep. First a little dog goes 'Bow-wow-wow!' Then a big
> dog goes 'Boh-oh-oh!' Then two little dogs begin to quarrel & snap at
> each other . . . And here comes the drum & fife band, just as I am
> writing. The drum goes 'Bang-bang-bang,' & the fife goes 'Tootle-
> tootle-tootle,' & just when they are opposite our house they make such
> a noise that the windows shake. I am in a rage with them, & should
> like to rush out & fight them with my big walking-stick.

These tribulations made him consider moving out.[100] In 1868, Henrietta Lyttleton of London's Belgrave Square took umbrage at a trio
of German musicians, the third such group to appear on her street
that day. She had given them 'the usual sign to go away' (one
wonders!), but this dismissal was countered by a neighbour throwing
them money and the music played on. The hand that threw the
money belonged to a woman in a house that had previously been
the subject of a complaint by Mr Lyttleton to the police court. It
was musical retaliation.[101]

A case heard at the start of this period threatened to open the
floodgates for neighbour litigation. In 1889, Justice Kekewich delivered his verdict in *Reinhardt v Mentasti*. In converting a Piccadilly
house into a hotel, the Mentasti brothers had erected a stove in a
previously unused basement room. Placed against the wall next
to their neighbour's wine cellar, the heat from the stove ruined
Mr Reinhardt's choicest wines. Judge Kekewich ordered that the
obnoxious stove be removed. The issue at stake was not the reasonable behaviour of the neighbour, but injury to property.[102] Reporting
the case, the *Daily News* was at pains to note that 'it would be
wrong to suppose that the law is eager, or even willing, to grant
protection against the troubles inflicted by one's neighbours'. It
was the extraordinary nature of the damage that led Kekewich

to his conclusion. However, ordinary noises were merely 'inevitable accompaniments of town life, and, whatever be the consequences to nerves and temper, the sufferings they cause are allowed to go unaddressed'.[103] The *Leeds Mercury* was horrified by the verdict – and fretted about a flurry of 'injunctions and interpleaders at the instance of neighbours with fads of different kinds'. A more measured response was delivered to the readers of the *Morning Post*. Litigation, costly and uncertain, would not be used wantonly to 'seek legal redress for trivial inconveniences' as a result of the case.[104]

On 22 June 1894, Mary Chastey and her sister Ellen, who had run a lodging house on Exeter's Southernhay West since 1892, noticed that the dentist next door was filling his backyard with a range of buildings. The dentist, John McKno Ackland, built two new low buildings and raised the height of another building to sixteen feet. According to the Misses Chastey, the effect of this building work was to dampen their basement and make the rooms at the rear of their house undesirable for tenants, on account of the dark and the reduced ventilation. The kitchen staircase was dangerously darkened. The house, formerly free of smells, became stagnant as 'the effluvia penetrated the court-yard into the dwelling house'. The Chastey sisters took their case against the dentist to *nisi prius*, supported by a former tenant, Judge Edge, who inspected the rooms and noticed a new closeness to the air. They were awarded an injunction and £10 damages, and Ackland was instructed to remove the buildings, or come to a financial agreement with the Chasteys. The Court of Appeal overturned the decision and the dentist was found to have committed no legal wrong in reducing the ventilation to the backyards. Eventually the case came before the House of Lords, who suggested a bigger award of damages (£300) to the Chasteys. The sixteen-foot-high addition still stands today.[105]

In crowded city centres, especially in areas occupied by costers and hawkers, near both the wholesale markets and their own sales pitches, neighbours also had to put up with the clutter that came

Fig. 19 John Galt took this photograph of backyards of workers' homes in Spitalfields, East London *c*.1900. This picture reveals proximity.

with sales; produce waiting to be sold, or past being saleable, wagons, hand-carts and donkeys could all get in the way.[106] Often these sellers could not be accommodated in new properties because landlords ruled against warehousing in properties, and so they crowded into the older slum dwellings. On streets lined with carts and barrows, 'a pony or donkey entering or leaving by the front door of a house is no uncommon sight'. A 'number of barrows and a donkey cart' indicated the presence of costers, as did the empty boxes of the fish curers who lived near Billingsgate Market.[107]

In 1883, someone in Half Nichol Street in London's East End had constructed a tall pigeon loft in the backyard (see **Fig. 19** for a similar construction, erected in London's Spitalfields).[108] The height was needed because there was no space to spread the bird accommodation sideways in the tiny yard. Gus Elen, a 'coster comedian' who found music-hall fame in the 1890s, sang about the living conditions of ordinary East End folk. He described in a mock-boastful fashion his garden (really just a yard) and its view. 'If It Wasn't For The 'Ouses in Between' (1894, written by Edgar Bateman and dedicated to George Sims, who argued for housing reform) hears this mock-cockney pretend that his garden, planted up with 'turnip tops and cabbages wot peoples doesn't buy', is the epitome of rural bliss. 'The neighbours finks I grow 'em and you'd fancy you're in Kent.' Without 'the 'ouses in between', you could 'see to 'Ackney Marshes'. In this garden of rotting market produce and a donkey with 'imitation 'orns' (which he is teaching to 'moo just like a cah'), the mockney pretends to enjoy a little *rus in urb*. After poking gentle fun at urban smallholders, Gus Elen himself retired to Thurleigh Avenue, a quiet street in Balham, and bred poultry.[109]

In 1895, a stipendiary magistrate heard how George Hoodley King, a naturalist living on Great Portland Street in London, bred snakes that had a habit of slithering over to the neighbour's house before they reached clients such as the Duke of Wellington and the Countess of Aberdeen. Mrs Taylor, next door, was so scared that she became under the care of a doctor and did not seem to believe King's assertion that the unwelcome visitors were not venomous. Giving evidence in court, King's wife rather cheekily suggested that the snakes were attracted by the large number of black beetles infesting the Taylor residence. The matter had already been raised with the sanitary authorities, who had not identified a nuisance. Nonetheless, the magistrate hummed and hawed about whether this case should come under the Public Health Act (1891) and decided that it did. He made an order for the snakes to be kept securely, and awarded Taylor costs.[110]

UPSETTING NEIGHBOUR ARRANGEMENTS

Suburbia grew up in this period. The semi-detached houses that spread out across the country were filled with possessions that could make the neighbours jealous. There was less social mixing, and social workers stepped into the poor areas. Nellie Benson deplored the lack of interaction between rough and respectable, and Octavia Hill tried to raise the standards of the rough, while the Fabians nosed around poor Lambeth houses. New model dwellings had too many rules for those who needed to work at home and, for some, the suburbs were too far from their workplaces. Overcrowding persisted, resources were stretched and some relationships turned nasty.

An increasing desire for 'encapsulation' in this period saw households disappearing 'behind the garden hedge or yard wall'. Back-to-back dwellers found it more difficult to do this – having no private external space, some water closets were installed in basements, reducing the need to share exterior spaces with neighbours.[111] By-laws banning back-to-backs gradually gave more people access to some outdoor space behind their homes, which promoted individualism and domestic containment. Some people protected their domain with high fences, while rough householders often unashamedly dumped stuff in view of the more respectable neighbours.

We moved into this chapter with the Joneses, and we will move out with one of them; one very hard to keep up with. Lee Jones was the man who asked his neighbour to move a piano in 1891. Two years later, he had formed the Liverpool Food Association after a visit to the slums triggered his interest in the diet of the poor. The society provided cheap meals for children as they left school, and the lady attendants brought food to invalids at home. He renamed his society the League of Welldoers in 1909, as part of a general protest against state intervention, timed to coincide with a landmark review of the Poor Laws. Jones believed that philanthropy should suffice and that it negated the need for an increasingly professional and overpaid cadre of social workers.[112] Others also expressed concern that the formalisation of welfare services (hitherto provided freely amongst the poor) would 'upset neighbourhood arrangements'.[113] Nonetheless, social work continued to develop side by side with philanthropy and mutual aid. Various liberal reforms, including the 1908 Children's Act, the 1906 Provision of School Meals Act, and the

1908 Old Age Pensions Act, marked a watershed in welfare provision that set the foundations for mid-century developments. The 1911 Unemployment and Health Insurance Act formalised the economic activities of the friendly societies by making them responsible for much of the administration of the health insurance scheme.[114] Many women became social workers, and their work (which was often unpaid) lifted some of the burden on people to help their poorer neighbours. The state gradually eased neighbours aside.

5

Semi-detached Neighbours (1919–1944)

Between the First and Second World Wars, suburban development proliferated and much of it was semi-detached. Approximately two million such houses were built, about twice the number of terraced houses and four times the number of detached houses.[1] In 1918, Lloyd George had called for 'Homes fit for Heroes', and the following year the Housing and Town Planning Act gave councils the main responsibility for providing low-rent housing.[2] More than a quarter of the four million homes built between 1918 and 1940 were local-authority properties.[3] New housing estates of the period can be roughly divided into two sorts – council-built working-class flats and houses, and middle-class semis built speculatively for sale. By 1922, Little Collingwood Street, whose inhabitants had posed for a photograph at the start of the twentieth century, had been flattened to make room for the Collingwood Estate. Bullen House, a foreboding five-storey block of flats built by London County Council (LCC), stood over the spot where the residents had looked into the lens two decades earlier.[4]

Watling in Barnet was another new estate. The first residents arrived in 1927, and within a year there were more than 2,000 families, all new neighbours.[5] Not all the people who were displaced when slums were demolished were rehoused in new properties. The new homes were often occupied by people already adequately housed, and their houses were then filled by the former slum-dwellers. Displacement severed neighbourly bonds that had developed over generations. Neighbour was wrenched from neighbour, and new neighbour relationships were formed en masse on the estates. In 1931, a columnist in the *Manchester Guardian* warned that

> the municipalities of Lancashire are now breaking the last retreats of traditional neighbourliness up in an admirable frenzy of slum-clearance . . . poverty is made endurable by company, and they find it hard to accept sometimes that a new house with a garden has also a next-door neighbour to do and to be done by when need presses.[6]

The introduction of rent controls, which froze rental income at 1914 levels, caused the private rental market to shrink and boosted owner-occupation. This was reinforced by building-society loans that enabled increasing numbers of people to buy homes. Although by the end of the 1930s two thirds of homes were still privately rented, home ownership started to become a popular alternative in that decade.[7] Cheap credit allowed house-holders to move to the edges of towns and settle in semis with keyhole porches and sunburst gates. The middle-class semis quickly became cannon fodder for the architectural aesthetes. Osbert Lancaster, who labelled them 'by-pass variegated', noted 'how carefully each householder is provided with a clear view [via bay windows] into the most private offices of his next door neighbour'.[8] Their uniformity irked George Orwell, who saw 'long, long rows of little semi-detached houses . . . The stucco front, the creosoted gate, the privet hedge, the green front door'.[9] In fact, the privacy and opportunities for individual expression enjoyed by these suburban pioneers would have been liberating compared with the tight intimacy of the terraced streets that many had moved from.

The semi quickly became the most desirable type of home for people on middle incomes, and new plan variations were intro-duced. One design partnered the two front doors in the middle with the stairs ascending the party wall, with only two rooms adjoining the neighbouring house, thereby exposing the occupants to less noise.[10] On the other hand, having the doors at the ends effectively removed the need to exchange pleasantries with the neighbours when fumbling for a house key.

As early as 1920, some people were expressing doubts about the quality of the 'Hutches for Heroes'.[11] The lack of men and materials, coupled with high demand, meant that many homes were erected quickly by builders working long hours. George Hicks, the president of the National Federation of Building Trade Operatives, feared that some of the properties were too close together, and would eventually deteriorate into slums. The party walls were so thin that 'one could almost hear one's neighbour change his mind'.[12] The author of an article in the *Manchester Guardian* described the experience of living in the 1930s new-builds: 'we never learnt to suffer gladly the ruin of our evening by the proximity of our neighbour's wireless set on the other side of a thin wall'. In 1935, the author of the article returned to a solid late-nineteenth-century terrace and appreciated the thicker walls. Although flanked by neighbours, 'in three years', he remarks, 'we have heard neither their wireless sets nor their voices from any of our rooms'.[13]

AT THE MERCY OF ANYONE WHO MOVES IN ABOVE

Council and private estates were different. Councils placed limits on changes that tenants could make to their homes. Shared gardens would be cultivated and maintained by the council and doors were repainted at the same time, often in uniform colours. While such controls and conformity signified exclusivity in the Grosvenor Estates of Mayfair, they had a stigmatising and frustrating effect when councils imposed them in poorer areas.

Divided neighbourhoods are common in history. Class suspicions, or even different aspirations within the same class, can be enough to split communities. In December 1934, the residents of a suburban area of Oxford found their path to the shops blocked by brick walls topped with rotating spikes, known as the Cutteslowe Walls. The walls were built by the Urban Housing Company, worried that their houses would not sell with council tenants as neighbours.

Neighbours on either side of a wall were of a similar social status; the difference was that on one side there were private owner-occupiers and on the other local-authority renters. Despite legal challenges (and various attempts to remove them), the walls stood (in a variety of forms) until March 1959, when Oxford City Council compulsorily purchased the land underneath and demolished them.[14]

'The gravest threat to privacy', according to a Mass Observation report, 'comes when two or more families live in the same house.'[15] The slackening pace of house-building, plus population shifts during the First World War, had seen a temporary rise in lodging.[16] People living in divided houses and flats needed to take special care not to annoy their neighbours. A Kensington woman put her finger on the problem: 'the only trouble is you're at the mercy of anyone who moves in above'.[17] The Mass Observers found that the 'desire for privacy, for keeping oneself to oneself, is a powerful motive in modern society'. The best sort of neighbour was 'sociable, but not inquisitive', and would be from the same social class. Some thought that 'er next door was too common; others that 'im over t'road was a snob. Michael Young noted that the massive Becontree Estate was more mixed than most settlements, because the policy of the LCC was not to segregate incoming residents by class. This progressive policy was unpopular. One woman from Roehampton told the Mass Observers that

> they should separate the different kinds of people. Our next-door neighbours are common and use very bad language. The rough people should be put together. I don't want to have a lot to do with my neighbours, but I want to *like* them.[18]

In 1927, a Becontree Estate tenant wrote to the LCC complaining that the 'Smug Suburbia' classes (of which he was a self-proclaimed member) were housed 'cheek by jowl' with 'the brute force class' from the East End tenements. The latter, he thought, were untrained in 'the theory of citizenship'. So much for 'Homes for

Heroes'. Our correspondent was proud of his garden, but described it as being 'at the mercy of a group of boys . . . yelling battling football fiends' who 'all belong to Class 2 and have no right outside my place'. Although grateful for his council house, he was saving up for a place of his own.[19]

The Mass Observation study revealed people's vehement dislike of shared porches and pathways. Cleaning regimes were complex; some neighbours cleaned the porch too much, others too little. Some felt a pressure to clean just because they thought their neighbours would want that. Awkwardness was compounded when porch-sharing neighbours did not get on. The uncertainty triggered by a knock at the door could cause consternation – which household did they want? Autonomy was desired and cherished. This meant having one's own front door. A resident of the Becontree Estate told of a fight on the step; one of her neighbours was 'slapped across the face with a wet flannel' by her porch-sharer. The wife of a bus driver in Roehampton disliked 'having the side entrance so near to the next door one', adding to the interviewer, 'not that I don't get on with them, but you know my meaning, don't you?'[20]

Fig. 20 shows Wide Yard, off York's Hungate, in the early 1930s, an area prone to flood and blighted by slaughterhouses and chicory works.[21] A woman is washing in a dolly tub, with a mangle. By the 1940s, using outdoor spaces for domestic activities such as washing clothes, or even hanging them, was becoming stigmatised. A woman in Fulham thought that chopping wood on the doorstep suggested a declining neighbourhood.[22] Competition for space could turn nasty in these crowded yards. One man recalled fights over clothes lines in the mill towns. 'I once saw a woman advance on her neighbour with a carving knife, only to pass by and cut down a clothes line.'[23]

The Mass Observation report also showed that by 1940, few households still shared a toilet. It was no longer considered acceptable to most people.[24] An earlier study featured poor 'Mrs J', who had to pass eleven toilets and ash bins to get into her Rochdale cul-de-sac. When she sat down to eat, 'someone from a back door

Fig. 20. Wide Yard, York, about 1933.

opposite will come out and flush the WC . . . so it is not very
private'.[25] Sharing a toilet with neighbours was tough for families
with youngsters, whose bladders do not always communicate well
with their brains. Walter Greenwood and his chums interrupted
their neighbours' motions by waiting until the shared toilet was
occupied and then, 'armed with a slat from an orange box at whose
end stood a candle stump fixed in its own grease', they would slide
it through the emptying flap and toast the occupant's bottom.
Becoming a victim of 'arseon' was only one of many risks faced
by neighbours sharing a toilet.[26]

BEING NEIGHBOURLY TO YOUR EQUALS

Wealthy people did not share basic amenities and could select areas
to live in according to the types of people who lived there. In some
areas, groups of like-minds would settle together. In the 1880s,
Chelsea's Tite Street had become home to friends James McNeill

Whistler and Oscar Wilde (as well as John Singer Sargent and Algernon Mitford). When Whistler and Wilde's 'vigorous and volatile' friendship turned sour, it must have become awkward being neighbours.[27] In contrast, the Mall Studios in Hampstead seemed a more harmonious area; amongst the artists there in the 1930s lived Ben Nicholson and Barbara Hepworth, Henry Moore and Cecil Stevenson. The critic Herbert Read also lived nearby and called the area a 'nest of gentle artists'.[28] Ben Nicholson's sister, Nancy, and Robert Graves, her new husband, joined a different set – the literati on the hill – when they moved to Dingle Cottage, at the bottom of John Masefield's garden on Oxford's Boar Hill in 1919. Nancy set up a business with one of their neighbours (the Hon. Mrs Michael Howard), a grocer's shop that opened briefly in 1920 next to the house of the Masefields. Constance Masefield disliked the tourists who came to the shop and the business collapsed, causing some ill-feeling amongst the illustrious neighbouring families. Graves saw much of Masefield, in his garden shed, writing 'Reynard the Fox'. Other neighbours included Masefield's predecessor as Poet Laureate, Robert Bridges, who, according to Graves, dominated the neighbourhood 'with his bright eye, abrupt challenging manner, and a flower in his buttonhole'. In 1921, when Graves had moved to Islip, his friend T.E. Lawrence wrote to him declaring, 'I think it's good to be out of your cottage; Mrs H [Mrs Michael Howard] and Mrs M [Constance Masefield] and the Laureate [Robert Bridges] were three overpowering neighbours.'[29]

In *Point Counter Point*, Aldous Huxley has the young working-class socialist Frank Illidge declare that 'The rich haven't got any neighbours.' In contrast, for the poor, living cheek by jowl, there was 'no refined and philosophical ignoring' of the neighbours, and in extremis, 'there can be no question of refusing' to help. Illidge described his mother's reciprocal childcare arrangement with Mrs Craddock next door. On posher streets the rich 'never perform a neighbourly action' or expect neighbourly help, because they can pay for help; they 'hire servants to simulate kindness'. When nurses and governesses were paid to care, there was a lack of concern and

knowledge between rich neighbours that was compounded by the
physical detachment of big houses on generous plots. Addressing
his comments to Walter Bidlake, a young journalist, Illidge states:

> Each of you is boxed up in his own secret house. There may be tra-
> gedies going on behind the shutters; but the people next door don't
> know anything about it . . . Ignorance is insensitive bliss. In a poor
> street misfortune can't be hidden. Life's too public. People have their
> neighbourly feeling kept in constant training. But the rich can never
> have a chance of being neighbourly to their equals . . . [30]

Oral histories from former residents of York's Hungate slums
revealed how neighbours would 'muck in' if a mother fell sick and
would feed her family.[31] James Douglas, writing in 1934, said that
neighbourliness was 'one of the advantages of poverty . . . Poor
folk nurse each other when they are ill. They tell their troubles to
each other.'[32] Bristol neighbours helped a frail and deaf widow by
employing her as a 'knocker-up' in the mornings, remembering
how she had nursed their family members in the past.[33]

Are we therefore to pity the unloved rich who lacked real neighbours? Indeed so, according to the reminiscences of a retired social
worker, laid up in bed and nursed by her maid-of-all-work. Her
mind drifted back to her days of visiting in the slums, and she
remembered the 'little acts of kindness and of love' done there in
the name of neighbourliness. There, a 'busy mother thinks nothing
of sitting up all night with a sick neighbour', of cleaning, caring
and arranging funerals, all 'as a matter of course'. Affluence bought
privacy. Households with staff and gadgets failed to realise the
plight of households 'without these auxiliaries when some disaster
overtakes them'. Some believed that care and concern in the slums
is 'a calculating selfishness' geared to build up credit when their
own times get hard. Our social worker disagrees, seeing only
altruism.[34]

Batch baking, large broths and conserves would be shared, and
food was often swapped, lent and borrowed.[35] Northerner Richard

Hoggart described his experiences of neighbourly relationships in Hunslet, a suburb of Leeds. He contrasts working-class and middle-class habits in the first part of the twentieth century.[36] His description of working-class relationships as very local and based on mutual exchange and support is similar to Keith Wrightson's portrait of neighbours four centuries earlier. Neighbours would borrow a glass of milk or a bowl of sugar. Ted Willis, who later created *Dixon of Dock Green*, was about to tuck into his tea in 1920s Tottenham when his mother plucked it from the stove and took it to a family of six nearby. Young Ted was walloped for complaining and told, 'Stop whining! You're hungry. They're starving.'[37]

Poorer neighbourhoods were more tightly knit; but tight knitting has greater tension. Jerry White's account of Campbell Bunk is equivocal; support was motivated by both altruism and self-interest. White concludes that the 'machinery of mutual aid was fashioned out of sympathy for the plight of others; and from the rational assumption that all might sooner or later need assistance themselves'.[38] These complicated unwritten obligations could be suffocating. A young woman in a Surrey village declared her neighbour to be 'a horrid woman' who she pretended to like.

> The awful part is that she's such a dirty woman when she gives you a cup of tea, the cup's dirty. I used to refuse all the meals, but I had to go in at night and have a cup of tea to keep her quiet. She took my bread for me, and paid the butcher and baker and all that, so *I couldn't fall out with her* [author's italics].[39]

This despised neighbour, we go on to learn, is also a 'scandalmonger' with an especial interest in illegitimate pregnancies.

NOT AS NEIGHBOURLY AS BEFORE

Households could share toilets, cesspits, washing lines and quite a lot of personal information. 'Popping in and out' was common in one area of Bristol, but unwritten conventions prevented visiting in the early afternoon and chats only resumed once the children were back from school.[40] Visits were often brief and with a practical purpose. Even children would often wait outside, on the doorstep, rather than go into a neighbour's house. In his childhood, Hoggart would knock at a neighbour's door and call, 'Is your Joe in? Can he come out?' He did not expect to go into the house, but would wait on the pavement for Joe to appear.[41] Middle-class neighbours were linked through their children. The parents of school friends arranged babysitting circles, took in parcels, fed pets and watered plants.

Involvement with neighbours, either from a desire to be helpful or an urge to be inquisitive, was supposed to be more prevalent in the north of England. Southerners were thought to keep themselves to themselves.[42] However, many did not conform to these stereotypes and there were wide variations between neighbourhoods and streets. Carrie Telford, remembering Lambeth in the 1920s, contrasted the 'white curtain streets' – Roupell, Whittlesea and Thede – with rough-and-ready Ethelm Street.[43] Stella Davies' home in Moss Bank, Crumpsall, backed on to a rough street. 'We were not allowed to speak, much less play, with the children in the street.' On the other side of her house lived a family with a nursemaid – '*They* were not allowed to play with *us*.'[44] A newspaper article from 1931 declared that it is 'certainly true that even Lancashire is not as neighbourly as she was, but there are still hundreds of dim streets and dark alleys where neighbours are a godsend and their help kills the sting of poverty'. People did not bake or wash for a sick neighbour 'as they once did' (thus contradicting the ex social worker quoted earlier), although they were still willing to run errands, care for children and provide coal for the hearth. Looking back a generation, the article's author sees neighbours sharing pans big enough to cook a sheep's head; the reciprocal nature of early-twentieth-century neighbouring is stressed:

If you had pegs, you were probably short of a roasting tin. If you had a posser or dolly, you were most likely without a stiff brush for swilling the backyard flags, or perhaps a flat iron. Nobody had everything, and there was something like communal use, if not ownership. One small-tooth comb did for the street, and, if the street was not too long, one cobbler's last for reironing the row's clogs.

The author thinks that poverty is less blatant in 1931 and so the 'demand on neighbours not so inclusive and exacting'.[45]

By the early 1930s, neighbours tended to share extras, not basic domestic equipment; they were handing down clothes but not sharing combs. Back in 1911, Asquith's Liberal government introduced national unemployment and health insurance schemes, which had by 1920 covered most manual workers. The scheme lost funding when masses became unemployed in the depression, and in 1931 it was replaced by means-tested unemployment benefits. The 'dole' was made the responsibility of local authorities in the 1929 Local Government Act, via Public Assistance Committees.[46] Increasing state intervention in financial crises, plus the swelling ranks of social workers in the 1920s, suppressed neighbourly responses to the plight of those living nearby.

A case heard at Manchester County Court tested the boundaries of kindly neighbourliness. The case centred on a claim by Adelaide Hanley of Junction Street for £10 from her former neighbour, Ernest Nicholls. Mrs Hanley and Mrs Nicholls had been school friends and were neighbours in Junction Street in 1925 when Mrs Nicholls' daughter contracted scarlet fever. Hanley was a nurse and arranged to care for the girl every day. She considered herself to be professionally engaged. However, the Nichollses claimed that they understood the services had been offered in the 'feeling of neighbourly friendliness'. While Hanley was tending the girl, her own son was cared for by a sitter. The judge declared that the services rendered had gone beyond acts of neighbourly kindness and set up a timetable of payments from the Nichollses to their former neighbour.[47]

Neighbours continued to help each other in emergencies. The number of hospital births rose from approximately 15 per cent in

1927 to over 50 per cent in 1946.[48] Numbers of health visitors also swelled and access to welfare clinics improved dramatically.[49] The involvement of neighbours in childbirth contracted. In the poorest areas (and in rural areas especially), changes were slow. Responding to a proposed scheme for home helps in 1943, Mrs N.K. Taylor from Bexhill-on-Sea penned a letter to the *Picture Post* expressing a plea for such a scheme to include 'maternity-trained home-helps' (middle-aged female volunteers). Noting that most young mothers giving birth at home 'have to rely . . . on relatives or neighbours', Mrs Taylor said she had been both a neighbour needing help, and a helping neighbour. She had twice found herself 'having to rush in and do duty as midwife'. In 1917, the Women's Cooperative Guild identified a need for home helps, and hoped these would do away with 'crude arrangements' with 'gossiping neighbours'. Jane Lewis has argued that 'in prescribing middle-class ideas of responsible motherhood . . . policies often discouraged already existing patterns of mutual aid between women'. In some neighbourhoods these persisted, however. *The Motherhood Book*, published in 1935, listed various necessities that would have simply been unavailable to many working-class women, who shared amongst themselves even the most basic equipment such as bowls and jugs.[50]

Childbirth can be planned, but other events are more sudden and surprising. The *Manchester Guardian* reported how a family got to know their new neighbours in an emergency shortly after moving in. A girl had accidentally locked herself in her bedroom. In the effort to free her, the family had 'made many acquaintances with or without ladders or a knack with locks'.[51] Neighbours were often first on the scene of domestic disaster. John Jones of Chester injured his head trying to rescue his neighbours from a fire in 1929. He rushed out of bed when he heard the commotion and in the course of saving the grandmother fell from a bedroom window.[52]

Residents of the new Watling Estate were pushed together in response to antagonism from the established neighbourhood that surrounded their homes. A letter in the *Hendon and Finchley Times* in December 1927 that criticised the interlopers led to the formation of a Residents' Association. It published the *Watling Resident*, which first appeared in May 1928 and said, 'Beyond our immediate neighbours we know no one on this great estate . . . The Watling Residents' Association hoped to bring together those whom convention forbids to introduce themselves'. Watling comprised many people from similar circumstances in St Pancras and Islington. Although they had not been near neighbours before, they at least had 'a common geographical background of experience.'[53]

Neighbourhood solidarity was common in the 1930s. Tenants refused to pay rents en masse for facilities that were too stretched and conditions that were insanitary. They would only do so when landlords provided better facilities or reduced rents, or the courts compelled them to pay. Rent strikes were not new – several were staged before the First World War, but these mostly failed.[54] Campaigns in London in the late 1930s were more successful. Two hundred and forty families living in model dwellings in Bethnal Green decided that their homes in Quinn Square were no longer models of anything good. Taps were shared by four households and toilets by two. A playground in the centre of the square had been built over, reducing light and air; the toilets were lockless, the roof washhouses were unusable and the rooms were damp. An unemployed tenant 'on the Means Test' faced eviction. The tenants 'sensed the danger' and blocked it. At a meeting they discussed rents, agreed they were too high and decided not to pay. The landlord undertook to make repairs, and promised that legal action would not be taken against any tenant without prior consultation with the Tenants' Association.[55]

Further east, the housewives of the Hanbury Buildings in Poplar's Ming Street spent several weeks picketing the doors, armed with brooms, to prevent the bailiffs from getting in. Their refusal to pay landed twenty-six tenants in Bow County Court in November 1939. An architect giving evidence for their defence said that conditions were the worst he had seen; water closets were separated only by sheets of corrugated iron, and were described as 'disgustingly insanitary . . . things have got so worn that all the cleaning in the world would do no good'. The judge decided that most of the tenants could lawfully withhold money.[56]

THEM AT NINETY-SIX

In the mid 1930s, the journalist Hugh Massingham decided to make a journalistic foray into the East End slums. He masqueraded as a rent collector and took a room. The neighbours quickly became suspicious, whispering about him and suspecting him of spying on them. An overcrowded family thought he was a sanitary inspector. A prostitute feared he was collecting information against her. Each neighbour recognised the position of power that a person with knowledge of their secrets might have. Massingham faced collective hostility; he was watched and rebuked, his milk bottles were 'filled with watered carbolic acid', and rubbish was hurled through his window. It culminated when a neighbour broke in, smashed his crockery and did 'his business in the frying pan and left it in the middle of the table'.[57]

Massingham explained that in summer, people occupying upper floors 'did not stay indoors if they could possibly help it'. Instead, they crowded on to the streets to keep away from the bugs and the stifling heat.[58] One man counted twenty-three people sitting on chairs outside their homes along one street in Preston. Another thought the 'ruddy street was full of chairs', with more out than in.[59] In a photograph of Washington Street, Nottingham (**Fig. 21**), from the early 1930s, the women have hung washing across the street. The officious-looking man in the black hat is a stranger amongst the female neighbours. He will have to risk his dignity by ducking under the linens. The women stare at him warily, waiting until he has passed to continue their conversation.

Commentators condescended that gossiping was symptomatic of the wasted lives of the poor. Carrie Telford remembered the gossiping women of 1920s Lambeth, on shabby Ethelm Street, 'their arms folded, their sleeves rolled up. Outside the doors jawing to one another, you know.' Respectable women did not join in.[60]

Fig. 21 Washington Street, Nottingham, 1930s.

Constance Harris surveyed the social conditions in Bethnal Green between 1925 and 1926 and was especially critical of 'slatternly women who stand for hours at the street door, with arms akimbo, and dishevelled hair'. Harris suggested that 'tittle tattle, and ennui' found 'an outlet in idling and gossiping in the streets' and criticised the dilatory nature of the women's lives.[61] Malicious gossip was condemned. In his autobiography, Walter Greenwood recalled back-biting Mrs Flarty. This unpopular character was to be seen 'with sweeping-brush in hand . . . perpetually appearing on her doorstep on the look-out for somebody with whom to discuss other people's affairs'. She spoke of neighbours not by name, but by house number, 'them at ninety-six'.[62]

A Market Drayton widow supporting five children on the dole wrote anonymously to the *Picture Post* in 1939 arguing that widows should get higher contributions. She wrote, 'I hate to receive PA [dole from the Public Assistance Committee] and do not wish my neighbours to know.'[63] Similar reticence was evident in another letter written to the *Picture Post* that year. 'Quite nice looking', 'Miss—— Lancs', with 'a sweet temper' and fond of children and animals, wondered if the public might help her find a husband, but added 'please will you keep my address out . . . as all our family read the PICTURE POST, then we lend it to next door'.[64]

Stanley Spencer painted his Cookham neighbours. He loved the 'unhappeningness' of Cookham and the way neighbours helped each other when the River Thames flooded. He wrote in 1945 of his 'small house', Cliveden View, 'I don't feel inclined to leave it. It is very quiet; you don't hear any wireless from the cottages near.'[65] In his later years he forged a close relationship with a neighbouring family to whom he would go for meals and to listen to the radio.[66] In one painting from a series called 'Domestic Scenes' of 1935–6, Spencer captured cherished moments when Annie, his elder sister, would pass gifts and flowers to her cousin over the hedge that separated their houses.[67]

I AM ASHAMED TO BE SEEN GOING IN

Just as Britain joined the Second World War, the *Picture Post* carried an advert for Rinso, which depicted a domestic battle for the whitest washing being fought amongst the nation's housewives. 'Neighbours stare with envy', apparently, at Mrs Howell's laundry.[68] The suburban semi offered many of these opportunities for keeping up with the Joneses. Front gardens were the arena for competitive display. Outdoor activities usually took place in back gardens because the fronts were too exposed. George Orwell thought suburban gardens were nearly identical, apart from a bare patch in the middle of the lawn, which indicated the presence of children.[69] These were more private spaces, whose fences could be augmented by trellis near the house, allowing people to take the air in their pyjamas without being spotted by neighbours.

A 1938 Paint Marketing Council campaign exploited shame and neighbour envy. A smart behatted couple exclaim, 'Our front door DOES want doing . . . *I'm ashamed to be seen going in.*' Householders were urged to consider the indignity of a dingy and scruffy house – a lick of paint might make all the difference.[70] The families settling into the new housing estates got lino, curtains and furniture on hire purchase to avoid falling behind their neighbours. Hearing a 'wireless next door' in the homes built for heroes on the Watling Estate resulted in an 'obligation to bring home a wireless'.[71]

In his *Gardener's Bed Book*, published in 1929, Richardson Wright returns to that vintage chestnut, the old Joanna. The introduction of the piano made ownership of instruments more accessible, and piano-playing became a widespread aspiration for the socially ambitious. Wright suggests that 'parents subjected their children to music lessons' as part of the jig that was 'keeping up with the Joneses'.[72] An advert placed in the *Picture Post* in 1938 declared that a Barnes Piano 'is the admiration of your neighbours' and included details of a hire-purchase scheme.

The Royal Mail made a short film in 1934 to promote the Post Office Telephone Service. The Petts and the Potts were introduced living in adjacent semi-detached houses amongst the 'Paradise Building Plots'. The Petts' daughter practises the piano in 'Peacehaven'. Next door, in 'Kismet', the childless Potts live a suave and languid existence. Mr Pott and Mr Pett also work in adjoining offices and leave work simultaneously but studiously ignore each other. The Petts get a telephone, which transforms their lives; groceries are delivered and outings planned. Mrs Pott enviously watches her neighbours leave for a picnic in a taxi. Eventually the men start to acknowledge each other after work. The film ends with a convoluted tale involving a burglar who is thwarted by the initiative of Miss Pett dialling 999 on the new family telephone.[73] The Petts and the Potts could have saved money, as other neighbours did, by having a shared party line fitted. The advantage was a cheaper connection, but this was at the cost of some convenience and privacy. If one party picked up their phone and found it was in use by the other, the accepted practice was to return the handset to the cradle and wait. This considerateness was indicated to the other party by a click, but it was possible for a sharing neighbour to hear a gossip-worthy snippet on the line before bowing out.[74]

WHO IN LAW IS MY NEIGHBOUR?

James Atkin was born in 1867. His future wife, Lizzie, was born 'within twelve days and 100 yards' of James. However, Atkin is not here to represent neighbourly love. Atkin was a judge, and he handed down a landmark judgement in a negligence case that came to be known as the 'Neighbour Principle'. He sought to ensure that people consider caring for others (such as customers) as if they were a neighbour. Atkin puts it like this, 'Do unto your neighbour as you would that he should do unto you.' He asked, 'Who in law is my neighbour?' and gave the answer, 'Persons who are so closely and directly affected by my act that I ought reasonably to have them in contemplation as being so affected when I am directing my mind to the acts or omissions which are called into question.' This principle remains the classic test for liability in negligence cases.[75] If a person does not ensure they keep their property sound (through negligence), it could become a nuisance to the neighbours.

After the mid twentieth century, more people wanted to move to the countryside and rising car ownership made this easier. Some rural migrants started to complain about the sensations of rural life. In October 1935, Gerald Montagu, the owner of a poultry farm in Thorpe near Egham in Surrey, gained new neighbours. Not the Capulets, but the newly-wed Leemans. Montagu was the son of Lord Swaythling and he also had a little place in London's Belgrave Square. Thorpe Cottage did not turn out to be a quiet place for Mr and Mrs Leeman to start their married life. The cottage was one hundred yards from an orchard in which several hundred birds, including cockerels, were given free run. The Leemans were woken at two o'clock in the morning and could not return to sleep until after seven o'clock. They slept 'with cotton wool in their ears and the windows closed'. Constance became ill. Bernard Bruton, the previous owner of their cottage, claimed that he did not leave the property solely because of the noise, although he did compare the clamour to that of a 'football crowd cheering a cup-tie', and another witness described the noise as 'three cornets, two of which were out of tune'. Various witnesses for the defence (all countrymen) said they were scarcely disturbed or woken by the fowl. Justice Greaves-Lord ruled that Montagu should reorganise his poultry within a month. A farmer twenty-five miles away offered a more remote home for the cockerels, allowing the Leemans to sleep peacefully.[76]

Not everybody sought quiet; they wanted sonic normality, and normality is a subjective thing. Ruth Durant kicked off her absorbing account of the Watling Estate by revealing 'The Problem' on the Estate:

> One afternoon in the autumn of 1927, early in the history of the Watling Estate, a woman banged loudly at the door of her neighbour. When it was opened she cried out: 'What has happened?' 'Why,' said her neighbour, 'what should have happened: what is the matter?' 'Everything is so terribly quiet,' said the first woman, still frightened to death.[77]

Another woman, who had been rehoused in Kentish Town, complained that her new neighbourhood was not friendly enough because 'There's nothing going on. As I say, I like a jolly good fight to watch. Mind you, I don't want to be in it.'[78] This theme of anomie in the sanitised world of the new suburb is one that recurs in many places and through into the 1970s.

ALL NEIGHBOURS ARE NOT LOVESOME[79]

Over time the sources of noise have come and gone, but dogs have always been constant companions. Mrs E. Palmer of Kingswood in Bristol wrote to the *Picture Post* in September 1940 to tell everyone about her 'nice dog with a silky golden brown coat'. He 'playfully chases round, sometimes over my neighbour's garden plants, where there are a few old cabbages and stuff'. When the neighbours object to the antics of her nice dog, she chains him up, but then he 'barks and whines and the neighbours object even to that' and become 'not very polite'. The advice from *Picture Post* was straightforward and gratifying to her neighbours – 'Change either your dog or your neighbours.'[80]

Children were a common source of neighbourhood noise and nuisance. Their inconsiderateness and ebullient playfulness could annoy. The diary of Sydney Spencer, Stanley's brother, reveals a scrape with a neighbour. Both brothers 'got decidedly punctured by Mr Parsons catching us on his tin sheds and swearing at us, throwing the walnuts [they were scrumping] at us'.[81] A report into 'Noise in the Working Class Flats' commissioned by the Ministry of Health in the mid 1930s suggested that pipes should be located 'out of the reach of children, for their noise of impacts against a pipe can be carried to considerable distances'.[82] During the Second World War, some citizens were relieved when children were evacuated away to spoil the peace of the countryside.[83]

The Mass Observation study of 'People's Homes' found that neighbour noise was only a significant problem for people in flats. The Mass Observation team wondered if noises might get on people's nerves in the new flats 'precisely because their "nerves" were already somewhat edgy from having to live in an unaccustomed proximity to their neighbours'. Some suggested that post-war buildings should be more soundproofed. One tenant complained that 'you never get any peace . . . you can hear every little noise next door . . . You can hear all that's going on, but you've got to make allowances.' Some people were inhibited, fearful of disturbing their neighbours. One resident complained that the 'sliding door to the bathroom is bad. It makes a noise, and we can't use the bath late in the evening because of disturbing others.'[84]

Littlehampton, a Sussex seaside town, was the unlikely birthplace of a series of poison-pen letters. This local difficulty came to the attention of the nation in 1921 when Rose Gooding, a woman twice convicted for writing letters to her neighbours, had her convictions quashed on appeal. More letters had circulated while she was imprisoned, making it clear that she had not been the author. A laundress, Edith Emily Swan, the daughter of a painter and plumber, had lived on Western Road since her birth in 1891. Swan and her siblings could be the children in the photograph in **Fig. 7** on page 69, which was taken outside their house. Swan had sought to incriminate Gooding, her neighbour, but was herself eventually charged with defamatory libel after 'indescribably filthy' letters had been received by another neighbour. Letters continued to circulate, and one woman assaulted another, whom she incorrectly suspected of being the author. Following a sting operation, involving stamps doctored with invisible ink by the Post Office, a subsequent trial in 1923 found Swan guilty of sending libellous letters containing 'indecent words' to Charles Gardner, a sanitary inspector who lived on the street. What is not clear is why Swan, a resident of the street from birth, would want to frame one neighbour and send filthy letters to others. Letter-receiving neighbours claimed to have been on friendly terms with her. When Justice Travers Humphreys, the prosecuting counsel in the trial, published his memoirs, he suggested that Swan, a spin-ster of thirty, had become 'unhinged probably as the result of repressed sexual instincts', and also hinted at feelings of social and moral superiority. Gooding lived with her sister, Miss Russell, described by Humphreys as having 'somewhat loose morals', with illegitimate children to prove it. The Gooding family, headed by William, a seafarer of uncertain employment, was judged by Humphreys to be a 'slightly rougher class than the Swans, Miss Swan in particular being a noticeably modest decent type of woman'. Humphreys concludes that 'in the restricted circle in which she lived and moved, Edith Swan was a real public danger'.[85]

A series of letters written between 1937 and 1942 in Pinner epit-omises the mean-mindedness of some neighbour relations. Maud and Herbert Hatch lived in a large house next to the vicarage in Pinner. In the summer of 1937, whilst the vicar, the Reverend Eric Barnes, was on holiday, Maud started to write letters about the rebuilding of the vicarage. The Hatches had recently installed a new window, but on scrutinising the plans for the new build, they discovered it would be blocked by his garage. Complex negotiations via a firm of solicitors and a churchwarden called Mr Hogg resulted in the moving of the window, and changes were made to the vicarage plans, on the understanding that the Hatches would make 'no further objections to the building . . . now or in the future'. In December 1937 the churchwarden expressed his hope that 'these differences are settled' and that 'friendly relations' could be restored. However, in April 1939, Herbert Hatch wrote to their holy neighbour about his barking dog. In 1942, they were again at loggerheads, and Maud wrote to Hogg ('as a friend') letting him know her regret that she felt compelled to engage a solicitor after Rev. Barnes had 'blacked out the light of one of our windows and refuses to do anything about it'. Mrs Hatch claimed that poplar trees growing near the boundary threatened the structural integrity of the Hatch property and their pipework, and blocked light to their drawing room. She asked for five trees to be felled and crassly appealed to war sentiment, noting that it was 'not only unkind but unpatriotic to shut out your neighbour's light in these days when we are asked to save every scrap we can'.[86]

BLITZ SPIRIT

Advertisements during the war often had a didactic message. An advert for blackout curtains appealed to a sense of responsibility towards the neighbours. 'Blackout makeshifts', it shouted, 'are depressing – they are dangerous to you and your neighbours – they are a positive nuisance.'[87] In 1941, Exide Batteries warned people, 'Never allow your radio to play too loudly. Remember that your neighbours may be on war work and will want to sleep in the day.'[88] Not everybody wished for such considerateness; Peter Bowles's autobiography reveals how his grandfather would listen to the wartime wireless news in the evening using a tumbler pressed against the neighbour's wall.[89]

The gas-masked Southend neighbours in **Fig. 22** chat over a fence in a beautifully staged photograph taken in March 1941. Joyce Storey

Fig. 22 Neighbours in Southend.

recalled the huddles of women who chatted on her street during the 1940s, 'with the metal polish tins still in their hands'. Indulging in neighbourly tattle had long been seen as something akin to being a spendthrift; they made an unprofitable use of valuable time. Don Haworth noted that two women were tut-tutted when they put down their pails of chamber-pot waste to talk when en route to the ash tip.[90] Such censure was exacerbated during the war.

The war probably saw an intensification of neighbourly relations, because in emergencies neighbours were often first on the scene. Many families were split up, causing lonely people to seek solace with neighbours. One *Manchester Guardian* journalist noticed a 'social reformation' in his suburb: 'with the threat of invasion co-operation and resourcefulness have flourished amazingly. Mere friendliness has blossomed into communal effort.' People brought their snowbound neighbours provisions, and teas were passed over the fence (it was better to heat only one kettle). Bartering also helped vary the neighbours' diets.

> Mrs Y. who keeps hens, successfully barters two eggs for enough spinach for four from her neighbour, while Mrs Smith is heard making a pact with Mrs Jones that when either has sufficient material to make cake or buns she shall spare the other a portion of the finished product.[91]

Noting that 'some neighbours are loath to lend' gardening equipment, a letter to the *Picture Post* in 1943 suggested that Neighbours' Gardening Clubs be formed, to organise the distribution of tools, mowers and thinned seedlings.[92] Women met in each other's houses while husbands were away fighting, or manning the ARP lookout posts. Communal knitting would be a way to share materials and gain companionship whilst also being useful to the war effort – churning out socks, mittens and helmets for fighters and evacuees.[93] Amy Riley, a retired teacher from Brighton, was one of the Mass Observation diarists during the war. In April 1942, she mentions the talk about food shared during knitting get-togethers:

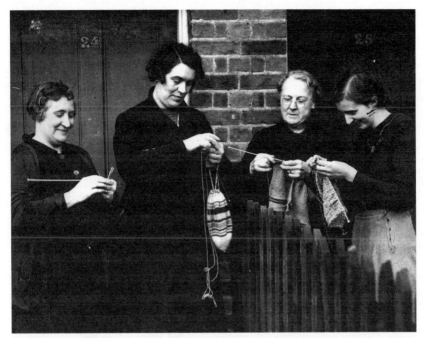

Fig. 23 Women knitters in Bayford, Hertfordshire, 1940.

This rationing makes for neighbourliness; some one [*sic*] said they go to each other saying 'What can I get from you this week? I have more tea than I want.' And if one goes away for [the] week-end she tells her milkman to leave her milk with Mrs So-and-So.[94]

This photograph in **Fig. 23** is also staged; women did not stand on their doorsteps knitting because it would have spoilt the tension in the garment. Knitting is for sitting. Like the photograph of the gas-mask-wearing women, this image was propaganda created to cultivate neighbourly feelings and communal effort in wartime.

Some Good Neighbours schemes had been established in towns in the interwar years – Mrs Walter Wild presided over one set up in Manchester in 1934 to provide respite care for parents or carers of the infirm and old. Mrs Hardy founded the Voluntary Unofficial Aunts in the north for similar purposes.[95] The war years saw Good Neighbour groups forming for civil defence. Most were fire-watch schemes. In 1940, in Hull, a League of Good Neighbours was set up, overseen by air wardens. In every residential street there was a householder who would provide a kettle, spare blanket, hot-water bottles and 'an open door'.[96] By February 1941, the *Manchester Guardian* was able to state patriotically (although probably also exaggeratedly) that enemy bombs had not seriously affected war production 'because of groups of "good neighbours" who have raced to the help of every factory which has been bombed'. One task performed by these groups was to stock tarpaulins to protect buildings with damaged roofs.[97] Increasing numbers of these fire-watching schemes were established across the country. By April 1941, 100,000 Mancunians were involved.[98] A young civil servant living in Vincent Road, London, described his local association in his Mass Observation diary, picking out details from the first communiqué. Names of male neighbours, and their house numbers were listed – put into three fire-service crews. Welfare providers and first-aiders were identified, as were pail, ladder and hose storers, and everyone was reminded that 'All your neighbours are concerned in your welfare and it truly is a case of "All for each and each for all".' The civil servant noted that 'before this thing started father knew very few people in the road – 2 or 3 chaps "to talk to" – 2 or 3 more on nodding terms . . . but now knows nearly all the men in the street'.[99]

'Excited speculation about the dawning of a new democratic spirit rooted in neighbourly responses to the threat of bombing was commonplace in the autumn of 1940 – even *The Times* ran an enthusiastic leader on the subject', explained James Hinton in his account of Mass Observation diarists during the war. In July 1940, Matthew Walton, one of the diarists, planned a communal shelter with his next-door neighbour. Walton enjoyed the community spirit brought out by the endeavour and wrote: 'My neighbours have lost that air of suspicious respect for me as a schoolteacher, and grant me instead the friendly respect of a good worker.' The raids were infrequent, however, and neighbours started to ignore the sirens. The little-used shelter flooded. Walton tired of pumping water from it and resigned from the shelter committee.[100]

Fig. 24 Neighbours putting up Anderson air-raid shelters in their gardens during the Second World War. In this photograph of neighbours erecting their garden shelters, taken sometime in 1940, there was still a party wall between the neighbouring families, even at the end of the garden.

Some communal Anderson shelters were constructed in the middle of the street, especially where gardens were too small for household shelters. People also crowded on to London Underground platforms. Some challenged the right of neighbours to bring pets (including a 'monstrous tabby' and a 'cage of love birds') into shared shelters.[101]

The street warden visited Nella Last, another Mass Observation diarist, in October 1940. He asked about the Lasts' ability to provide equipment such as buckets, ladders and blankets, and informed Nella that he thought she and 'Mrs Atkinson next door would keep open house if we had bad trouble', flattering her (he thought) that, 'you're both kind of soothing bodies'. Nella was amused. Derek Orchard in East Finchley remembers that his family 'became very friendly with our neighbours, especially following the outbreak of the war, as one does at times of crisis, with Air Raid Wardens and

Fire Watch teams being set up in the area'.[102] However, the *Picture Post* featured a letter in May 1941 from a W.H. Berry from High Road, Chadwell Heath, describing the apathy surrounding neighbourhood fire-watch crews. The writer shamed the 'thousands of idle folk in so-called "safe" areas who wait for their neighbours to form fire-parties but never think of doing anything themselves'.[103]

An earlier edition of the *Picture Post* carried the story of three neighbouring families from Sudbury who combined efforts to share catering. Each made two meals per week. Meals were cooked in one kitchen but then eaten privately (except Sunday lunch, which was shared at Mrs Turner's house).[104] In an exhibition on fuel economy opened by Major Gwilym Lloyd George in December 1942, a cooking demonstration suggested that housewives should offer to cook something for their next door neighbour whenever the oven was on.[105] These ideas were not universally embraced; H.T. Jackson of Hook Road in Epsom thought the scheme for communal eating would 'break up the sacred and indissoluble unity of the family'. Jackson 'would as soon take my family to feed out in a common trough'.[106] Maybe his neighbours would have preferred that. A Manchester businessman quoted in a Mass Observation report from November 1942 expressed a similar sentiment: 'Cooperation would not work. I would not let *my* wife cook or wash for the people next door.'[107] Some thought that co-operation was only for the poor and decried the exhortation to sit round a fireside conserving fuel with their neighbours, one chuntering that 'it would have to be a damned good neighbour'.[108]

As a boy, Derek Orchard lived in a cul-de-sac of two dozen similar houses in East Finchley, next door to an Austrian couple and their son during the war. The families chatted over the garden fence on Sundays. One day the police chief informed Orchard's father that radio signals had been intercepted during an air raid, and these were traced to the house next door. Mr Orchard helped the police trap the enemy spies, and before long, radio equipment was discovered in the neighbour's fridge. The Austrians were taken away and a magistrate's clerk from Macclesfield moved in.[109]

In July 1940, Harold Nicolson, from the Ministry of Information, acted to reassure the public that government warnings of the likes of 'loose lips sink ships' were not threatening conversations between neighbours over the fence: 'We have no wish to restrict human converse or to damp neighbourly gossip . . . We want people to be more friendly and neighbourly than they have been'.[110] Other departments gave contradictory advice. The Ministry of Food appealed for people to 'rat on a neighbour' they suspected of black-market profiteering. This led J.T. Newton of 20 Hookstone Chase, Harrogate, to put pen to paper and express his annoyance to the editor of the *Manchester Guardian*. Newton wondered if Lord Woolton realised the 'destruction of neighbourliness and goodwill that will follow any large attempts of the public to act as informers', and thought this was proper work for the authorities, not neighbours.[111] In her wartime recollections, Dorothy Tildsley remembered that the fear of being shopped by neighbours as a user of the black market led people to hide luxuries, even if they were legitimately obtained. Sir Stafford Cripps continued the policy of neighbour ratting in the post-war period, offering rewards for information about breaches of currency regulations. Unimpressed, J.B. Pick wrote to the *Picture Post* that

> we shall shortly be able to collect lump sums for informing on those neighbours who use a drop of red petrol, get an extra slice of meat, receive a food parcel from Ireland, forget their identity card . . . There will be no need to struggle against totalitarianism. Totalitarianism will have won.[112]

This period saw upheaval in society and on the home front. Neighbours had become more separate in the interwar period and were temporarily drawn back together during the war. For some, sharing resources and facilities with their neighbours was still a financial necessity, but for most, increasing privatisation was apparent. There were still disputes on some streets; problems triggered by envy, contretemps over barking dogs and crowing cocks. Emotional, practical and material support continued to be provided to those who lived nearby, and this would have intensified during the rough war years. Richer people in their private-estate semis acquired shiny new things to show off to their neighbours, while the poorer people still made do, lent and borrowed. The Liberal administration extended state help, the profession of social work developed and some roles previously undertaken by neighbours were carried out by social workers. At the outbreak of war, most social workers were women, and were relatively low-paid. The profile of the profession was boosted by their war efforts; they had an active role in the evacuation of children and rehousing the bombed-out. The war revealed the poverty of some evacuated children and the absence of support for many older people. The post-war period would see the government fully fledge the welfare state, which had a revolutionary effect on the material relationships between neighbours in the decades that followed.

6

A Separate House for
Every Family (1945–1969)

Housing in the slums had been cramped and fetid. The residents deserved better. Old friendships were exchanged for spacious accommodation in new tower blocks and peripheral estates. Ties of mutual aid that had strengthened in the crucible of war dissolved as people retreated into their homes. When normality returned, neighbours grew distant.

Between 1945 and 1969, just under two million semi-detached houses were built, which was nearly twice the number of flats.[1] In 1945, the wartime coalition government had pledged 'a separate house for every family that wishes to have one'. The post-war Attlee government strived to meet the commitment, and over one million new local-authority homes were built in the following six years. The number of properties rented from local authorities doubled between 1945 and 1951, bringing publicly owned houses to 15 per cent of the total stock (up from 1 per cent in 1914). The Conservatives' successful election campaign recognised people's desire to convert their increased personal wealth into property by invoking the 1920s ambition to create a 'property-owning democracy'. They pledged to build 300,000 houses each year.[2] Although the majority of these houses were built by local authorities, increasing private housing continued to be a policy priority for the party. Across the country, on an unprecedented scale, people settled into new homes, and began the delicate process of getting to know their new neighbours.[3]

As the economy recovered in the mid 1950s, many areas were scheduled for development. Early projects were traditional family homes, but soon system-built multi-storey tower blocks were in vogue, with council decisions biased towards them by government subsidies. The high-rise building boom culminated in 1968 with the partial collapse of the Ronan Point tower block after a gas explosion, and the blocks were further stigmatised by a lack of maintenance in the recession of the 1970s. Private home-ownership became psychologically central to an Englishman's status as a fully fledged citizen, and by 1970, half of all housing stock was in owner-occupation.[4]

There is a popular misconception that the people who lived in slums were all rehoused en masse. Some were, but the vast majority were not. A 1954 study compared the experiences on two estates, one in Sheffield and the other in Liverpool.[5] To populate the Sheffield estate, the inhabitants of a slum were relocated there together; 6,000 people had been moved in the ten years up to 1936, sometimes entire streets at once. Neighbours in the old street were neighbours on the new estate. Their shared anxieties and common memories helped to generate a sense of 'belongingness' evident on the estate.[6] Three houses along Salford's St Stephen's Place were condemned as in danger of collapse, and the families were rehoused to new flats in Eccles New Road on the Langworthy Estate. Two families – the Partingtons and the Mackins – remained neighbours in their new homes, several miles from where they had lived before. Mrs Mackin told the *Manchester Guardian*, 'we've still got our good neighbours'.[7] However, wholesale neighbour transplantation was far from the norm; the estate in Liverpool grew without it.

When people were rehoused, emotional bonds could be dislocated. In 1957, the sociologists Michael Young and Peter Willmott found that family ties in London's Bethnal Green had been very strong, so strong that for one boy a 'grandmother's neighbours [were] so well known as almost to be his own'. If one family got on bad terms with their neighbour, their relatives automatically shared that antipathy. Once the families moved to Debden in Essex, many kinship ties loosened. 'People's relatives', they noted, 'are no longer neighbours sharing the intimacies of daily life. Their new neighbours are strangers'.[8]

Two bronze statues erected in new estates at this time both subliminally promoted and romanticised neighbourly bonhomie (**Fig. 25** and **Fig. 26**). The first, *The Neighbours* by Siegfried Charoux, has had a prominent position in the Highbury Quadrant Estate, Islington, since 1959. The second, *Neighbourly Encounter* by Uli Nimptsch, was sculpted using two local children as models, and was placed in the centre of the Silwood Estate in 1964. The children straddled a fence that marked the boundary between Bermondsey and Deptford. *Neighbourly Encounter* is currently missing.

YOU MUST SAY PRIVATE THINGS IN A WHISPER

A post-war clash of neighbourhood planning ideologies was prefigured in 1944, when two opposing plans were drawn up for the

Fig. 25 *The Neighbours* by Siegfried Charoux, Highbury Quadrant Estate.

Fig. 26 *Neighbourly Encounter* by Uli
Nimptsch, Silwood Estate.

Woodchurch Estate in Birkenhead. The Conservative-run council
selected the orthodox plan of their Borough Engineer, Mr B.
Robinson, in preference to a more radical scheme by Professor Sir
Charles Reilly, even though the Reilly plan was very popular with
the people who were going to live on the new estate. Robinson's
plan was 'intended to allow the estate's residents to keep away from
each other as much as possible'. Separate houses sat on curving
roads in a garden-suburb arrangement. In contrast, Reilly's design
clustered houses around forty-four greens, to mimic a necklace of
villages, and included communal features designed to foster 'neighbourly living', such as a shared hot-water system that required the
residents to agree preferred temperatures. Reilly rejected suburban
layouts, with their houses that 'look away from each other and so
do the people'. Neighbours could meet around his greens, 'see one
another, and retain the friendliness of the little streets'. Supporters
of Robinson's plans felt that the working-class residents would not
play cricket on the greens but instead turn them into slabs 'of

hardened mud, with footballs whizzing past the noses of the incautious'. Conservative councillor Guy Williams was not convinced that Reilly's design would foster community spirit, remarking that 'if a man doesn't feel community-minded, he should thank God for a 5-ft hedge round his house'. A child psychologist, Lawrence Wolfe, was a fervent supporter of the Reilly plan. He regarded the 'isolationist way of life' (as promoted by Robinson) as 'disastrous' for the family and for society, and firmly denied that the conditions for 'co-operative spontaneity' were antithetical to privacy. He believed that families would share the village greens for recreation and mothers would naturally arrange a rota for supervising children. Reilly's plans were later applied in Bilston and Dudley in the Black Country, but the communal aspects were compromised.[9]

Looking further into the homes than Reilly, the self-build guru Walter Segal had strong views about the internal layout of dwellings. In 1948, he announced that bathrooms 'should not be placed between two bedrooms without sound-insulating partitions on either side', and nor should bedrooms be placed on either side of a party wall without sufficient insulation. 'Neighbourly feelings', Segal tells us, 'are not enforced by a kind of planning which allows the windows and balconies of one flat to be overlooked by those neighbouring.' Segal also argued for separate private accesses in newly built flats, because people living in flats should not be forced to overhear conversations at their neighbour's door.[10] The historian Marcus Cunliffe, an advocate of flat-dwelling, wrote to the *Manchester Guardian* in August 1950 explaining that the common perception was that all new flat developments had 'such thin walls that all the neighbours' noises, decorous and indecorous, filter through'. Cunliffe felt that too little was done to sell the idea of living in flats, and too little fuss was made of 'good flat developments'.[11]

In the mid 1950s, Jennifer Longford (then Jennifer Stevenson) lodged with a family she called 'the Johnsons' (Mary and Joe, with three children and another lodger, Maureen). Joe had adopted the role of the house husband, and Mary rested a lot. Under the

pseudonym 'Margaret Lassell', Longford wrote up her notes eight
years later, calling the book *Wellington Road*. It is an exquisitely
sensitive study of personal relations and social circumstances. The
Johnsons were a troubled family, and they lived amongst other
troubled families on Westfield Road (renamed Wellington Road for
anonymity). Their street was part of a post-war housing estate on
the outskirts of Bristol (not, as reviewers speculated, in Liverpool,
Manchester or Hull).[12] Longford mentions various neighbours – the
Stevens on one side, and Mrs Dawson and her children on the
other, with the Binnells opposite. Although the Johnsons were on
fairly good terms with the Stevens, Longford never saw either of
them in the Johnson house. When the two couples met accidentally
during an evening at the cinema, they exchanged greetings in the
queue and on the bus home, 'but no more'. Until he got chummy
with another family, Joe would go to the Stevens to get change for
the gas meter. Arthur Spring, who lodged 'a few houses away', was
a regular visitor. Spring came on Sundays to play cards, bringing
sweets for the children, but specified that three-year-old Elizabeth
wore knickers (she often did not). *Wellington Road* gives us a peek
into the life of a lodger, but hopefully Longford's experience was
unusual. The house had three bedrooms, but Longford's rent
brought her a share of Mary's bed, rather than a room of her own.
Mary viewed this set-up as ideal. She liked company in bed, and
not sharing with Joe made good family-planning sense. This sounds
logical, and possibly bearable in exchange for a low rent, until
Mary's job, as a prostitute, is factored in.[13]

In 1953, the sociologist Leo Kuper published a study of Thimbler
Road (given the soubriquet 'Braydon Road'), a neighbourhood of
houses built around greens on the edge of Coventry. Like Reilly,
Kuper aimed to discover something about the 'potential contribu-
tion of the town planner to more intimate relations between
neighbours, through his control of the physical environment'. The
Thimbler Road houses had steel frames that allowed noises to
permeate neighbouring properties. Mr Hilton worked nights and
had asked if the walls were insulated against noise before accepting

his house. He was told they were, but he soon found they were not. Furthermore, the open-plan arrangement of the plots, with undemarcated gardens and uninterrupted surveillance between the houses, conflicted with the growing desire for domestic privacy in the 1950s. Kuper noted that these factors conspired to create 'an awareness of neighbours even within the inner sanctum'. The cul-de-sacs gave nowhere to hide, and all the neighbours were 'readily taken in at a glance'. Contact between the neighbours was further enhanced by a 'limited number of routes to the outside world'.[14] This had enduring benefits for one couple. Ray Coleman and his bride-to-be, Mary, met as teenagers living next-door-but-one on Thimbler Road. The Colemans celebrated their diamond wedding anniversary in May 2011.[15]

The Thimbler Road residents had communal front gardens, and their back gardens were divided symbolically, with strands of wire stretched between concrete posts. These were common in contemporary council housing estates, and allowed children and pets to roam. Open gardens with negligible barriers have never been popular with English householders. Fencing gives a break to wind, protection to plants, and provides privacy. Back in Thimbler Road, the downstairs toilet was uncomfortably close to the neighbouring garden, and Mr Brown said that some women would not use the toilet if there was a man in the garden next door. Women disliked the visibility of their washing line, and one had even been ridiculed for the infrequent changes of her bedlinen. Gradually householders erected sturdier fences. One family augmented their fence to deter a side neighbour from stepping over it and coming around uninvited. Another decided to put up a partition between their garden and that of the side neighbour, after complaining that 'every time you open the back door, you see your neighbour'.[16] On the Sheffield estate, foot-high walls of cement blocks were built, but these did not contain dogs and upset green-fingered residents. Indeed, they were said to 'merely provide a useful opportunity for children to improve their sense of balance'.[17]

Some council estates allowed residents to be more private, like

the huge Becontree Estate in Dagenham. Houses were surrounded
by privet hedges that were trimmed by a team of gardeners, and
tenants received a handbook that rhapsodised about their front
door as a 'gateway to your particular castle'. 'You can close it like
a fortress against the outside world', the tenants were informed.
The front gate was the first barrier in this fortification, and the
tenants were told to shut it quietly, as 'banging is bad for the latch
and annoying to the neighbours'.[18]

NO NEIGHBOURS POPPING IN

Although the worry about what the neighbours might say was
losing some potency, there was still a lingering sense of propriety
behind the net curtains. Jack Dawson, the son of the widow next
door to the Johnsons on 'Wellington Road', asked Joe (who was
acting as his wife's pimp) if he could sleep with Mary. Joe had
replied, 'Do what you like', which annoyed Mary; 'it was because
the Dawsons were neighbours that it mattered'.[19]

In a study of neighbours on the new estates built in the mid
twentieth century, H.E. Bracey found that 'calling on neighbours
unannounced is not considered a virtue . . . steps are quickly taken
to curb excessive neighbouring of this kind'. English householders,
Bracey added, 'clearly recognised that neighbours constitute a threat
to privacy'.[20] Likewise, when the sociologist Philip Abrams interviewed neighbours, he found that good neighbours were often
identified as people who could be relied on, but who did not pry.
An intrusive neighbour was a bad neighbour; 'A good neighbour
is someone who is friendly but not nosey and knows when not to
come.'[21] With the aim of *Exploring English Character*, the anthropologist Geoffrey Gorer surveyed 10,000 people in the early 1950s
through a questionnaire placed in a Sunday newspaper. He
concluded that the typical neighbour relationship in England 'can
probably best be described as distant cordiality'. Thirteen per cent
of people claimed to dislike their neighbours' inquisitiveness, and
those in the lower-working and lower-middle classes were 'particu-

larly liable to think they are being spied on, and to resent it'. One middle-aged working-class man from Cheshire described meddling neighbours as people whose 'noses are longer than their arms'.[22] Young and Willmott found that their subjects wanted more privacy when they moved from Bethnal Green to Debden. Limits were placed on contact. One neighbour was heard to say, 'I don't think you can go to a neighbour if you want anything personal.'[23] Wolfe worried that the 'poor creatures of suburbia' who kept themselves to themselves might withdraw so much that they read too much into 'a look, a gesture, or a casual remark' and got the hump with their neighbours.[24]

Writing about north-west England between 1940 and 1970, Elizabeth Roberts found galloping privatisation caused by greater affluence and female employment. In traditional neighbourhoods you were expected to help a neighbour and no neat rules of reciprocity applied – person A might help person B; person B helped person C. Roberts saw increasing separation between neighbours and a concurrent increase in privacy and domesticity. Having filled their homes with the fruits of the consumer society, people tended to stay indoors. Previously much 'effortless sociability' occurred whilst women performed tasks such as donkey-stoning their front step. In Dagenham in the early 1960s, Peter Willmott found that women who went out to work had less to do with their neighbours. A Mrs Ralph soldered coils in a factory, so did not have 'time to stand and jaw. I don't very often see them [neighbouring women] except on Saturdays up at the shops.' Other women who were interviewed by Willmott relied on neighbours so they could work. Mrs Jordan, over the road from Mrs Palmer, bought groceries for her neighbour and looked out for the children after school.[25] By the 1970s, some neighbours had forgotten the etiquette of 'effortless sociability' (i.e. that chats were limited by chores and contact should end with the start of the next task). A woman interviewed by Roberts explained how she was forced to get a job to avoid a lonely neighbour who outstayed her welcome, taking up all of her free time.[26]

Neighbourly relations were often conducted outdoors, in neutral spaces. When a woman from the next street sought advice from Joe Johnson about her rent, they spoke 'on the front doorstep'. Longford explained that people 'who come in for a purpose rather than a visit, are not asked to sit down, or given a cup of tea; though visitors from a distance never go away without one'.[27] Even in the relatively open and long-established area of St Ebbe's in Oxford, the sociologist John Mogey noticed that there was, by the 1950s, a tradition of not entering a neighbour's house; people chatted on the streets.[28] One of Kuper's interviewees said, 'I don't believe in going into each other's houses – you can keep friendly without that.'[29] According to Gorer's study, fewer than one in twenty English people claimed to know their neighbour 'well enough to drop in without an invitation', and entertaining a neighbour with a meal was 'very exceptional'.[30] On the Liverpool estate, Mrs James's approach to neighbouring was to 'have few in the house and never to make cups of tea for them'.[31]

Elizabeth Bott studied family and social networks, including the Newbolts of Bermondsey. Mrs Newbolt valued the area for the lack of social pretensions. 'When things are la-di-da', she confided, 'you feel out of place.' The Newbolts' neighbours were of a similar social status (Mr Newbolt was a semi-skilled factory worker). Bott noticed overlapping roles; a neighbour might also be a friend, a work colleague or a relative. The Newbolts were friendly with the neighbours, but 'took it for granted that a friendly relationship with a neighbour would end if the woman moved away', just as Maud Pember Reeves had noted in Lambeth half a century earlier. To fit in, Mrs Newbolt was expected to gossip and be gossiped about, 'no gossip, no companionship'. Neighbour relationships were regarded as female ones. Bott notes, 'Mr Newbolt looked rather shocked when I asked him if he saw much of his neighbours.'[32]

One of Kuper's subjects suggested that some areas of the country were more inviting to neighbours. Most people on Thimbler Road in Coventry talked to neighbours on their doorstep. Sociable Mrs Cotton, the wife of a bricklayer, was the exception that proved the rule. She kept her door open and was 'often heard bawling to her children across the cul-de-sac'. Neighbours thought she was 'too villagey' for the area and she moved out. One Thimbler Road resident contrasted Lancashire neighbours (who would 'just lift the latch and walk in, and stop and talk') with Coventry, where 'they're just kept on the doorstep'.[33] An estate on the other side of the Pennines in Sheffield challenged the notion of a north/south difference. There, neighbours who were too chummy were mockingly called the 'in-and-outers' because they were always in and out of each other's homes.[34] These comments reveal fluidity; the ideal neighbour did not conform to a fixed set of behaviour – perfection depended on what a person wanted from their neighbour (whether that was involvement or detachment).

FAIR-WEATHER FRIENDS

The British welfare state, in a form we would recognise today, was built by the Attlee government. It replaced some services that were previously provided by neighbours through mutual aid. Legislation enacted between 1945 and 1948 gave a fixed weekly benefit for each child, after the first, up to sixteen years old; tightened up the local-authority provision of care for children; provided financial help for the sick, unemployed, elderly and pregnant; funded those below the minimum subsistence level and established the National Health Service.[35] Some local authorities embraced the new spirit of paternalism and added a layer of care on top of Whitehall's national foundations. In Oxford, the council engaged women as home helps to cook, care, and clean for those in need.[36] The *Picture Post* reported on a meals-on-wheels service in 1948: 'it's a godsend when a neighbour asks you to drop in around lunch-time . . . But these days, neighbours can't afford to extend such invitations often.' The Erith Mobile Meals Service was described as 'a kind of Travelling Neighbour', dropping off hot meals at the doorstep.[37]

The post-war period saw an increase in the numbers of people taking up professional positions in the newly formed welfare state, in the emergency services and in other careers. Social workers established themselves alongside other welfare-state professionals in medicine and education. The professionalisation of caring replaced compassionate obligation with mechanistic objectivity and measured concern; fewer roles were a neighbour's responsibility, as midwives, firemen and undertakers stepped in.

Home births were still common. In *Call in the Midwife*, East Ender Jennifer Worth has described her experiences as a midwife in the 1950s. She helped in a midwives' clinic that was held in a church hall. This had been the only clinic in the Docklands area until an eight-bed maternity unit opened at Poplar Hospital in 1948. Worth attended home births, and was 'used to managing in fairly primitive conditions', usually accompanied by neighbours and relatives.[38] The *Picture Post* reported the birth of Janet Levington in the front bedroom of 63 Widdicombe Road, Mottingham in Kent, on 4 August 1946, 'and the only unusual thing about the birth, to the parents and neighbours, is that we record the fact'. Half of the Kentish babies born at the same time as Janet were born at home.[39]

Neighbours were still on hand to help save people from fire. In February 1954, Walter Warburton of Council Street, Hulme, heard screams from the house next door. He investigated and was driven back by flames in the doorway. He then rescued Josephine Conlon and her young stepbrother Leonard from an outhouse roof.[40] Neighbours sometimes helped the fire brigade to extinguish fires. Sidney Blankley, whose Chesterfield house ignited in 1957, said 'the neighbours were wonderful. But for their efforts the damage would have been much more extensive.'[41] In 1948, Britain's fire brigades were brought under local-authority control. The design of fire engines improved, and after 1955, several authorities obtained new high-speed diesel engines.[42] Knowing that the engine was racing across town full of capable firemen turned neighbours into bemused, concerned or ghoulish bystanders. Not always, though. The photograph in **Fig. 27** shows an incinerated back-to-back on Langford Street, Leeds, in March 1966. The Wheatleys had dropped

Fig. 27 Langford Street, Leeds. The aftermath of a fire in 1966.

their baby into the arms of a neighbour, while another neighbour intercepted an ambulance as he ran to phone the fire brigade. Nobody was injured.[43]

Neighbours were no longer expected to help out in *every* crisis when their taxes paid the state to do it, although, of course, acts of caring and concern did continue. Mary Johnson was helped by Mrs Binnell during Elizabeth's birth. Mary was a little ungrateful and complained that there were children everywhere and she could not wait for them to leave.[44] A middle-class woman from Halifax told Geoffrey Gorer, 'I disapprove of my next door neighbour'. She explained that her neighbour had offered to help out when she was due to give birth, and said that she should knock on the wall to summon help, with the bitter caveat, 'I aren't forced to hear you!'[45]

People still looked after each other's children. A Pathé News clip from 1950 showed a canny rig-up of radio and microphone apparatus that allowed a neighbour to monitor a child next door, whose parents were out, from the comfort of their own armchair. Syd Little grew up with rowing parents. After his mother stormed out one day, Mrs Mare from next door took over parenting until harmony returned. This tumultuous childhood did not stop Syd entertaining millions on the television as the diminutive half of the comedy duo Little & Large.[46] Bereaved parents who had lost three young sons in a fire in their council flat in Middleton, north of Manchester, had decided to start afresh by emigrating in 1963. It was the kindness of their neighbours that changed the Wardles' plans. Mr Wardle said, 'we never knew neighbours could be so wonderful. We thought we would be alone, but people haven't been able to do enough for us. We feel we just can't leave now.'[47]

Despite this counterpoint, neighbourly duty did change from the mid twentieth century, in part due to the expansion of the welfare state. This was not necessarily a bad thing. People could elect to support their neighbours, motivated by genuine care rather than a sense of social obligation, or in expectation of reciprocal favours. In a crisis a person could turn to the state or pay for help, rather than depend on neighbours. By the time Gorer surveyed neighbours in 1955, only 8 per cent of English people would 'entirely' rely on their neighbours in a crisis, and to the question 'Do you think you could rely on your neighbours in a pinch?' 10 per cent replied that they would not rely on them at all.[48] On the Sheffield estate, over 65 per cent of people with more than four children would ask for help in a serious illness, but only about 40 per cent of childless people said they would.[49]

Affluence allowed people to buy things rather than borrow from or share with neighbours. Elizabeth Roberts discovered that in the 1940s, many favours had been offered or received from neighbours without payment. By the 1970s, people preferred to pay for these services. Laying out of the dead is a good example.[50] The Co-operative movement started offering undertaking services in the 1920s. By the late 1930s, hearses had become motorised.[51] Developments were slow to change habits in some areas; in the early 1950s, neighbours on the Sheffield estate still performed the laying-out of dead residents, and some took responsibility for collecting money for wreaths.[52] Nonetheless, full-time funeral directors gradually took over work that had been done by both neighbours and part-time undertakers. Looking at Banbury during the 1960s, Margaret Stacey and her team of researchers noticed that neighbours rarely pulled together to deal with the practicalities and emotions of bereavement. Relatives, not neighbours, cared for the grief-stricken.[53]

Stuff was exchanged more rarely and grudgingly than before. Over on Thimbler Road, residents disapproved of borrowing things, although a few did not mind lending stuff. Bracey discovered that estate-dwellers disliked the idea of loaning food, but thought the exchange of garden tools acceptable.[54] For Mogey's Oxford residents, borrowing money was not respectable, 'especially if you do not repay promptly and in full'.[55] Asking for repayment was awkward. One householder said, 'Never borrow, then you'll never be under any obligation to anybody.'[56] Joe Johnson of 'Wellington Road' even refused to lend his neighbour the evening paper, muttering, 'Whatever paper they ask for we haven't got. You know, if you lend them one, you'll never see it again.' Not all of his neighbours were as mean, and magazines were passed around. When the Binnells asked Joe for half a loaf, some sugar and milk, only 'til morning', he uncharitably refused, claiming 'their morning never comes', and told his lodger that he would not settle in the street if he could afford to buy a house, because 'there's always someone wanting to borrow something'.[57] One of the residents of the Liverpool estate in 1954 listed the items her neighbours had asked to borrow in one week; they included a pram, an electric fire, a tablecloth and money for coal. Previously, the woman had lent a gas fire to a neighbour and then spent two years trying to get it back before eventually discovering it in another neighbour's house.[58] By the mid 1960s, researchers were noting differences in exchanges according to social and economic status. In Banbury in Oxfordshire, while poorer families still 'tended to exchange basic commodities' such as the proverbial cup of sugar, wealthier families exchanged advice, plants and tools.[59] The state and personal wealth nibbled at the edges of people's gladness to be active neighbours.

GOOD NEIGHBOUR SCHEMES

By November 1945, Alison Settle, writing in the *Observer*, decried the loss of neighbourliness, which she specifically referred to as 'friendly help . . . between woman and woman'. She blamed the 'keep-myself-to-myself spirit of the vast suburban sprawl' for reducing 'the cordial exchange of small services between neighbours', and proposed a 'Help Your Neighbour Campaign'.[60] Two years later, in the harsh winter of 1947, Settle worried about old people being 'crippled' by privations and asked if the wartime Good Neighbour plan could not be operated nationally – to shop for, visit and change library books for the elderly.[61]

Settle's wish came true by 1963, when many communities were forming Good Neighbour schemes to help the elderly, plug gaps in state services and retrieve habits of neighbouring lost only recently. One scheme was staffed by housewives, schoolchildren and handymen, and co-ordinated by a vicar. 'Anything from sitting up with a sick person to mending a fuse for someone who is infirm will be tackled. Tasks will be allocated between those best fitted to undertake them', reported the *Guardian*.[62] A Burnley scheme aimed to provide one good neighbour for each of the 1,000 streets of the town, and was intended to help the 'old and lonely'. This council-promoted scheme was designed to bring people needing help to the attention of the authorities, rather than to have a team of jobbers. Volunteers were asked to 'keep a close but unobtrusive eye' on vulnerable people. Mrs Bruggen from the council said, 'we don't want them to be regarded as snoopers or spies prying into private lives, but just to be on hand at times of need'.[63] Many schemes were organised by churches. A 1966 guide, *The Caring Community*, highlighted that

There are almost everywhere constant opportunities for simple acts of friendliness, particularly in thickly populated areas where people do not necessarily know their neighbours; where, for example, short-term help over shopping or transport is often required during sickness or by elderly people, and where loneliness abounds.[64]

Good Neighbour schemes were a return to the community-based help we see in Keith Wrightson's work on the pre-modern period. These schemes were an organised form of the help and care neighbours had traditionally given each other automatically.

Protecting children became a less communal affair during this period, as traditional neighbourhoods were broken up, families dispersed and the dangers presented by cars pushed children into their gardens. Parenting was especially home-based amongst the middle classes and the more comfortably off working-class children, who were usually watched over just by their own parents (mostly mothers) and paid help. The chef Nigel Slater remembered his 1960s childhood in Penn in the West Midlands, where

No one in our road was unemployed . . . Few, if any, of the women worked. Everyone had children of more or less the same age . . . There were no babies, no single mothers, no young childless couples. No blacks, no homosexuals, no foreigners . . . Neat, calm, polite, distant, with only the children ever setting foot in one another's houses.[65]

On Thimbler Road, the Rowans, thinking their son was getting 'very rough', confined him to play within the wire barriers in the garden. When he became timid, he was sent out to toughen up on the street.[66] A single mother in Blackburn interviewed by the author Jeremy Seabrook in the late 1960s said that the neighbouring children did not play with her children (whose father was in prison), saying 'Oh, I'm not playing with you, we haven't to play with you.'[67] Conflict over the behaviour of children cropped up frequently in the 1954 study of a Liverpool estate, with some neighbours expressing shock about foul language. One boy was kept indoors to shield his ears. Complaints to parents about behaviour could be met with hostility.[68] Similar troubles faced the tenants on the Sheffield estate. 'I dread school holidays', said one mother. 'I have more quarrels and lose more friends than in the whole rest of the year.'[69]

Smaller helpful gestures still occurred, like looking after house keys. A photograph of Crompton Street in Leeds, taken in 1964, shows a chalked message on the front door of number 10, giving details of where a key can be obtained.[70] Money was still passed between neighbours, and in some places collective buying schemes were set up. The Johnsons were involved in the 'postal store agency', with goods bought on commission. Mary was the agent, but Joe did all the work, taking over from a woman opposite when she 'got into a muddle with it'.[71] Some neighbours still provided short-term loans to their neighbours. Meg, who lived in rooms beneath Winifred Foley in London's Lisson Grove, acted as the house banker; 'she had never refused a borrower, never charged any interest, and often had to be persuaded into accepting repayment'. When the Foleys moved to a new council flat, Winifred felt 'something was missing'. That something was the tenement community feeling. 'Nobody was bringing a cup of tea to my door, nobody was having a chat on the landing . . . There was no nosey vital Meg chatting upstairs.'[72]

PETTY SAVAGERIES BETWEEN NEIGHBOUR AND NEIGHBOUR

Some neighbours were not very neighbourly. Joe Johnson was assaulted by a neighbour whose ball he refused to return and started having blackouts eighteen months later. A different neighbour refused to help Mary, who was struggling with Joe's blackouts, saying, 'you can't keep coming in and out of here, wanting something'. Mary was bewildered, because she had never been in the neighbour's house before.[73]

Women fought on the Liverpool estate. Mrs Haliburton worried about the 'bickering and fighting' and added, 'I have seen women out with pokers and hammers.' Asked about the cause of the skirmishes,

Mrs Haliburton opined, 'women on this estate have so little to do and suffer from sheer boredom'. Moreover, they chat over the fence, share secrets, 'and then they quarrel knowing that each has the other in the palm of her hand. Often they come out with everything they know about each other.' Mrs Haliburton thought social mixing was to blame and recommended segregation according to occupation, income and culture. The Haliburtons' neighbour of eighteen months, Mr Isaacs, said he and his wife did not try to be neighbourly, although they did like the Haliburtons.[74]

Two songs from 1968 sneered at insufferable neighbours from the perspective of youth. The lyrics of 'My Pink Half of the Drainpipe' by the Bonzo Dog Band are disjointed with asides to imitate neighbourly small chat between semis. The younger neighbour is bored by prolix precision about tomato plants, pets, family holidays, drill attachments and turf, and finds solace in a pink property boundary that he might paint blue.[75] The Small Faces song 'Lazy Sunday' also reveals the social gulf between old suburbanites and their younger neighbours. From the start, the singer expresses a wish to get on with the neighbours, but they bang on the wall and complain about noise. Like the Bonzos, the Small Faces also ridicule suburbanite neighbours' preoccupations. 'Lazy Sunday' was inspired by one of the songwriter's own feuds with his neighbours.[76]

In his enthusiastic sales pitch for the Reilly plan, Lawrence Wolfe argued that 'possession often becomes obsession', which in turn developed into suburban 'house-madness'. Wolfe described the symptoms:

It hurts them when anyone so much as touches *their* fence, *their* privet hedge, or *their* gate. A neighbour woman has the temerity to fasten one end of her clothes line to *their* fence, so they cut it off, letting her washing . . . fall into the mud.

This 'house-madness' would not occur in the life of Reilly, where co-operation was cultivated through sharing facilities. Families would not develop undue attachment to the bricks and mortar of their own houses, when there were more communal aspects to their living environment. It was thought that this sense of community would neutralise territoriality and do away with 'petty savageries between neighbour and neighbour that are so common in the isolationist street'.[77]

A modern-day Romeo and Juliet story played out in the village of East Farleigh in Kent. In 1957, the Capons had moved from London and settled into Squirrels Cottage, the property adjoining The Cobbolds, which was home to the Lott family. Trouble soon broke out. There was a falling-out over the Capons' dog and chickens, and 'other petty things'. The families stopped talking for five years. Eventually there was a thaw in relations, and by 1965 two of the children had fallen in love. When seventeen-year-old Jennifer Lott's father discovered her relationship with twenty-one-year-old Adrian Capon, he banned their tryst. Adrian touchingly told the *Daily Express* that 'he cannot stop me loving her', adding that it was 'impossible for us not to see each other because our gardens are adjoining'.[78]

A sycamore came between Cheshire neighbours in 1951. Charles Darbyshire Cheetham, of The Nook in Cheadle Hulme, challenged his neighbour's right to grow a 'very large tree' three feet from the boundary. The neighbour, Charles Whatmough, sued Cheetham for trespass after he lopped the tree, claiming it had interfered with light to his property. The offending sycamore was also alleged to have disturbed an asphalt path to The Nook, and threatened its drains. The Vice Chancellor of the Lancashire Chancery Court was unimpressed and slapped down claims of thrice-yearly leaf removal from gutters on account that leaves fell only once a year. He was not having any of it. 'It is rather a trumpery dispute', he harrumphed. 'If every neighbour could get an injunction against the adjoining owner because the roots of his trees came into his ground there would not be a single householder in England who did not get an injunction . . . I mean it is the first thing a tree does.'[79]

It was not just trees causing bother; nuisances could come from within homes too. Half of dwellers in steel-framed houses claimed to lose sleep due to noise in a 1948 survey, compared to one fifth in brick houses.[80] In Thimbler Road, paired neighbours complained of sounds coming through the thin steel walls. One heard 'the neighbour's wife scratching at her grate with a poker', although fireplaces were not located on party walls, and others heard water cisterns refilling. One woman found that her neighbour's vacuuming interfered with her wireless, so she vacuumed hastily, assuming that hers did the same.[81] Wireless interference due to a neighbour's electrical devices was sufficiently common by 1954 for GEC to market the 'Bride's Iron', which had such a quick action on the thermostat that 'there is no irritating interference with radio or television programmes – either for you or your neighbours'. The following year, a selling feature of one typewriter was that is was 'noiseless' and could therefore be used 'in a small flat, a terraced house; your neighbours won't mind'.[82]

Mrs Leek knew that her immediate neighbour on Thimbler Road, Mr Donnolley, worked different shifts to Mr Leek, and so kept quiet 'so as not to disturb him'. More anxiety was noted from residents about uncontrollable noises from within their own homes, 'as for example, bronchial coughs, babies crying at night, or a Welsh husband who joins in with the singing on the wireless' (Mr Leek, perhaps?). Various noises were mentioned, including 'shoes dropped at bedtime', piano music, bedroom rows, and making up afterwards. 'You can even hear them use the pot; that's how bad it is,' remarked one resident, adding, 'It's terrible.' 'It makes you feel that *you* must say private things in a whisper', whispered one interviewee. Another woman knew when her neighbour had visitors because they spoke loudly; 'they may be used to brick houses', she speculated. Some quirks of layout and material caused problems to the neighbours. Rooms were mirrored in the semi next door, which meant that activities could clash and annoy. Each night, 'the connubial heads lie, each on their own side of the partition', except those heads working a night shift. Mrs Haynes, in cleaning the mirror hung on the party wall, caused banging that was answered by angry knocking from the neighbour. Mr Haynes counselled his wife to ignore the overreaction.[83] A survey of 1948 found that the radio was the source of most intrusive neighbour noise, despite broadcasts of polite reminders to keep the volume down, especially in summer when windows could be open.[84] Mrs Dudley, a resident of Thimbler Road in Coventry in the early 1950s, had established a friendship with her side neighbour, but had since quarrelled over the noise made by the Dudleys' three children. Proximity enhanced the potential for nuisance; 'If we'd been a bit further apart, we'd still have been friends' rued the Dudleys' neighbour.[85]

People seriously troubled by nuisances could still pursue an action against their neighbour, or get an injunction to stop the problem. The 1960 Noise Abatement Act built on the 1936 Public Health Act and placed limits on noises that might annoy neighbours. The 1947 Town and Country Planning Act nationalised the right to develop and tightened procedures. A part of the planning committee's task became the reluctant arbitration between neighbours at logger-heads over conversions and extensions. Most people only encountered the planning system as a neighbour, either one hoping to develop, or one wanting to thwart their neighbour's developments.

KEEPING UP WITH THE NEIGHBOURS

Mrs L. Guthrie of Blackpool put pen to best paper in 1957, telling the *Picture Post* that 'In my experience "The Joneses" have been stimulating neighbours. And thanks to them, several minor dreams have been fulfilled.'[86] Willmott and Young found suburban one-upmanship in London's Woodford; one interviewee noticed that

as soon as next door knew we'd got a washing machine . . . they got one too. Then a few months later we got a fridge, so they got a fridge as well. I thought all this stuff about keeping up with the Joneses was all talk until I saw it happening right next door.

Another Woodford resident bought a new car and boasted, 'that'll be a knock in the eye for *them*'.[87] In a different study, focusing on Debden, the same researchers were told that new rugs were hung on the line as flags of prosperity.[88] Working alone on the Becontree Estate, Peter Willmott noticed that 'for every Mr Andrews who already has a "flat-top refrigerator and washing machine", and every Mr Salmon who has a suite in "uncut moquette", there are a dozen others at Dagenham who want the same'.[89] I want an uncut moquette suite too; whatever it is.

Kuper observed that the similar exteriors of the Thimbler Road houses meant that there was more emphasis on possessions as a way of displaying taste and individuality to the neighbours. Interiors could not be neglected, because they were also visible. Mrs Dudley feared being judged for her bare stairs and hall, and kept her curtains partially drawn to hide her shabby possessions and decor. Curtains were popular purchases, and people fretted whether to display the pattern inwards to the room or out to the street.[90] Infectious consumerism was not just a disease of the middle classes. Many items could be got on the never-never. The wife of a London labourer noticed that her neighbour bought a new Hoover and a studio couch to keep up, 'and she's still paying for it'.[91] Before the 1950s, most neighbours were as poor as each other, but mid-century rises in prosperity for some, coupled with credit, meant that more labour-saving devices were sold, creating more competition and an expectation to keep up. Young and Willmott were surprised by the 'striking' influence of largely anonymous neighbours on the purchases made by the subjects of their study.[92]

There was a big increase in car ownership between 1947 and 1966, from nearly 200,000 to over 950,000.[93] For many men (probably an underexamined group in all neighbour studies) the car became a bonding tool. Colin Luckhurst, writing in the *Guardian* in 1963, found car ownership to be the ideal solution to 'the hurdle of social awkwardness' he had experienced with his neighbours since moving from the south to the north. Until he took possession of his 'sixth-hand Austin', neighbourly contact had been limited to talk about the weather and garden plants. 'Neighbourly conversation, edged with suspicion, went no farther.' Luckhurst detected 'social feelers' on the first Sunday the Austin sat outside his house. Once-grunting neighbours 'became voluble over body rot and petrol consumption . . . Social contacts boomed, and first name terms were soon established in the intimacy of under-car examination.'[94]

Televisions became increasingly common in the 1950s. Many households bought one to watch the coronation. The Househam family of Meanwood Terrace, Leeds, invited their neighbours in to view it.[95] Mary Johnson's parents were visited regularly by their neighbours, who watched their television set and ate their tea.[96] Those acquiring a TV after 1960 could also keep up to date with the antics of ITV's *Coronation Street*, in which the Tatlocks lived next to the Barlows along a terrace that was to see numerous inter-street marriages. Researching *The Home and Social Status* in 1955, Dennis Chapman found that relatively few terrace homes had aerials ('visible evidence of television'), but many council houses did – in fact, more than private semi-detached houses. Detached dwellers were considered 'mildly eccentric' if they did not own a set.[97] By 1967, a colour television cost 35s. per week to rent. Colin McIver in the *Guardian* noted that this was 'not a prohibitive level for the "one upmanship" market, anxious to impress the neighbours'.[98] A study of the penetration of appliances in Britain since 1950 has shown that items such as televisions (whose presence is signalled by antennae) became more widely purchased than appliances for housework, such as washing machines and fridges, which 'have limited value for status display, and are normally tucked out of sight'.[99]

YOU ARE THE NEIGHBOURS

Willmott and Young and Gorer found that manual workers living in middle-class areas were most likely to complain about snobby neighbours. Perhaps with some justification if the complaint of one resident was typical: 'All these East Enders in the road. The noise and the ice-cream papers and the wireless on all day.'[100] L.M. Poole, writing for the *Guardian* in 1960, was quick to defend herself against accusations of 'snobbishness' when she described the 'communal isolation' of being a professional living in a council house on a new housing estate. Most of the neighbours were working class, and Mrs Poole struggled to bond with them. Noticing that her 'accent, tastes' and ideas created a barrier, she thought a lack of 'cultural contacts' was the problem. She hid her 'guilty secret', that her husband was a librarian, fearing that knowledge of it would entrench the separation. At home with a baby, Poole rarely saw her neighbours, and spent her days dreaming of living in a 'private estate house' near the library. She reserved her sharpest criticism for the 'few families' who allow their children to truant, or who 'switch on a radiogram full blast at 12.30 a.m., and those whose littered gardens are undug'.[101]

Race relations became an issue for neighbours by the end of the 1960s. A rapid rise from the 1950s in the numbers of West Indian, and later Asian, immigrants had triggered questions about neighbouring skills. In 1966, the *Guardian* reported that twice-weekly Good Neighbour classes were being planned for Pakistani workers at a mill in Cheshire.[102] Race issues had been sharpened after the 1964 general election, when Patrick Gordon Walker, the Labour spokesman on foreign affairs, lost his Smethwick seat following a racist campaign by supporters of the Conservative candidate, Peter Griffiths. His followers had chanted the slogan 'If you want a nigger for a neighbour, vote Liberal or Labour.' Gordon Walker had opposed the 1962 Commonwealth Immigrants Act, which tightened regulations and placed limits on immigrants entering the country. Griffiths never convincingly disassociated himself from the sentiments expressed in the slogan. He was quoted as describing it as being 'a manifestation of the popular feeling. I would not condemn anyone who said that.' The pre-election rumour mill was clogged with falsehoods, including that 'Patrick Gordon Walker sold his house at Smethwick to the blacks'. Housing had been a key concern in the constituency throughout the decade, which was marked by shortages. There had been protests in 1961 at a proposal to move a Pakistani family into local-authority flats on Christ Street. When Malcolm X visited the town after the election he said, 'I wait for the fascist elements in Smethwick to erect gas ovens.'[103]

Like many other Midland constituencies, Smethwick was home to relatively high numbers of immigrants. A few years later, in a nearby constituency, Enoch Powell infamously foresaw rivers of blood. Days before the introduction of the 1968 Race Relations Act, he advocated voluntary assisted repatriation. He used the example of a Wolverhampton woman who was said to be the only white woman living on her street. Running a boarding house, this woman 'saw one house after another taken over. The quiet street became a place of noise and confusion.' She claimed that her white tenants moved out. Refusing to let rooms to immigrants, or sell the house for a low figure, she claimed that her windows were broken, excreta was pushed through her letterbox, and she suffered chants of 'racialist' from her neighbours.[104] Most of the attacks, however, were not on white neighbours. After two Chinese laundry owners were attacked in St Helens in 1963, and the windows of the house where the manager and some staff lived were broken, the *Guardian* asked the man next door for a comment. William McGibbon described his Chinese neighbours as 'very good, pleasant and quiet neighbours'.[105]

Six years later, Jeremy Seabrook made a study of a summer in Blackburn. He found a community mourning the loss of old neighbourliness; of sharing food and caring for children. The same city was wary about an influx of migrants to work in local trades. When interviewed, John Johnson admitted that he did not know how he would feel if an Indian or Pakistani family moved in next door. Others muttered about ghettoisation, fly-tipping, backyard chicken slaughtering and gaudy paintwork: 'They haven't got our ways.' One woman was sure she would 'hate living next door to them . . . because of the smell of the cooking'. Seabrook noticed the irony that people were objecting to behaviour in immigrant families that seemed remarkably similar to the 'old communal working class ways of life', when neighbour helped neighbour. Surveying a street on a summer evening, Seabrook saw immigrant families in the doorways and seated on doorsteps in much the same way that families are shown using the streets in photographs from the early twentieth century; only the faces Seabrook saw were darker. 'Fifty years earlier there would have been tired mill workers in the same attitudes of relaxation and repose.' In 1969, while Seabrook was capturing Blackburn attitudes, a new term, 'Paki-bashing', was being coined on the Collingwood Estate in Bethnal Green.[106]

Racial issues continued to blight some areas of the country, and caused friction and disharmony. Integration was not always easy, and conflict was increased by the spread of urban myths. Seabrook was twice told the apocryphal story about Pakistani workers colonising the attics of every house down various (unnamed) Blackburn streets. Such rumours were rife elsewhere too, but details were always fuzzy.[107] I would like to give the last word on this subject to the female half of a mixed marriage, who claimed in 1964 to have repeatedly heard the phrase 'I'm not prejudiced, but what would the neighbours think?' She retorted, 'If you believe in something enough, you don't give a hoot what the neighbours think. After all . . . *you* are the neighbours.'[108]

After the war, houses became more comfortable and were filling with stuff. People wanted to show off their shiny new things to neighbours, but in doing so tried not to invite requests to loan them out.[109] From the early 1960s, the availability of more jobs for women and the contraceptive pill reduced family sizes. Lodging declined, and with more room indoors, fewer people were seen on the streets. Traffic clamour and danger extinguished even more sociability on the streets. English people did not have a tradition of inviting neighbours indoors, and with diminishing chances to meet at street corners or on doorsteps, there was less contact between neighbours. The welfare state removed a sense of obligation to help neighbours in distress. Detachment led to loneliness and in the mid 1950s, doctors reported a high incidence of 'suburban neurosis' on new housing estates.[110] Do-gooders fought these fissile forces with Good Neighbour schemes, but their efforts failed to pull people permanently back together.

7

Detached Neighbours (1970–2010)

Fig. 28 'Semi-detached' by Michael Landy, Tate Britain, 2004.

In 2004, Tate Britain exhibited 'Semi-detached', a replica of the pebble-dashed home of Ethel and John, the parents of the artist Michael Landy (**Fig. 28**). Installed in the exhibition hall, the semi-detached house became fully detached. By lifting the house out of its context, and away from its twin, Landy made visible the way many semi owners have separated themselves, refusing to see themselves as part of something bigger. Landy's house neatly sums up a modern attitude: houses are separate, even when attached. Ideal houses are surrounded by space and are just for one family, who can shut out the world behind their own front door. Half of the detached houses standing at the turn of the twenty-first century were built since 1969, while only a sixth had been built before 1919.[1]

Chairing a Parliamentary Committee on privacy in 1972, Kenneth Younger described the modern middle-class family as 'relatively soundproofed in their semi-detached house, relatively unseen behind their privet hedge and rose trellis'. Compound this with the ubiquity of the car, and citizens can develop a sense of being more hidden than 'any sizeable section of the population in any other time or place'.[2] Problems occur when this privacy forms barriers to society – allowing people to become socially isolated and lonely, like the archetypal housewives on the edge of 'suburban neurosis'.[3]

Since 1970 there has been a continuing rise in the percentage of households owning their own homes. The 'right to buy' council houses swelled owner-occupation in the 1980s and beyond. Each year between 1981 and 2006 saw an increase in owner-occupiers, the overwhelming majority of whom lived in houses rather than flats. In 1981, a third of households rented from a local authority, but this had plummeted to approximately 10 per cent by 2000. The same proportion rented privately in 2000, a massive reduction from the start of the twentieth century. Owning a home can bring a greater sense of rootedness and territoriality. In 2006/2007, owner-occupiers had lived in their homes an average of nearly twelve years, compared to private renters at just under two years. This has an impact on neighbourliness, for better or worse.[4]

It is likely that many more people are annoyed by neighbours than appear in statistics. This anomaly is caused by the legalities of property selling. A seller must disclose any problems they have reported as being caused by neighbours; copies of letters sent and details of complaints logged need to be supplied. As neighbour wrangles could at worst affect the sale of a property, or at least reduce the price, many homeowners affected by nuisance will not report their neighbours. They bite their tongue. A survey from 2010 suggested that over 60 per cent would move home rather than confront a nuisance neighbour.[5]

Thirty years after tower blocks became stigmatised, high-rise flats began to appear again in many cities, although this time round they were often occupied by childless people. Many are 'professional sharers', who split the accommodation costs and try to live together. The notes left by flat-sharers to each other suggest that this can be awkward. These notes are collected in the pages of I lick my cheese by Oonagh O'Hagan. One reads, 'THE WASHING UP YOU DIDN'T DO IS IN YOUR BED. CHEERS, AL.' A particularly cringe-worthy one asks that the person who has left 'crusty' black knickers 'with silver streaks' in the bathroom to 'kindly remove them'.[6] Other notes result from friction around food-stealing, running out of toilet roll, using noisy equipment late at night and diluting toilet-ries to conceal 'borrowing'.

KNOWING THE NEIGHBOURS

People of my generation might assume that street parties started with the Silver Jubilee of 1977. Dressed in red, white and blue, I sat at a trestle table laid with jelly and ice cream. Moss Lane in Bram-hall, Cheshire, was festooned with some rather pathetic bunting. Here I am (**Fig. 29**), in my Aran jumper (it was a cold day up north) with my sister and my mother. I was only four, and did not know then that this event was merely another in a sequence of national events celebrated with flags and dressing up. I was a baby when some streets came out when Princess Anne wed Mark Phillips in 1973. Even further back, neighbours celebrated peace in 1919 with teas and parties, and again for VE and VJ Days in 1945. Streets had come out for the Coronation of George V in 1911 and for his Silver Jubilee in 1935. They were back out for George VI's coronation in 1937, the Festival of Britain in 1951, and the coronation of Elizabeth II in 1953. There was no street party on my road for the wedding of Prince Charles to Lady Di in 1981, but other neighbours cele-brated together elsewhere.

Fig. 29 This is me and my sister in our Aran jumpers in June 1977, to celebrate the Silver Jubilee with neighbours on Moss Lane, Bramhall, in Cheshire. I am looking at the camera, and my mother is behind me.

In 1977, our family knew many of the faces about us (although we cannot remember their names today). These were the leafy suburbs of a fairly affluent neighbourhood (Bramhall gentrified further once the Cockaynes had left). I was a child and so not aware of any rifts or intrigues, although my dad heard rumours of a swinging network involving the more bohemian end of our street. Writing thirty-four years later, I live in the suburbs again, and although I would recognise many neighbours if our street hung out bunting, I think I would be able to put far fewer names to those faces.

News reports often linger on the anonymity of neighbouring. In July 2010, when a young mother died tragically at home in Merseyside, one neighbour said, 'I didn't know her very well. It's so sad that we don't know our neighbours anymore.' Another, noting that the dead woman 'seemed happy and carefree', also told reporters that she 'had kept herself to herself'.[7] The idea of not knowing the neighbours is not novel. In 1897, a witness in a court case startled the defendant by answering his question 'Do you know me? I don't know you mister' with 'Why, I live next door to you.'[8] However, the extent of this unfamiliarity does appear to be deepening. A survey carried out in 2009 suggested that a third of people under twenty-five did not know their neighbours' names. The same study suggested greater familiarity amongst those over the age of sixty-five, with only 4 per cent from that age group not knowing their neighbours' names.[9] Polling by YouGov in 2010 identified that nearly half of the adult population thought they knew more about the daily activities of their favourite celebrity than about their neighbour. Changing mentalities have seen celebrities become the legitimate targets of our prying as neighbours have stopped being so. The poll showed that an average of 39 per cent never visited a neighbour's house. This figure obscures age differences; 60 per cent of 25-to-34-year-olds never visit, compared to only 28 per cent of over-55-year-olds, and so the picture may not be so bleak. As people age and settle, they involve themselves more with the lives of those around them. Visiting the neighbours has never really been part of the English experience anyway, and the same poll reported much more positive things about the practical help that neighbours have given. Nearly a quarter said they had cared for a neighbour's plants or pets in the last year, and the same proportion kept a spare key for a neighbour. The *General Household Survey* published in 2000 suggested that most people had done a favour for, or received a favour from, a neighbour in the past six months. It also revealed 'generalised trust' amongst neighbours, with 58 per cent saying that they could *trust* 'many or most' of their neighbours, a higher figure than the 46 per cent who *knew* 'many or most' of their neighbours. Two thirds had taken in mail for neighbours who were out.[10] I have lived in my house for five years and am slowly gathering names as I take in parcels and overhear snatches of conversations. Not knowing the name of a neighbour is no barrier to cordiality. I say hello to several of my nameless neighbours and share small talk about the kids and the weather. Perhaps the most striking response to the poll was to the question 'Are there any elderly or disabled people in your neighbourhood whom you keep an eye on, to see if they need help?' Two thirds replied no (including 80 per cent of 25-to-34-year-olds). Had this question been asked of neighbours 300, 200, or even 100 years ago, a much more positive response would have come back.

However anonymous neighbouring seems these days, the opinion of the neighbours in assessing the reputation of victims and perpetrators of crimes is still valuable. Reporters will canvass neighbours' opinions when a tragedy has occurred, especially when the location of the crime was near their own doorstep. For example, in the murder of Jill Dando on her street, or after the atrocities committed by Fred West in his own home, the views of the neighbours were highly relevant. Even in less infamous cases, where the crime has been committed elsewhere, journalists still seek a soundbite from ashen-faced neighbours. 'He seemed like a normal bloke to me . . .' they reassure themselves in a report about a suspected serial rapist, '. . . he kept himself to himself.'

GROWING TOGETHER

A community garden has been created at the other end of the street from the home of the 1920s Littlehampton poison-pen letter-writer (see Chapter 5). Neighbours from the lower end of Western Road spent two years designing and building the garden – securing permission from the council, receiving funding from a variety of bodies and tapping into the collective enthusiasm and skills of the street (**Figs. 30** and **31**). The garden end of the street is more ethnically and socially diverse than the eastern, uphill end. A greater proportion of the residents at the garden end rent their homes from private landlords, while the eastern end has more owner-occupiers.

The neighbours turned a bleak patch of unloved land, the site of fly-tipping and vehicle repair, into a small, colourful fenced garden. Any neighbour with time and motivation could become

Fig. 30 The Beach Town community garden,
on the corner of Western Road, Littlehampton, 2011.

involved in the planning, design and building. A variety of skills
were cultivated in the process – with one neighbour tracing the
owners of the land, some steering the project through council
procedures, and another doing the plastering. Most neighbours
helped with the planting and paving when they could, and some
even operated heavy machinery. Not everyone on the western end
of the street become involved (although most were supportive and
encouraging), and some neighbours took a more active role. The
result is an eclectic mix of styles, reflecting the range of tastes that
different participants brought to the project. This makes the space
welcoming to all – it is not one person's vision, but the result of
communal, neighbourhood action. Any neighbour can add plants
or pots. A bright red rose was planted in memory of one of the
neighbours, who died while the garden was being created. A sculp-
ture of shells and pebbles by an unknown artist appeared one day.
The garden is fenced and gated, but is kept open all hours.

Fig. 31 The Beach Town community garden, Littlehampton.

Now that construction is complete, the caretaking is mostly in the hands of the neighbours whose properties immediately over-look the garden. This could become a source of friction in the future, especially when new residents move in. It could be argued that these neighbours gain most from the garden's existence. There has been little vandalism in the garden, although the mosaic 'B' of 'BEACH TOWN' was removed one day, leaving the sign reading 'EACH TOWN', an act interpreted by one neighbour as a state-ment. Inevitably, there was some rancour as the project developed and the garden grew; there were fallouts and intrigues. On the whole the neighbours involved felt that they got to know each other much better through their participation. Being on site meant that people were visible to each other and available to chat, in a similar way to neighbours in the past gathering around the shared pumps and privies. Other people on the street stopped to talk and brought cups of tea. This created opportunities for them to share non-garden concerns and to become involved with each other's

lives in ways they never had done before. The garden is not especially well used; few neighbours sit in it regularly. That is not really
the point of it, however. It is an improvement on what it replaced.
It is a symbolic space – it tells those who walk past that people
care about it, they have invested in their street.

ENGLISHMEN IN CASTLES

A home is normally now a family's biggest financial asset. Homeowners are disturbed by situations that might affect property values,
such as unkempt gardens, abandoned cars and overgrown hedges.
A few years ago, the property developer Sarah Beeny presented
Streets Ahead on Channel 4. Through arguments and recriminations,
Beeny persevered to get neighbours to work together to improve
the appearance of their street. The premise was that if all frontages
looked better, the whole street would be more desirable and therefore each house worth more. Some neighbours refused to join in,
and others only managed a couple of hours of half-hearted spade-
work before laziness overcame them. This often left a dogged few
to do all the work, while cursing the freeloaders. A few streets did
manage to pull together – and participants remarked that they had
got to know neighbours much better through the process. Michael
Fitchew from Norfolk Road in Walthamstow said, 'I didn't realise
that I would enjoy meeting the neighbours so much . . . the project
brought out a real Blitz spirit.'[11] Beeny herself was disillusioned by
the lack of interaction between neighbours. Interviewed at the
time, she talked about her own neighbourhood: 'They don't come
for supper or anything, but you ask how their kids are, and chat
like you would in a village. Now I see that mostly that doesn't
happen. People work all day, then come home and shut the door.'[12]
   Much of the active neighbouring in the past was carried out by
women, but an increasing number of women go out to work. In
1971, about 56 per cent of women worked; by 2008, this figure was
closer to 70 per cent.[13] Fewer neighbours have time to spare for
casual meetings; this was summed up in a comment made in the

1980s: 'I'm at work so I can't say I'm very neighbourly. And I have other home commitments in the evening. I know people to say hello to and people would help you if you needed it.'[14] Most people out at work during the day have only sporadic exchanges with their neighbours, perhaps when gardening or cleaning the car at the weekend. Retired people and parents at home with children have more opportunities to establish deeper relationships with their neighbours.

Back in July 1962, the police distributed leaflets in Bradford urging people to ask their neighbours to keep an eye on their homes while they were on holiday. A senior police officer is reported to have said, 'If people will be good neighbours we can prevent a lot of crime and avoid distress for many holidaymakers.'[15] Neighbours were not placed in this caretaking position so frequently in the past, because holidays were less common. American-style Neighbourhood Watch Areas were adopted in the UK from the 1980s. Mollington in Chester was the location of the first English scheme, established by residents beleaguered by burglaries.[16] There are now many across the county.[17] Francis Fukuyama has argued that this is not a formalisation of neighbourhood warmth but is symptomatic of a pervasive sense of distrust in society.[18] Signs of Neighbourhood Watch (see **Fig. 32**) are more evident in some areas. In 2005, a survey by the building company Linden Homes showed that three-quarters would investigate if they heard a neighbour's burglar alarm, but many admitted this was only because the noise would disturb them.[19]

The modern planning system ensures that neighbours are notified about proposed building works so that they can query or oppose development plans at the application stage. Neighbours making applications are able to identify challengers, so there is a potential for animosity. When the owners applied to extend a house on Whateley Road, East Dulwich, in 2008 (this was the street where Richard Adkins and Henry Pybus fought in 1900; see Chapter 4), the neighbours adjacent objected, as did people whose garden backed on to theirs. The rear neighbours worried about a loss of

Fig. 32 Neighbourhood Watch signs in Littlehampton.

privacy, the next-door neighbours about a loss of outlook and light. Planning permission was granted.[20] Until the passage of the 1992 Access to Neighbouring Land Act, adjoining homeowners had little right to go on to their neighbours' land to maintain their own property. Now a court order can be obtained to secure access.

The gardens of working-class houses had typically allowed little privacy, with neighbours sharing outbuildings and privies, and back-yards that could only be reached by walking through a neighbouring yard. In these backyards, demarcations of space were missing or imprecise. Many council-house gardens were originally fenceless, or had wire dividers, like those erected on Thimbler Road in Coventry. When council-house owners were granted the right to buy, strips of communal garden were divided up into individual plots. Lynsey Hanley recalled the fenceless gardens of the Chelmsley Wood estate ('The Wood') in Birmingham. Eventually 'the tedium of fetching footballs from one end of the green expanse . . . to the other became too much, and tenants were allowed to erect dividing fences'.[21] In modern times, garden sharing is not so readily tolerated; people want visible separation. Where I live, the words 'bisected garden' (i.e. walked through by neighbours) on the particulars can knock several thousand off the value of a house and cause some buyers to shun them.

Fences seem to be getting higher. As a child, I could easily see the elderly neighbours next door as I 'entertained' them with my puppet shows, and I was not a tall child. In friends' gardens I remember the Thimbler Road-style wire dividers, or squat wooden fences with trellis tops. Photographs of gardens in the early twentieth century suggest they either had high brick walls, low wooden fences or simple wire divisions. More recently, most gardens have panel fences at least five feet high. I cannot see over; I am not a tall adult.

Some disputes between neighbours concern the boundary: a sense of being robbed of land, or an infringement of privacy. June Iddon, in her seventies, was convicted in 2008 after she broke a neighbour's arm with a spade during a long-standing boundary dispute. After her neighbour had secured permission to move a fence that blocked his access to a driveway, Iddon took umbrage. In court, Iddon ('built like a sparrow', according to her lawyer) claimed she had blacked out during the incident, but her neighbour's daughter described seeing her wield the spade with 'the strength of ten men'.[22] Many cases are caused by a disagreement over the location of the boundary, which can arise after a misinterpretation of the plan or careless refencing. Some are more complex, however, and develop from the lack of a clear boundary when neighbouring houses were constructed. Two sets of Surrey neighbours had been friends for twenty years in 2005 when plans to erect a fence on a strip of land plunged them into enmity. The conflict escalated and a costly legal battle ensued. The squabble related to the parking of cars. Previously, a driveway used to park cars belonging to both houses was not separated by a fence. When one neighbour applied to divide the drive, the other neighbour objected because the fence would mean they would not have room to manoeuvre. The Kingston County Court ruled that an assumed boundary from 1935 gave the fence-seeking neighbour 'squatters' rights' over the strip of land. After stating his intention to erect a fence, then sell his house, this neighbour told a reporter: 'We used to get on very well. We would exchange house keys when we went away . . . Now we don't speak. We ignore each other.'[23]

Raising the height of a fence may trigger the chagrin of a neighbour because it implies that they are not to be trusted to obey the rules of neighbouring and so need fencing out. A scuffle took place in 2010 between two Stockport semi-detached neighbours, apparently over a panel that had been erected on top of a fence between their gardens. One man died and his neighbour was arrested but not charged. One of their neighbours (who wanted to remain anonymous) said of the dead man, 'He was just a quiet bloke.'[24] A tragic boundary-related conflict played out over a small privet hedge between two Lincoln neighbours in 2003. The hedge separated two gardens on Webster Close, a cul-de-sac of 1930s semis, and one neighbour was angered when the other reduced the height from feet to inches. A tussle over the hedge-trimmer triggered a violent response in one man, who shot his neighbour dead. After the shooter hanged himself while on remand, an inquest into the deaths noted that there had been some long-standing animosity between the pair.[25]

Boundaries made of trees can form the equivalent of the Victorian spite walls, growing to ridiculous heights and blocking the light to neighbours' windows. Neighbours of David Alvand recently rejoiced when he lopped and topped a crowd of leylandii at the front of his Plymouth home. The trees had grown to thirty-five feet after Alvand had lost a legal battle to enclose his property with a high wall. Alvand claimed that his neighbours victimised him.[26] An Englishman who sees his home as his castle will adopt a fortress mentality and resent trespass not only by people, but even by tree branches, animals and toys. In the 1940s, Charles Reilly and Lawrence Wolfe had urged planners to counter this 'house-madness' in their post-war developments, but their warnings went largely unheeded. There are currently estimated to be 100,000 'hedge rage' disputes across the country, and they became the focus of an addition to the Antisocial Behaviour Act in 2005. People now have the right to challenge neighbours whose hedges are high, although council charges put many off initiating proceedings.[27]

NEIGHBOURS FROM HELL

Neighbours in dispute can report a nuisance to the council or housing association, initiate court proceedings, seek arbitration, or take it up with the neighbour directly. This range of options is more formal and bureaucratic than ever before – although many have echoes of the London Viewers, police and law courts, manorial courts and civic authorities we encountered in earlier chapters. In the past, there was frequently confusion about which authority (if any) had the jurisdiction to deal with nuisance neighbours. Nowadays, routes for redress are a little clearer, but many people simply call the boys in blue.[28]

'Neighbours from hell' has become a cliché, attracting attention in the media.[29] Households are generally smaller and quieter than they used to be. Sounds coming from next door are more audible in quiet surroundings and people want more control over their domestic environment than the people we met earlier in the book could ever have had. With so many raucous sources of noise to be irritated by, it might seem odd that a survey of 2007 (by the insurers Cornhill Direct) identified wind chimes as the most irritating neighbourly noise.[30]

Jean-Paul Sartre told us that 'hell is other people', and annoyances are most likely to occur when neighbours do not share the same lifestyle; for example, if one works nights or students live next to the elderly.[31] Student houses are especially considered to have a negative impact on the neighbourhood.[32] Students have different body clocks to young families or old couples. Some student neighbours, however, are great, and will babysit, take in parcels and volunteer in the local community.

A stereotypical Sunday-afternoon suburban scene features men surreptitiously eyeing up cars being lovingly buffed by their neighbours. In 1995, a newspaper advertising campaign for a car asked, 'What will the neighbours think?' and thought that they would be impressed by their latest model, which might match the curtains.[33] A few years later, a competitor asked, 'What does it take to impress the neighbours these days?' and implied that their new car would 'get those net curtains twitching'. 'Why keep up with the Joneses', the advert asked, 'when you could overtake?'[34] In modern Britain, however, cars turn the neighbours red with anger as much as green with envy. Mostly, the trouble stems from parking. Some of this conflict arises from the misapprehension that a householder has a right to park on the street directly outside their home. Kerbside bickering can degenerate into violent conflict. Such cases are most common in communities with limited parking, such as narrow urban terraced streets. These feuds can develop with sinister conclusions, as in the case of Krystal Hart, a pregnant secretary killed in London in April 2007 following a protracted dispute with a neighbour about parking.[35] More recently, a Rochdale man was attacked with a golf club by a neighbour who was irate about parking. This conflict had a long history; in 1994, the attacker had believed that his neighbour had deliberately parked his car an inch too far in front of his terraced house. Over a period of years, the attacker had thrown bricks and paint, and 'deliberately positioned a puppet in his car with its middle finger up' so it faced his neighbour's house. The attacker's solicitor described the culminating golf-club attack as 'a moment of anger', adding that his client 'is not a Victor Meldrew character'. He was sentenced to ten months after pleading guilty to causing grievous bodily harm. At sentencing, the judge added that 'it's a common experience that, with the increase in cars in areas where people live close together, there will be disputes over parking of cars'.[36] Some of the streets we have visited in previous chapters now have parking problems. As on many other streets, in Beaconsfield Road in Ipswich, some cars park far on to the pavement.[37] Thimbler Road residents occasionally struggle to find a space to park in cul-de-sacs designed for households with fewer cars, and the narrow roads in the area are known as the 'Canley curse'.[38]

A different parking story has played out along Prebend Gardens, the tree-lined Chiswick street once home to the catfighting ladies in Chapter 4. In the early 1970s, Anne Smith (now known as Anne Naysmith), a concert pianist, was ejected from her rooms in 22 Prebend Gardens. Thereafter, she slept in her car, and battled to get back into her lodgings. Ms Naysmith was 'accepted and even loved by many' of her neighbours, some of whom became recipients of tomato chutney she made from produce grown on a makeshift allotment. Refusing handouts from neighbours, Ms Naysmith, aka the 'Rag Lady of Chiswick', lived off private funds. Something compelled her to stay near to her former home and offers of alternative accommodation were rejected. In 2000, a local couple put their house on the market and initiated a campaign to rid Prebend Gardens of Naysmith's car, writing to neighbours claiming, 'the fact remains that the car is a health hazard'. Many neighbours refused to unite against her, but the council towed the car away in 2002. Three neighbours had tried to obstruct the removal team and stopped only when threatened with arrest.[39]

An even newer neighbour nuisance arrived from the Antipodes in the form of the garden barbecue. Andrew Oldham's disturbing but witty poem 'Why Guns will Never be Legal In Britain' reveals how the noise and smell of a neighbour's barbecue can infiltrate a house and drive out the occupants. Oldham depicts neighbours who have a barbecue whenever it is sunny and invite loud family members.[40] Interviewed in *Pennine Life*, he explained that the ubiquity of summer barbecues makes them a nuisance: 'I don't want to smell what my neighbour is cooking everyday or hear why they hate each other.'[41]

Animals can drive neighbours apart too; cats foul borders and dogs bark at night. Neighbours in Nordelph, Norfolk, were close friends until one of them bought a Rottweiler–mastiff cross. One woman was scared of the dog, and her husband begged his neighbours not to keep it. The dog stayed, arguments ensued and eventually the owners were shot, hospitalising them both. The neighbour was found guilty of attempted murder. A policeman described the incident as 'a neighbourhood dispute that got completely out of hand'.[42] Remember the couple fearful of the 'artful' monkey in the next-door garden in 1872, which the Greenwich Police Court were powerless to deal with? Well, a hundred years later, the Surrey neighbours of William Wheeler lived in fear of his puma and two leopards, especially after Dax the puma mauled a boy (Wheeler said Dax just wanted a cuddle). At that time, keeping a puma was not a punishable offence, but legislation was drawn up a few years afterwards.[43]

Some nuisances return to rear their noisy heads. In 2008, neighbours of Peter Stoodley in Shepton Mallett were annoyed by his cockerels crowing 400 times per hour, sometimes starting at half past two in the morning and audible through closed windows. When Stoodley breached a noise-abatement order served by the district council, he was given an Antisocial Behaviour Order (ASBO) banning him from keeping livestock.[44]

In the early-modern period, neighbours reported watching Mary Wallys, Clement Underhill and Mary Babb having sex. This lascivious prurience was mirrored by a case heard in Newcastle Crown Court in 2009. A recording of Mr and Mrs Cartwright's bedtime activities was played to the court. Mrs Cartwright had already been served a Noise Abatement Notice in 2007, and was subject to an ASBO, but according to neighbours, the noise had not abated. Giving evidence, one neighbour explained that she was often unable to sleep due to the 'unnatural' noises, which were reported to last for hours, occur regularly and measure up to 47 decibels in a neighbouring property. One of the neighbours had described the sounds made by the Cartwrights as being 'like they are both in considerable pain'. Listening to the noises heard next door, a council official likened them to overhearing a murder.

Mrs Cartwright unsuccessfully argued that the case undermined her human rights and invaded her privacy. Recorder Jeremy Freedman said, 'we are in no doubt whatsoever about the level of noise that can be heard in neighbouring properties . . . It certainly was intrusive and constituted a statutory nuisance.' Sentencing Cartwright in 2010, Judge Beatrice Bolton (who has since herself become embroiled in a neighbour dispute over her dogs and the use of a shared garden)[45] said that she had seemed to make 'no attempt to silence' herself. When an environmental health manager had approached the Cartwrights about their noise, Mr Cartwright had appeared embarrassed, but Mrs Cartwright 'seemed to find it quite amusing'.[46]

Thirty-five years earlier, the Brick Development Association had considered the sounds of sex. Thin partitions of timber and plasterboard had proliferated in modern buildings and these did not enjoy the same noise-suppressing qualities as brick walls. Impetus for the campaign came when Anthony Cadman, the director general of the association, went on a fact-finding tour of housing estates, and found himself assailed by neighbours who could hear the Joneses 'at it' through the thin walls. A Milton Keynes couple heard every detail of their neighbours' sex life each Friday night. Cadman was especially concerned about neighbouring children; 'it's very upsetting', he said, to hear children saying, '"Mum, we heard Mr and Mrs Jones at it again last night."'[47]

Having a problem neighbour can be a route to obsession and hypersensitivity. This is illustrated by a neighbour row from Bolton in Lancashire, between the Hoggs in one half of the semi-detached house, and the Foggs in the other half. The Hoggs had lived in their half for twenty-six years, first as tenants of the council, and then as owners under the right-to-buy scheme. The Foggs moved next to the Hoggs in 1986, and for a while the two families chatted amicably over the garden fence. Eventually the Hoggs started to get annoyed by knocks heard at strange hours, plants being moved about and other pranks. A study of neighbours carried out by Colin and Mog Ball a few years earlier revealed how irritations can be misunderstood and how party walls can magnify molehills into mountains. 'Little things like that tend to make me edgy and I feel very irritated and aggressive', confided one of the Balls' respondents. The Hoggs felt under siege and became preoccupied, putting barbed wire around their garden and mounting a vigil. They started to call the police out, and this angered Ms Fogg next door. Incensed, she took a baseball bat to the Hoggs' door. Eventually the Bolton Mediation Service became involved and they uncovered misunderstandings. The pranks had been carried out by Ms Fogg's babysitters (whom she sacked), and the banging noises that had started the conflict were traced to a loose floorboard in the Fogg house. Relations thawed.[48] This case reveals the ways that incidental noises from next door can be misinterpreted by neighbours as deliberate and mischievous. The neighbours become obsessed, and can eventually become the bigger nuisance themselves.

FASCINATION STREET

Even if we no longer know our own neighbours as well as we once did, the English still retain a fascination with the idea of neighbours. We watch them on the television and not through lace curtains. In 1985, the BBC brought us a terraced street to rival Wetherfield's *Coronation Street* in the form of Walford's Albert Square (*EastEnders*), and in 1982, Channel 4 had introduced us to the residents of Brookside Close in Liverpool (*Brookside* ran until 2003). Situation comedies often exploit the tensions that exist between neighbours who have different lifestyles. *Love Thy Neighbour* (Thames Television) ran from 1972 to 1976 and was based around a suburban white couple finding themselves the neighbours of a black couple. The stupidity and bigotry of the white male contrasted with the sophistication of his more educated black neighbour. It exemplified a common tension in society at that time and aroused controversy. Thames Television's *George and Mildred* (1976–9) turned from race to class and followed the Ropers after they left their flat and moved to a modern housing estate, next door to the Fourmiles. Jeffrey

Fourmile was a snobby estate agent who considered himself superior to the Ropers and fretted that their presence would devalue property values. The neighbours who featured in *The Good Life* (BBC, 1975–8) were old friends, but their friendship was tested when one couple (Tom and Barbara Good) rejected consumerism to enjoy the 'good life'. The Goods converted their Surbiton garden into an allotment, generated electricity from methane and kept livestock (including pigs and a cockerel called Lenin), to the consternation of the Leadbetters, their conventional next-door neighbours. In *Ever Decreasing Circles* (BBC, 1984–9), married Ann Bryce is attracted to her suave next-door neighbour, Paul Ryman. Paul is the opposite of her husband, Martin, who is an anally retentive pedant who co-ordinates the Neighbourhood Watch. Angus Deayton is no stranger to life next door (and in real life he was one of Douglas Adams' London neighbours).[49] His key roles in sitcoms have been as the next-door neighbour. In *One Foot in the Grave* (BBC, 1990–2000), he was Patrick Trench, the neighbour of Mr and Mrs Meldrew. *15 Storeys High* (BBC, 2002–4) was unlike the other sitcoms, as the location was not suburban, but a city tower block. It featured the relationship between two contrasting flatmates – misanthropic Vince and eager-to-please Errol – and often showed glimpses of lives lived in the other flats.

Since the eighteenth century, status has become increasingly bound up with domestic display. As goods and services became more readily available in the consumerist culture of the modern world, neighbours resorted to the conspicuous display of products to gain a sense of superiority over their neighbours. *Keeping up Appearances* (BBC, 1990–5) featured Hyacinth Bucket (pronounced 'Bouquet', but only by Hyacinth), a status-obsessed social climber who spends much time trying to impress the neighbours.

The most manifest evidence of one-upmanship between neighbours comes once a year with the Christmas illuminations. Some neighbours team up. Thirty homes in a Dorset cul-de-sac draw crowds during the festive period and the residents have an official switching-on ceremony. Another street, in Burnham-on-Sea, also lights up the neighbourhood; one resident estimated that there were a hundred thousand lights along Trinity Close in 2009. Mostly this is harmless fun, and these streets also collect money for charity. In Burnham-on-Sea, the luminescent bling raised money for a charity set up in memory of a neighbour.[50] Lights, however, can shine too brightly for some. In 2006, a man from Berkshire's Sonning-on-Thames was ordered by a court injunction to scale down his illuminations to prevent the annoyances his neighbours had endured in previous years, when coachloads of spectators had arrived to marvel. Neighbours complained of noise, petty crime and disruption. Some resorted to sedatives.[51]

LOVE IS BLIND, BUT THE NEIGHBOURS AIN'T

Relationships between neighbours that start with a friendly salutation and a cup of borrowed sugar can end up in bed. For single people, this should have few complications (besides some awkwardness should the relationship dissolve), but when married people lust after a neighbour, the situation can become difficult. In 2008, an advert for a broadband service showed a woman sleeping with her next-door neighbour. The hapless husband bursts in (the neighbour having hidden) and rings 'Bob next door' to tell him about the cheap package. A mobile rings from within the wardrobe.[52] Florence Welch, the flame-haired siren who fronts the band Florence + the Machine, grew up with the four children next door when her mother fell in love with a neighbour. Welch has described her upbringing, once the two families amalgamated, as 'chaotic'.[53]

The culture of swinging was popular in the 1960s and 70s. Journalist Liz Hodgkinson came out in the *Daily Express* as a wife who swapped. She described evenings she and her husband spent with the couple next door in the 1970s. Relations became 'increasingly intimate' until they took each other to bed. Looking back in 1993, she wrote that both couples found the aftermath embarrassing: 'we had to cope with confronting each other on a daily basis . . . After sex, you are no longer merely friends.'[54] The presence of pampas grass (the swingers' signature plant) on a front lawn suppos-edly advertises availability to amorous cruisers.[55] Several of you might now be wondering why your aunt has some. Swinging is currently enjoying a revival (so they say), but it is no longer a neighbour thing, since the internet has given rise to regional, national and even international swinging clubs.[56] While swinging might have had suburban roots, nowadays pampas totems blow redundant in the wind.

In 2009, the neighbours of a pornographic film studio located in a cul-de-sac in Bradley Stoke, near Bristol, protested about the business. The film-maker claimed to 'get on very well with my immediate neighbours', but many of his neighbours staged a protest, voicing concerns about property values and the moral tone of the area.[57] In another cul-de-sac, this time in Bedfordshire, clients visited Claire Finch for topless massages with 'happy endings'. Finch was upfront with her new neighbours when she moved into her bungalow in 2000. 'I told everyone that I worked from home with a group of six older women selling sex . . . Nobody seemed to mind. In fact, my old neighbours were delighted', said the refreshingly frank Finch. Her relatively discreet business did not seem to annoy the neighbours, and one elderly woman, who allowed clients to park on her drive, even joked to Finch, 'Send them to me and I'll give them a rub down.' Finch was charged with brothel-keeping but was cleared of the offence. Three neigh-bours testified on her behalf, and the jury heard that Finch was a decent and caring neighbour.[58]

GOOD NEIGHBOURS, NOT GOOD FRIENDS

In 1972, the discovery of two long-dead women in their homes, one in Liverpool and the other in Portsmouth, exposed holes in the frame-work of social care. The director of the charity Age Concern called for more neighbour nosiness, and asked neighbours not to assume that every elderly person had relatives watching out for them. 'Part of the reason why some neighbours leave elderly people alone', he speculated, 'is that they don't want to become involved and they feel showing interest may take up too much of their time.'[59] After Margaret Thatcher had announced the death of society, she went on to say, 'there are individual men and women, and there are families . . . It is our duty to look after ourselves and then to look after our neighbour.'[60] In 2010, there were twenty-one Good Neighbour schemes in Suffolk alone, and these were very similar in character to the schemes established in the 1960s. Teams of volunteers offered transport, ran errands, befriended the lonely, read out loud, filled in forms and odd-jobbed. According to Springline, a Good Neighbour scheme in Lincolnshire, volunteers are 'just doing things that good neighbours do for each other'. The Rowntree researchers found that the schemes often suffer a mismatch between volunteers and the needy. The schemes were weakest or absent in the solidly working-class neighbourhoods that needed them most.[61] The volunteers were mostly middle-class women, and the cost (in time) of volunteering was prohibitive for many people in the most deprived areas. In 1998, the Rev. Richard Taylor of Benwell planned a scheme to move a 'nice' family on to the Pendower estate in Newcastle to run a community centre and offer advice and support; to be a 'Christian presence on the estate'. Eventually some of the volunteers were paid and a community centre with a live-in resident worker was established in two semi-detached houses, now known as the Sunnybank Centre.[62] In its initial incarnation, this development was akin to the late-Victorian settlement houses, which were part of the settlement movement that peaked in the 1920s and saw middle-class people settle into poor areas to offer advice and support to those around them.

Good Neighbours schemes have never been able to replicate the sort of relationship of the old traditional neighbourhoods. For one, the help only goes one way. All is not lost, and a focus on hellish neighbours (who are the minority) takes attention from the loving and caring stories still enriching life on streets right across the country. Although households are now more self-reliant, neighbours are still often first on hand in an emergency. When a Spanish student was stabbed in her Thimbler Road house in Coventry in 1994, her neighbour made desperate (and sadly unsuccessful) attempts to revive her.[63] There are more prosaic stories too – such as that told by David Gourdie and Conny Armstrong, neighbours in Middle-port, Staffordshire, who refused to move out of terraced houses earmarked for clearance in May 2006 because they wanted to remain neighbours in their new accommodation. Gourdie was quoted as saying: 'We are friends and I help her out. We want to live next door to each other.' Armstrong said, 'I don't know how I could cope without David.'[64]

8

If Friends are Electric,
are Virtual Neighbours the Future?

Young children might still draw *Play School*-style detached houses, but they now have a new cultural influence, courtesy of the BBC series *In the Night Garden* (**Fig. 33**). Two families of tiny wooden peg people live in adjacent semi-detached houses in the middle of the garden at the foot of a tree. The Pontipines are a family of ten who wear cardinal red. Their neighbours, the Wottingers, also number ten and dress in blue. Theirs is not the best layout because the front doors are far apart and consequently the living spaces in each house will share a party wall. The numerous children in each house increase the potential for nuisance. The Wottingers are seen less frequently, but are waved to by the Pontipines. The families rarely interact, at least when the cameras are on them. There is no pampas grass.

Over the past five centuries, we have, on the whole, become less neighbourly with the people who live near to us. Pre-modern neighbouring was about 'place, personal knowledge, active reciprocity (with certain limits) and the avoidance of conflict (or at least its reconciliation)'.[1] Neighbourly relationships were founded on giving and receiving support, especially amongst the poor. Neighbours' lives became less entwined over time. By the mid twentieth century, ideal neighbours were most likely to be those who 'kept themselves to themselves' and expected those near them to do the same. Neighbouring has become more passive. A 1954 study of estate-dwellers noted that 'The majority like to be friendly with their neighbours,

Fig. 33 *In the Night Garden.*

offering help and expecting it in return in times of need, but avoiding too great intimacy.'[2] With the passing of another fifty years, friendliness has been replaced by distant cordiality. The team behind *In the Night Garden* have tapped into the zeitgeist.

We now have the ability to avoid our neighbours in ways that pre-modern neighbours could not. They were lucky to have glass in their windows, while some of us have triple glazing with a resin coating to block more noise. Disputes between neighbours are often now mediated by bureaucrats. Environmental-health- and town-planning-created structures for decision-making and unexpected laws that respond to moral panics, such as the 1976 Dangerous Wild Animals Act, have framed the limits of acceptable neighbourly behaviour. The civic authorities of the past lacked codified legislation, and often the informal intervention of clergymen, Justices of the Peace and other neighbours were the best defence against nuisance-makers. We might curse the council at times, but they do provide a safeguard against some of the worst neighbour wrongs – such as spite walls and dangerous chimneys.

Elizabeth Roberts studied neighbours in north-west England between 1940 and 1970 and thought that lives had moved indoors. The streets were the venue for 'effortless sociability'. Neighbours were friends and friends were mostly from the neighbourhood. Gradually friends spread out and met though prior arrangements. It was no longer odd or resented to be private, because most neighbours became the objects of 'distant cordiality'.[3] In 1969, one of Jeremy Seabrook's interviewees, a member of a tenants' association for one of Blackburn's largest council estates, consoled herself, 'I suppose people lead full lives now, they have a far wider circle of friends.'[4]

DO GOOD NEIGHBOURS BECOME GOOD FRIENDS?

I have not directly addressed the difference between 'friends' and 'neighbours'. Friendships are relationships based on similar (or complementary) outlooks, shared interests or backgrounds. Neighbour relationships are based on residential proximity and are therefore more forced. You cannot choose your neighbours – they come with the house – and unchosen relationships can be rocky ones. Asked in court in 1852 if he was a friend to one of the witnesses, a man answered 'no friend at all – only neighbours'.[5] A hundred years later, a woman living on a Liverpool estate claimed that she 'got on all right with everybody . . . they are neighbours rather than friends'.[6] We have some knowledge of our neighbours, even if this is just where they live. They remain neighbours until we, or they, move away. Friendships are more enduring and can survive physical separation.

It is difficult to judge how well we know our neighbours. Colin and Mog Ball were surprised how much their interviewees had pieced together from observing their neighbours' habits and patterns of movement.[7] People want different things of their neighbours.[8] A woman surveyed by Gorer in the 1950s thought that her neighbours were 'ideal' because 'they keep away', but to others, this sort of aloofness would have seemed unfriendly. Responding

to the same survey, an Essex electrician complained that the neighbours on one side were 'always finding fault with everyone', and
those on the other side annoyed him by calling him Mr and not
by his Christian name.[9] People vary in their attitudes to privacy,
with consequences for the type of property they feel comfortable
in. Some are less conducive to easy neighbouring than others; not
all families could cope with the tiptoeing needed to stay cordial in
Coventry's steel houses. A resident who had lived in a steel house
for five years recently said that he found it 'very pleasant', adding
'you certainly get to know your neighbours'.[10] The trouble is, some
people do not want to know their neighbours.

Kevin Harris, a neighbourhood blogger and community development consultant, has drawn up a useful spectrum of involved
neighbouring, which ranges from the provocatively negative to the
positively supportive. For one person a 'passively negative', non-
communicative neighbour might be ideal. Another may yearn for
an 'interactive and supportive' neighbour who mucks in all the
time, or a 'passively supportive' neighbour who helps only when
needed.[11] People are not fixed on this spectrum. They can have one
type of relationship with one neighbour, and a different relationship
with another. We change our ways and our needs through our own
life cycle, depending on how much we work, whether we have
children at home, whether we are healthy and as we age. As we
become a different sort of neighbour, we need a different sort of
neighbour. The key to good neighbouring is working out what
kind of relationship each wants.

Indeed, to keep on good terms, some neighbours have found
that they need to keep a distance. This is because home is where
we are most ourselves; the location for curler-wearing and cursing,
the place we relax and blow off steam. Neighbours live at the inter-
face between our private and public selves. They glimpse the
backstage of our lives from a few steps away. Colin and Mog Ball
found that neighbourliness 'requires the preservation of a balance
between two needs: to be alone and to contribute to the community'.[12] One of the reasons we talk to our neighbour on the doorstep,

and rarely in the house, is that we are not normally prepared for visitors. We keep them at arm's length to avoid exposing our backstage mess. Visitors who travel to us usually let us know when they will arrive, and when they will go. Neighbours might come unannounced, outstay their welcome and remain too long beyond curtain fall.

Some friendly relationships soured into enmity. Relations between two Thimbler Road neighbours started well in the 1950s; they were 'in and out all the time'. Then they quarrelled, and hatred developed either side of their flimsy fence.[13] Joanna Crimmins and Jane Varndell, both of St George's Place in Southampton, were once as close as sisters. They shared everything. By 1884, however, they had fallen out and Crimmins found herself in the Police Court for assaulting the next-door neighbour she once loved.[14] These stories can serve as warnings: too great an intimacy with a neighbour might lead to struggles in the future. Neighbours, unlike friends, do not disappear once links are severed. They remain annoyingly close. People who once sought each other out now ignore each other, or worse.

TALKING ABOUT THE NEIGHBOURS IS UNNEIGHBOURLY

People are inhibited when asked to talk about their neighbours, which complicates neighbour studies. Mitchell and Lupton found this in the mid 1950s on the Liverpool estate, where interviewees initially gave 'vague and ambiguous comments', and only gradually became more open and 'precise'.[15] 'Talking about the neighbours is not considered very nice', commented the Balls. Good neighbours protect each other's privacy, so ironically the best neighbours reveal the least to researchers.[16]

Neighbours can be faithful or fraudulent. How do we know if our peccadilloes will be broadcast? The apparently innocent chat on the doorstep might allow profligacy or benefit-scrounging to be detected. The government encouraged citizens to rat on each other during the Second World War. A widow who claimed National Assistance just after the war was reported by her neighbours when she took part-time work.[17] Now water companies encourage people to report neighbours flouting hosepipe bans. Any system that relies on neighbours snitching on each other will corrode community harmony.

Mrs Yates, the lady observed by her neighbours' servants through wine funnels in 1831, seemed to be decidedly out of step with her neighbours by saying she wanted to keep herself to herself. Nellie Benson, the social worker in the 1880s, thought this standoffishness was common (although inexcusable). By 1969, a woman living in Blackburn's city centre reminisced about the halcyon days when 'it was different altogether'. 'Now', she complained, 'you've to keep yourself to yourself, you can't be neighbourly.'[18] Already by the 1950s, estate-dwellers were equating neighbourliness with keeping oneself to oneself. Privacy is not a simple gain. The stereotypically modern view of neighbouring – hands-off, home-centred, keeping oneself to oneself, possibly status-driven – contrasts with the traditional old streets, when relatives lived nearby and a shop or a pub marked each street corner. Privacy is relatively easy to come by in modern houses, on modern streets, but it comes at a price. Many of us have lost our sense of place in an immediate community. Lawrence Wolfe, the champion of the Reilly Plan, foresaw this in 1945.

I LOVE THOSE NEIGHBOURS THT DNT PASSWORD PROTECT THEIR WIFI ;) x[19]

Before supermarkets and refrigeration, and especially in the countryside, sharing food amongst neighbours was an essential way to use up supplies. A slaughtered pig could not be consumed by a small family before it went rancid. They shared and received an exchange in kind, usually at a later date, when their neighbour had a glut. Our ability to store food and distribute it over a long distance means we do not need to negotiate consumption with our neighbour. Depositing goodwill in the neighbour bank was an insurance against misfortune when you needed support. Chapter 1 showed how neighbourly trust could prop up credit networks, and later people even supplied items for their neighbours to pawn. Similar arrangements continued in working-class neighbourhoods until commercial credit became available. These developments have seen neighbours having less involvement with each other. In 1969, Jeremy Seabrook was finding resentment about the effect of rising prosperity on neighbourliness in Blackburn. In the past, there was a 'consoling certainty that all their neighbours shared the same poverty'.[20]

Most of us depend much less on our neighbours than was common in the past. Anna Davin described Victorian neighbours as living within a 'network of reciprocal favours'.[21] These favours could keep a family from the workhouse or starvation. With mutual support and sharing no longer significant facets of neighbouring, the negatives of hazard and nuisance seem more prominent. The sociologist Richard Sennett has shown how, in spite of the stress on self-sufficiency being essential to maintain self-respect, relationships without mutual support can be hollow.[22] Modern people mostly enjoy physical and emotional distance from their neighbours, so why do neighbourly relations continue at all? It is because making a neighbourhood work well requires more than just individual action, or council control. Neighbours need to get together, and the Beach Town community garden in Littlehampton is a good example.

The items lent and borrowed by neighbours have changed. We are unlikely to see a meal-dash or a donation of sugar. Domestic utensils like pots and pans were the items typically lent and borrowed in the distant past. We now lend bulky items we don't love and that we use infrequently, like ladders. A 1981 advert for a lawnmower ended 'LEND IT TO YOUR NEIGHBOUR AND YOU MIGHT NEVER GET IT BACK'.[23] Thirty years later, we are more likely to own our own, and we probably lend less than ever before. The urge to own things means that we are less likely to lend and borrow. Drills, steamers, wallpaper-paste tables and garden strimmers languish in many sheds, to be used infrequently. Whilst it might benefit our pockets (and the environment) to share these items amongst the neighbours, this would require a complex level of organisation, although one that could be facilitated by the internet, should any neighbours want to try it. Sharing would also negate consumerism. We are reluctant to lend some items because they are fragile. Laptops, for example, which might also reveal some of our most guarded secrets.

There is a temptation to use a neighbour's wi-fi signal. The online *Urban Dictionary* has given this the name 'neighbornet'.[24] In 2007, just over a century after the catfight between the stockbroker's wife and the solicitor's wife over an unreturned ball on Chiswick's Prebend Gardens, a man was arrested on the same street under the 2003 Communications Act for tapping into an unsecured wi-fi broadband connection.[25] Today people prefer to look down on the Smiths than to keep up with the Joneses. Researchers have found that material things only make us happy if our neighbours have fewer or they are of inferior quality. Prosperity next door brings dissatisfaction.[26]

Consider the way we heat our homes. In the distant past, this was a shared endeavour – we might keep our coal supplies in a communal area, which needed to be kept clear so the coalman had access. The elderly needed help hauling fuel and sweeping their grate. Heating required negotiation with neighbours. Reilly's plan for shared communal heating would have meant that conversations between households were necessary, that each house was not fully self-sufficient or fully self-contained. The way most of us heat our homes now does not involve our neighbours at all – gas and electricity are silently pumped into our homes.

In 2008, the Conservative Party pledged that if they gained power, fuel bills would reveal to people how much energy their neighbours use.[27] This idea exploits a new trend: out-ecoing the neighbours; keeping up with the Greens. A recent study by a DIY retailer suggests that automobile envy is gradually being replaced by rivalry over water butts, solar lighting and compost bins.[28] Many people project an image of environmental consciousness that does not reflect the truth (recycling rates are usually much lower than they would be if reported habits were accurate). Your neighbours might be able to see if you are recycling correctly. Down my street, a red tag on the recycling bin of a neighbour indicates the presence of a contaminant. Tut-tut. Neighbours know if you line-dry your washing, have two cars, are part of an organic-box delivery scheme, use a nappy-laundering service, get milk delivered, or drive to the corner shop for a loaf of bread. These clues help us to assess whether things are greener on the other side of the fence.

DON'T BUY THE HOUSE, BUY THE NEIGHBOUR

A division between renters and owners occurred after the First World War, and contact has been limited (and for owners, often unwanted) ever since. The Cutteslowe walls were an extreme example. For most people, having a house that your family exclusively occupies is a cherished aim. George Gissing yearned for this self-containment, which brings security, privacy and the ability to personalise our surroundings. In 1810, an American tourist noticed that the English strove for the ideal of occupying a whole house because this saw them 'having a more complete home'.[29] However, subdivision has been the historic response to housing shortage. Sharers, lodgers and those they lodged with experienced a greater compromise in their ability to remain private than other types of neighbour. Few take in complete strangers when they can afford not to. Lodgers are neighbours with whom you have a financial relationship, mixing potent ingredients for dispute.[30] Gissing calmed down once he had his own front door.

Having babies, for instance, puts pressure on the household budget. To balance the books, lodgers were often taken in. This meant that many families had less space and privacy at exactly the moment they could have done with more. Frederick Willis described how the Roffeys let out the whole of the top floor when their family was young, gradually decreasing the number of lodgers as the family grew. 'The present young man, they hope, is the last of a long line of lodgers.'[31] Some landlord/lodger relationships were good. Dorothy Fiddler (the Preston mill worker murdered in 1875) was more than a cash cow to her landlady, who cared about her welfare. Modern sharing is now more likely to take place before marriage and child-rearing. Lodging has become less common, and the introduction of the contraceptive pill in the early 1960s meant that family sizes have shrunk too.

Building societies had little impact on levels of owner-occupation until the twentieth century, because previously many houses were bought to lease out. At the outbreak of the First World War, only 10 per cent of households were owner-occupied.[32] By 1970, this figure had risen to just over 50 per cent, and it is now around 70 per cent.[33] Paradoxically, the spread of home ownership has been coupled with increased social and geographical mobility, so homes are traded as commodities rather than necessarily our anchor in the community. As we trade our homes for profit, we get structural surveys and legal searches done, to safeguard our investment. The neighbours on either side can affect the value of our property, so it would help if they could be surveyed too, especially given the reticence of vendors to tell the whole truth about bad neighbours.

Charles Reilly's unimplemented 1944 plan for Birkenhead was designed to foster 'spontaneous cooperation' around village-style greens. The idea of claimed focal spaces was developed further by Oscar Newman in his book *Defensible Space*, published in 1972. He said that the lack of collective community action on modern streets caused problems. These could be solved if architects and planners create 'defensible spaces', which could be protected by neighbours with a range of real and symbolic barriers and using opportunities for surveillance 'that combine to bring an environment under the control of its residents'. Measures would include the positioning of windows so people can see their neighbours and the streets. If neighbours don't look out for each other, and cannot recognise each other, then their street is vulnerable to intruders.[34] The Beach Town community garden on Western Road in Littlehampton is an example of a 'defensible space' that was created by the neighbours themselves. The process of turning a scruffy and indefensible plot into a garden combines Newman's focus on space and Reilly's keenness for collective neighbourly actions.

NO LONGER HANGING OUT TOGETHER

I know more of the neighbours who live on the same side of my street (the evens) than opposite (the odds) because it is easier to hear and speak to them. I recognise more of the odds because I see them coming and going. Flat-dwellers might know the sounds made by the feet above them but not be able to connect them to a face. The places where neighbours get to know each other have changed. Now we talk over the (higher) garden fence or on the driveway. It used to be by the pump, on the street, down the pub or at the corner shop. The residents of Western Road in Littlehampton once met at a corner shop (it is thought locally to have

Fig. 34 The Golden City on the corner of Whateley Road and Landcroft Road in East Dulwich has been closed for many years. It was once a place where neighbours might meet, in the queue. Nowadays there are more upmarket eateries spread along nearby Lordship Lane.

inspired Ronnie Barker's BBC comedy *Open All Hours*). The shop is now in the hands of a national chain and is no longer the sort of place where neighbours meet. They are more likely to stock up in one of the town's supermarkets and just pop to the local shop for odd and ends.

At the very end of the nineteenth century, a German miner visiting England noticed how English people hung their linen out to dry in the street, 'thereby affording the neighbours an opportunity of forming their own opinion of them. Indeed, it is over their washing that neighbours in the same street become acquainted with each other.'[35] Booth's researchers also commented on London women who stood 'gossiping before their doors' after hanging out the 'weekly wash'.[36] Back-to-backs had no yard for drying, so laundry had to be aired in public, where it could be stolen, get dirty or obstruct the neighbours. Drying indoors was difficult in cramped and poorly ventilated properties. The Ministry of Health's *Housing Manual* (1949) revealed the changing sensibilities of the post-war period. Outlining preferred layouts for 'communal laundries', it suggested that they should have cubicles to 'allow washing in privacy'.[37] This was different from the shared coppers, dolly tubs, barrels and mangles that used to clutter spaces outside working-class houses. Since then we have seen more laundrettes, and our homes have welcomed increasing numbers of private gadgets – allowing washing and drying to be carried out completely indoors. The historian F.L.M. Thompson believes that the 'release from the necessity of doing one's dirty washing in public was literally the path to respectability'.[38] This means we find it easier to safeguard our privacy; our frilly pink unmentionables can go unmentioned by the neighbours and not be hung out for all to see. It does mean, however, that neighbours just don't hang out together any more.

We seldom meet our neighbours because we carry out our activities away from them in garages and behind fences. The community development consultant Kevin Harris argues that 'Neighbourliness requires neighbouring: mutual recognition among

Fig. 35 This image of Stocks Street, Leeds (apparently of the Elliott family at number 15 and their neighbour at 17 in the early to mid 1950s), shows washing hung outside the house; drying was an opportunity to chat to 'er next door.

residents through repeated informal encounters over time.'[39] Yet these opportunities have reduced.

Our experience of neighbouring is less scatological than ever before. People in the past knew their neighbours' toilet habits. Alice Wade blocked her neighbour's gutter with human waste in 1314 and Samuel Pepys encountered a neighbour's poo in his cellar. Sharing privies, and later water closets, was normal. In 1841, the Liverpool Health of the Town Committee calculated that an average of fifteen people shared each privy in the city's court dwellings.[40] Nationally the proportion of households that lacked their own toilet dropped from 21 per cent in 1951 to 1 per cent in 1991.[41] We neither wait until our neighbour is finished to relieve ourselves, nor see their remnants in a shared bowl. Unless the walls are particularly thin, we do not hear their motions. Families who moved from Bethnal Green to Dagenham in the twentieth century went from using a WC 'three flights down and shared with two other families' to having their own indoor toilet.[42] Today, most people will probably never use their neighbour's toilet. If caught short on a visit to a neighbour, you would most likely wait until you had made the short trip back to your own house than go there. Do you know what your neighbour's toilet looks like?

NOT KNOWING THE NEIGHBOURS

In the past, it was vital to establish a good reputation by acting in a neighbourly fashion. These days we can usually avoid our neighbours' misfortunes. Their lives are more detached from our own than at any time in history. Gossiping over the garden fence is an endangered neighbourly pastime. In the tight communities of the past, neighbours often had a multifaceted knowledge of each other that extended beyond the home to workplaces and social and religious settings. This encouraged more acceptance and understanding. Those who became crabby killjoys in their old age 'had also been known for most of their life-time, and neighbours could explain how their idiosyncrasies arose'.[43] With neighbours increasingly unable to identify each other, spending more time at distant workplaces, or enjoying leisure time away from home, the fear 'what'll the neighbours think?' has diminished and will continue to do so.

Compare the fear in early-modern society of being regarded as a corrupt businessman by your neighbours with the distance between business and neighbouring on modern streets. Today our creditworthiness is not judged by the neighbours and local reputation, but by faceless businesses and algorithms in computers. We do not have to spend time cultivating goodwill. It does not matter so much now what the neighbours think of us.

Our moral outlook has also changed. Looking at the early-modern period, Laura Gowing found that women's reputations were 'filtered through the lens of sexual propriety', as judged by the neighbours.[44] Today, despite the tough-love meddling that we watch on *EastEnders*, if we suspect a neighbour to be acting in a morally inappropriate fashion – maybe having an affair – we are unlikely to do anything about it.

Since the creation of the National Health Service, healthcare has been freely available, diminishing the value of neighbours as carers. They may still offer lifts or do shopping but will not generally sit at the bedside of an ill neighbour. Neighbours used to be essential at the beginning and the end of life; to help babies out and to lay out the dead. Before the mid twentieth century, a baby was more likely to be born at home in the presence of a female neighbour than in the presence of the baby's father. Now, the reverse is true. The vast majority of babies are born in hospital with the father present, not a neighbour. Consequently we invest less emotion in the lives of our neighbours' children and are therefore less forgiving of their nuisances.

Welfare gradually spread a safety net under struggling households. Philanthropy and social work have added to neighbours' redundancy. People once read letters to their illiterate neighbours, and sometimes drafted their wills and petitions. They kept an eye on the nippers next door because childcare was not an option for most working mothers until after the Second World War. Charles Reilly's plan for a twenty-four-hour nursery was astonishingly forward-thinking; too much for the conservative burghers of Birkenhead.[45] In contrast to the past, we are now only superficially aware of the problems our neighbours face. We may hear them shouting, or see them dumping a mattress in their garden, but our anger at their sociopathy is not tempered by empathy, because we do not know them.

What now, thy neighbour? Good Neighbour societies are founded on a notion that organisation will bring about a return to traditional neighbourliness. It will not. Close neighbour networks existed to mitigate the effects of poverty, disease and squalor. People shared adversity, and their bonds were usually stronger than those between the more secure neighbours. For generations, middle-class commentators marvelled about the ways the poor helped each other. While we have lost some neighbourliness, we have also lost the grinding poverty that nurtured it. What we have gained is a deeper sense of privacy. By the 1950s, neighbours who kept their distance were seen as good, not those who brought pies and sat for a chat. Restraint was welcomed more than reciprocity. Active neighbouring has declined, but latent neighbouring has remained. Most neighbours still trust each other and will help out in an emergency.

Who would want to return to traditional neighbouring, if that came with the hardship and lack of privacy that fostered it? Modern neighbouring has a different character because the context is different. We rely on neighbours less; we can be passive neighbours. We can choose to be private in ways that most neighbours of the past could not, in the wooden shacks of Bermondsey and the back-to-backs of nineteenth-century Leeds. The poor were exposed, but the rich enjoyed the luxury of concealment. The rich were denied unbidden neighbourly help, but they were less likely to need it. Now we can choose to live like the aristocracy who occupied Belgrave Square – with little or no support from our neighbours.

ABUSE IS ESSENTIALLY WHAT THE NEIGHBOURS THINK IS WORTH REPORTING

The car has severed neighbours on one side of many streets from the neighbours over the way. In 1972, 52 per cent of households had access to a car or van. By 2000, 73 per cent of households were mobile.[46] Cars cause parking conflicts, but can also be social glue for some (mostly male) motorists. Cars curtail the independence of children; they have changed the patterns of play. Playing children might have been a source of friction amongst neighbours in the past, but they were also a source of contact. Children living in 'home zones', where pedestrian activity is prioritised on a street with parts closed to traffic, play out more than children on streets that are merely traffic-calmed.[47] Echoes of Reilly's plan appeared in the Canley developments in Coventry, which include Thimbler Road. They have large shared green spaces at their heart. As a nation, however, we never have lived the life of Reilly. Instead, play has shifted to backyards and cul-de-sacs as cars have colonised the streets. Reilly's plan sought to reduce dependence on private vehicles and to separate them from areas of play, allowing collective super-vision of children.[48] I played on the street as a child. Few, if any, children play on my street now. I used to knock on doors wanting a penny for the guy or to be sponsored to do something. I would be wary of letting my own children do this. Am I right? Responding to Home Secretary David Blunkett's plan's to control 'sexual grooming' in 2002, Shami Chakrabarti of the civil rights organisa-tion Liberty worried that his solution went too far and could turn the offer of an ice cream to the child next door into a criminal offence. 'If', said Chakrabarti, 'you make people afraid that talking to your neighbours' children could be seen as an offence, you actu-ally make those children less safe.'[49]

On the whole, women have suffered most from bad neighbours, and gained most from good ones, because they have been more domestic. This gender balance is tilting as more women work. In 1900, less than a third of women worked for money; by the 1990s, this was nearer to two thirds.[50] This change will have seen fewer female neighbours at home during the day. Today, a woman's first experience of active neighbouring might come when she takes maternity leave, or stops working to care for her children. Children can still root women in their neighbourhood, but they can also be the cause of friction. A popular manual advises modern parents to leave their baby to cry in the cot, to 'fuss and yell for 10–20 minutes'.[51] 'Controlled crying' is tough. I found that it fought my maternal instincts and did not seem workable in our small terraced house with a thin wall separating us from the family next door. Hilda Jennings discovered that some of the young mothers she inter-viewed in the 1950s 'suffered from nervous strain owing to the need to keep the children quiet'.[52] In 1993, a discontented baby exposed her mother to a £5,000 fine for noise pollution. Jackie Whitehouse's ultimatum from the noise pollution officers at Cannock Chase District Council was criticised by MPs discussing the Noise and Statutory Nuisance Bill later that year.[53]

One woman interviewed at the end of the twentieth century

related that 'we did actually have someone, you know, who used to beat his partner up quite violently, and you try to turn a blind eye, don't you? You just listen to it because in this house you can't help that, at 2 or 3 o'clock in the morning.' It was only when the sounds became audible to their children during the day that these neighbours called the police. 'It was none of our business', asserted the woman; the well-being of her own children was the only spur to action.⁵⁴ Kevin Harris sees a tension between the ideal of privacy and the assessment of what it is to be a good neighbour.⁵⁵ Two thirds of reports of suspected child abuse made to the NSPCC come from neighbours or family friends. Neighbours will often not report a first suspicion, but wait an average of two months before bringing a child to the attention of the charity. In 2008, the head of the NSPCC's helpline said, 'there are many responsible neighbours who are looking out for these children. But we want more to join them and to call as soon as they suspect something'.⁵⁶ Social workers need to be careful to avoid creating tensions between a neighbour and the family they have reported.⁵⁷ Writing about one of the most notorious cases in recent history, known as the 'death of Baby P', Camilla Cavendish in *The Times* wondered what role the neighbours had played in bringing in the social workers or the police. She suggested that some neighbours fear 'drawing attention to themselves' and do not trust the professionals.⁵⁸

GOD SAVE YOU FROM A BAD NEIGHBOUR, AND FROM A BEGINNER ON THE FIDDLE

A former mayor of Blackburn, interviewed in 1969, summed things up nicely:

> With these blocks of flats you never meet the families . . . that nice neighbourliness has gone absolutely. Perhaps it needed adversity to produce it in the first place. People care for one another when they've gone through the mill themselves.⁵⁹

If we do not rely on our neighbours as we did before, if we do not have a mutually supportive relationship with them, is it any wonder that we might notice more of their irritating habits and attributes? Today, bad behaviour is less likely to be countered by good deeds. You might overlook an occasional noisy party for a neighbour who cares for your pet. Just think what you might have overlooked in the past if a neighbour nursed you through an illness. Without the caring, sharing and socialising elements of neighbour-ship, the inevitable annoyances can be magnified.

The most common noise nuisances today can be divided into the age-old (crying babies, noisy children, loud sex, arguments and barking dogs) and the modern (television, recorded music, electrical DIY equipment). People can take their concerns to the council, or share their pain on a dedicated website.[60] A domestic support group, the Right to Peace and Quiet campaign, was established in 1991, but became a victim of its own success when it was swamped with enquiries from householders. Val Weedon, who set up the campaign, is now an ambassador for a national noise helpline. Ironically, she started out in the music industry, working for the Small Faces, who sang about not getting on with neighbours who have 'no room for ravers'.[61]

We constantly calibrate our own neighbouring. Many still resolve nuisances by chatting to the neighbour. Some of us are still trund-ling pianos around, just like the neighbours of Lee Jones in Liverpool in 1891. Friends of mine (who were once my neighbours) recently fell into conflict with their current neighbour over the piano sounds heard through walls. After a strange war of music, with a CD of Miles Davis's *Kind of Blue* played at full blast, peace returned when the piano was moved away from a party wall. Most people try to limit the sounds and sights coming from homes so they do not disturb neighbours, or broadcast household secrets.

The sounds of merriment at night – oafish bellowing and girlie screaming – heard on many city streets, coupled with scare stories about the plight of some 'have-a-go-heroes', means that we are now more likely to turn a deaf ear to cries for help. This indifference was tragically demonstrated in Newport on the Isle of Wight in 2009, when Mark Wells suffocated in a storm drain after getting trapped trying to retrieve his key. He was thirty feet from his door. Before he succumbed, he shouted for help for up to an hour, but no one came. Neighbours thought they were hearing drunken antics and ignored his pleas. The coroner described the events leading up to the tragedy as a 'sad reflection on society'.[62]

GOOD NEIGHBOUR, GOOD MORROW

The consequences on neighbourliness of technological innovation and the decentralisation of work are hard to predict. Home-working may bring about a revival in neighbourly relations. Walk down the streets of Britain during the day and you increasingly see teleworkers typing emails to colleagues around the globe while keeping half an eye on the comings and goings of their neighbours; acknowledging them, greeting them and occasionally seducing them. Other techno-logical changes may have undermined neighbourliness. The anthropologist Kate Fox has argued that the mobile phone has replaced the garden fence. 'Most of us no longer enjoy the cosiness of gossip over the garden fence. We may not even know our neigh-bours' names, and communication is often limited to a brief, slightly embarrassed nod, if that.' Fox sees mobile phones promoting social-ising across distances in a fragmented and isolating world.[63] Nowadays, many people have a more dispersed circle of friends, and we keep up with them online and through texts. A 2010 YouGov poll showed that 41 per cent of those surveyed thought that online communica-tions mean people have more contact with friends abroad than with the person next door.[64] The Facebook wall has replaced the garden fence. Paradoxically, our personal lives are promiscuously exposed online, while being coyly concealed from neighbours. Eli Pariser, author of The Filter Bubble, does not think that the internet will 'make us all next-door neighbours'.[65] Hypermobility and instant-communication technologies have extended the range of human contact, running the risk of turning neighbours into strangers.

Not all digital-age developments drive neighbours apart. Residents' online forums, like the one in East Dulwich used by some Whateley Road neighbours, have provided platforms for neighbours to 'meet' virtually, discussing issues that affect their local environment. People thinking of moving to the area can post questions to their potential neighbours. In June 2010, an enquirer asked if the local half-houses are noisy and got several responses. One said that the 'walls are paper thin', but others countered that the flats were no noisier than a normal terraced house. One respondent wrote that she hadn't realised that her neighbours had a baby (as evidence of the noise-proofing). This response reveals one big difference between modern neighbours and those in the past. The modern neighbour is neither present at the birth of a new neighbour, nor aware of its existence for a 'few weeks'.[66]

Virtual worlds are opening up, where people live parallel digital lives as avatars. *Second Life* is an internet-based virtual world where 'residents' socialise, buy land, build homes, procreate and raise families. Even in their second life, residents can be hounded by annoying or inconsiderate neighbours; they interrupt conversations, their buildings can creep over borders and their tall walls can block views. Second-lifers do, however, enjoy one advantage over real-worlders. They can build a phantom wall (an 'invisiprim') that screens out the neighbours but is transparent on their side. If the real world offered an option to wallpaper out the neighbours, life would lose some of its lustre.

Notes

1 Becoming Neighbours (1200–1699)

1. W. J. Turner, *Exmoor Village* (London, 1947), p. 24. • **2.** MOA, 'People's Homes' (1943), File Report 1651, pp. 8, 393. • **3.** Segal, *Home and Environment*, p. 104. • **4.** Melville, 'Use and organisation of domestic space' p. 28. • **5.** Barty Phillips, 'Loathe thy neighbours', *Observer*, 11 September 1977, p. 22. • **6.** Robert Frost, *Selected Poems* (London, 1936), pp. 121–2. • 7. John Mapletoft, *Select Proverbs* (London, 1707), pp. 47, 101; *OED*, s.v. 'fence, n'. • **8.** 'Right answer to the wrong question', *The Times*, 15 September 1962, p. 10; *OED*, s.v. 'neighbour'. • **9.** Wrightson, 'The "decline of neighbourliness" revisited', p. 34. • **10.** Samuel Johnson, *The Dictionary of the English Language*, 2nd edn, 2 vols. (London, 1755–6), II, s.v. 'neighbour'. • **11.** Swan, *We Travel Home*, pp. 55, 79. • **12.** OBP, 26 November 1855, Henry Brown (t18551126-60). • **13.** Chris Phillipson, Miriam Bernard, Judith Phillips, Jim Ogg, *The family and community life of older people* (London & New York, 2001), p. 87; Bulwer and Abrams, *Neighbours*, p.18. • **14.** Michael Hoskin, 'Herschel, William (1738–1822) musician and astronomer', *ODNB*. • **15.** Pam Perkins, 'Godwin [formerly Clairmont; née de Vial] Mary Jane (1765–1841), translator and bookseller', *ODNB*. • **16.** The Papers of Randolph Churchill, The Churchill Archives Centre, Cambridge, http://janus.lib.cam.ac.uk. • **17.** Piers Williams *rev.* Peter Berresford Ellis, 'Johns, William Earl (1893–1968), children's writer and journalist', *ODNB*; P.B. Ellis and P. Williams, *By Jove, Biggles* (London, 1981), pp. 115–16. • **18.** MOA, 'People's Homes', p. 380. • **19.** Foley, *Shiny Pennies*, pp. 52–3, 56, 76. • **20.** Holme, *The Carlyles at Home*, p. 82. • **21.** Jenny Diski, 'Old Bag', *London Review of Books*, 32:16 (19 August 2010), pp. 16–17. • **22.** George C. Ives, *Obstacles to Human Progress* (London, 1939), p. 11. • **23.** Janet Backhouse, 'Luttrell, Sir Geoffrey (1276–1345), Landowner and patron of the Luttrell psalter', *ODNB*; Helen Castor, *Blood & Roses* (London, 2004). • **24.** Orlin, 'Boundary disputes in Early Modern London', p. 360 • **25.** Schofield, *The*

London Surveys of Ralph Treswell; Orlin, *Locating Privacy in Tudor London*, pp. 163, 167. • **26**. Vanessa Harding, 'Families and Housing in Seventeenth-Century London', *Parergon*, 24:2 (2007), 115–38, pp. 130–2. • **27**. William Baer, 'Housing for the lesser sort in Stuart London: Findings from certificates and returns of divided houses', *London Journal*, 33:1 (2008), 61–88, p. 69. • **28**. Ibid., pp. 70–9. • **29**. Schofield, *The London Surveys of Ralph Treswell*, p. 132. • **30**. Baer, op.cit., pp. 80–1; Craig Spence, *London in the 1690. A Social Atlas* (London, 2000), p. 90. • **31**. Ben Jonson, *The Works of Ben Jonson*, 7 vols. (London, 1756), VI, 237. • **32**. Schofield, *The London Surveys of Ralph Treswell*, p. 23. • **33**. Chew and Kellaway, *London Assize of Nuisance 1301–1431*, cases 309, 316, 325–38. • **34**. Loengard, *London Viewers and their Certificates*, pp. l–li, 70. • **35**. Orlin, 'Boundary disputes in Early Modern London', p. 360. • **36**. John L. Locke, *Eavesdropping. An intimate history* (Oxford, 2010), p. 3. • **37**. J. Ambrose Raftis, *Studies in the Social History of the Mediaeval English Village* (Toronto, 1964), p. 207. • **38**. Marjorie K. McIntosh, 'Finding language for misconduct: Jurors in fifteenth-century local courts', in Barbara A. Hanawalt and David Wallace (eds.), *Bodies and Disciplines. Intersections of literature and history in fifteenth-century England* (London, 1996), 87–122, pp. 92–3. • **39**. Orlin, *Private Matters and Public Culture*, p. 185. • **40**. Diane Shaw, 'The construction of the private in medieval London', *Journal of Medieval and Early Modern Studies*, 26:3 (1996), 447–66, p. 461. • **41**. Orlin, *Locating Privacy in Tudor London*, pp. 6, 154–5, 169–70, 173, 178–92. • **42**. Ibid., p. 174. • **43**. Duncan Salkeld, 'Making sense of differences: postmodern history, philosophy and Shakespeare's prostitutes', *Chronicon*, 3 (1999–2007), www.ucc.ie/chronicon/3/salkeld.pdf, 7–35, esp. pp. 31–2. • **44**. Laura Gowing and Patricia Crawford, *Women's Worlds in Seventeenth-Century England* (London, 2000), pp. 156–7. • **45**. Ingram, *Church Courts*, p. 245. • **46**. Sharon Wright, 'Broken cups, men's wrath and the neighbours' revenge: the case of Thomas and Alice Dey of Alverthorpe 1383', *Canadian Journal of History*, 43 (Autumn 2008), 241–51, pp. 242–4, 250–1. • **47**. Amussen, *An ordered society*, p. 123. • **48**. *Lawes of the Market* (London, 1595), sig. A7r-v. • **49**. Clare Williams (ed.), *Thomas Platter's Travels in England 1599* (London, 1937), p. 182. • **50**. Amussen, *An ordered society*, p. 98. • **51**. David M. Turner, *Fashioning Adultery: gender, sex and civility in England, 1660–1740* (Cambridge, 2002), p. 121. • **52**. *The true narrative of the confession and execution of the prisoners at Kingstone-upon-Thames* (London, 1681), p. 2. • **53**. *A true narrative of the proceedings at the Assizes holden at Kingstone-upon-Thames* (London, 1681), p. 3. • **54**. William Gouge, *On Domesticall Duties* (London, 1622), p. 228. • **55**. H.C. Johnson, *Warwick Quarter Sessions Records 1682–90*, Warwick County Records, 8 (Warwick, 1953), pp. 110–11. • **56**. George Webbe, *The Practise of Quietnes*, 7th edn (London, 1638), pp. 8, 183. • **57**. Cockayne, *Hubbub*, pp. 50–3. • **58**. Marjorie Keniston McIntosh, *Controlling misbehaviour in England 1370–1600* (Cambridge,

1998), pp. 60–2. • **59**. Reginald Scot, *The discoverie of witchcraft* (London, 1584), pp. 7, 34. • **60**. Guildhall London, St Dunstans-in-the-West Wardmote Inquest, 1558–1823, MS 3018/1, fol. 15v. • **61**. Somerset Archive and Record Services, Somerset Quarter Sessions, Petitions, Taunton Sessions, Wellington, Q/SPET/1/149, n.d. • **62**. Ingram, *Church Courts*, p. 31. • **63**. Hawkins, *A summary of the Crown-law*, I, 281. • **64**. Tusser, *Five hundreth points of good husbandry*, sig. 87v. • **65**. Gowing, *Domestic Dangers*, p. 129. • **66**. Wrightson, 'The "decline of neighbourliness" revisited', p. 26. • **67**. Ingram, *Church Courts*, pp. 331–2. • **68**. Daniel E. Doyle (ed.), *Saint Augustine. Essential Sermons* (New York, 2007), p.407. • **69**. Tebbutt, *Women's Talk*, p. 1. • **70**. Keith Wrightson and David Levine, *Poverty & Piety in an English Village. Terling, 1525–1700* (London, 1979), p. 111. • **71**. J. A. Sharpe, '"Such Disagreement betwyx Neighbours": Litigation and Human Relations in Early Modern England', in John Bossy (ed.), *Disputes and Settlements* (Cambridge, 1983), pp. 167–87, esp. p. 168. • **72**. Tusser, *Five hundreth points of good husbandry*, sig. 87v. • **73**. Gowing, *Domestic Dangers*, pp. 21–2, 98–129. • **74**. Ibid. pp. 98–9. • **75**. Christopher Hill, *Society and Puritanism in Pre-Revolutionary England* (London, 1964). • **76**. John Bruce (ed.), *The Diary of John Manningham*, Camden Society, 99 (London, 1868), p. 156. • **77**. Paul S. Seaver, *Wallington's World. A Puritan Artisan in Seventeenth-century London* (Stanford, 1985), p. 103. • **78**. Wrightson, 'The "decline of neighbourliness" revisited', p. 21; *idem*, *English Society*, p. 55. • **79**. OBP, 11 July 1688, Dorothy Harding (t16880711–14); see also OBP, 27 February 1696, George Bowyer (t16960227–12). • **80**. Craig Muldrew, *The Economy of Obligation. The Culture of Credit and Social Relations in Early Modern England* (Basingstoke, 1998), pp. 64, 113, 156, 160, 194. Muldrew cites Tusser on p. 164. • **81**. Tusser, *Five hundreth points of good husbandry*, sig. 87v. • **82**. Tebbutt, *Women's Talk*, pp. 19–20; Capp, *When Gossips Meet*, p. 50. • **83**. Steve Hindle, *On the parish? The micro-politics of poor relief in rural England, c. 1550–1750* (Oxford, 2004), p. 8. • **84**. Capp, *When Gossips Meet*, p. 38. • **85**. Keith Thomas, *Religion and the Decline of Magic* (London, 1971), pp. 552–69; Alan Macfarlane, *Witchcraft in Tudor and Stuart England* (London, 1970), pp. 170–6, 192–8. • **86**. Annabel Gregory, 'Witchcraft, Politics, and "Good Neighbourhood"', *Past & Present*, 133 (1991), pp. 31–66; Malcolm Gaskill, *Witchfinders: A seventeenth-century English tragedy* (London, 2005), pp. 71, 83, 97, 109, 139. • **87**. Hearnshaw and Hearnshaw, *Court Leet Records*, pp. 445, 465. • **88**. R.A. Buckley, *The Law of Nuisance* (London, 1981), p. 3. • **89**. Loengard, *London Viewers and their Certificates*. • **90**. Chew and Kellaway, *London Assize of Nuisance*, case 370. • **91**. Melville, 'Use and organisation of domestic space', p. 29; Orlin, 'Boundary disputes in Early Modern London', p. 361. • **92**. Thomas Donaldson, 'On the practise of architects and the law of the land in respect to easements of light and air', *Sessional Papers of the Royal Institute of British Architects* (1866), pp. 169–91.

• **93**. Cockayne, *Hubbub*, pp. 144–5, 244. • **94**. LMA, Viewers Reports 2, COL/SJ/S7/467, case 98. • **95**. Chew and Kellaway, *London Assize of Nuisance*, cases 214, 370, 419–23. • **96**. Loengard, *London Viewers and their Certificates*, pp. 49–50. • **97**. Hearnshaw and Hearnshaw, *Court Leet Records (Southampton)*, p. 416. • **98**. Matthews and Latham, *Diary of Samuel Pepys*, I, pp. 269, 274–5, 304–5. • **99**. LMA, Viewers Reports 2, COL/SJ/S7/467, case 69. • **100**. Cockayne, *Hubbub*, pp. 142–3. • **101**. Chew and Kellaway, *London Assize of Nuisance*, case 617. • **102**. Cockayne, *Hubbub*, pp. 111, 210–11. • **103**. C. S Knighton, 'North, John (1645–1683) college head', *ODNB*; A. Jessop (ed.), *The Lives of the Norths*, 3 vols. (London, 1890), II, pp. 284–5. • **104**. Joel Franklin Brenner, 'Nuisance law and the Industrial Revolution', *Journal of Legal Studies*, 3:2 (1974), 403–33, pp. 405–7. • **105**. Cockayne, *Hubbub*, pp. 134–6. • **106**. Norman Davis, *Paston Letters and Papers of the Fifteenth Century*, 3 vols. (Oxford, 1971), I, p. 244. • **107**. Gough, *History of Myddle*, pp. 107–8. • **108**. OBP, 19 February 1675, Stevens (t16750219–4). • **109**. OBP, 30 April 1679, no name (t16790430–3). • **110**. William Shakespeare, *The Winter's Tale*, ed. John Pitcher (London, 2010), I, ii, 189–95. • **111**. *The True Narrative of the Execution of John Marketman* (London, 1680). • **112**. Anthony Quiney, *Town Houses of Medieval Britain* (New Haven, 2003), p. 90. • **113**. Chew and Kellaway, *London Assize of Nuisance*, cases 362–6, 419. • **114**. Loengard, *London Viewers and their Certificates*, pp. lix, 102.

2 Terraced Neighbours (1700–1839)

1. Peter Whitfield, *London. A Life in Maps* (London, 2006), pp. 130–1; Guillery, *Small House in Eighteenth Century London* pp. 126–42. • **2**. Maurice Beresford, 'East End, West End: the face of Leeds during urbanisation, 1684–1842', *Publications of the Thoresby Society*, 60–1 (1988), pp. 74, 89, 93–6. • **3**. Alfred Werner (ed.), *The Sword and the Flame. Selections from Heinrich Heine's Prose* (London, 1960), p. 432. • **4**. 'Manners. The English, the Scots, and the Irish', *The European Review* (October 1824), pp. 62–8. • **5**. Guillery, *Small House in Eighteenth Century London*, p. 35. • **6**. Hawkins, *A summary of the Crown-law*, I, 229. • **7**. Cited in George, *London Life*, pp. 86–7. • **8**. I. C. Taylor, 'The Court and Cellar Dwelling: the eighteenth-century origin of the Liverpool slum', *Transactions of the Historic Society of Lancashire & Cheshire*, 122 (1971 for 1970), pp. 67–90. • **9**. Lawrence Stone, *The Family, Sex and Marriage in England 1500–1800* (London, 1977), esp. pp. 8, 255. • **10**. Amanda Vickery, *Behind Closed Doors. Homes in Georgian England* (New Haven and London, 2009), pp. 38–42. • **11**. Amanda Vickery, 'An Englishman's Home is his Castle? Thresholds, Boundaries, and Privacies in the Eighteenth-Century London House', *Past & Present*, 199 (2008), pp. 147–73, esp. pp. 162–73. • **12**. Christoph Heyl, 'We are not at home:

Protecting Domestic Privacy in Post-Fire Middle-Class London', *London Journal*, 27:2 (2002), 12–33, pp. 13–14. • **13**. For example, Plymouth Improvement Act 1825 (5 Geo 4 cap 22), pp. 413–14. • **14**. Thale, *Autobiography of Francis Place* p. 108. • **15**. OBP, 22 February 1738, Samuel Taylor and John Berry (t17380222–5 22). • **16**. OBP, 17 July 1717, Ann Hasle (t17170717–18); 9 July 1718, Jane Plintoff (t17180709–5); 11 January 1815, Catherine Tewner (t18150111–44). • **17**. David J. Seipp, 'English judicial recognition of a right to privacy', *Oxford Journal of Legal Studies*, 3:3 (1983), 325–70, p. 336. • **18**. 'Murder at Gosport', *The Times*, 26 July 1827, p. 4. • **19**. OBP, 6 September 1769, James Bannan (t17690906–52). • **20**. 'Arches' Court', *The Times*, 6 July 1824, p. 3. • **21**. *Trials for adultery: Or, the history of divorces. Being select trials at Doctors Commons*, 7 vols. (London, 1779–80), I, 1–7, 12–13, 27–37. • **22**. Sarah Burton, *A Double Life. A biography of Charles & Mary Lamb* (London, 2003), p. 252. • **23**. Wu, *William Hazlitt*, pp. 136–7. • **24**. Griggs, *Unpublished Letters of Samuel Taylor Coleridge*, I, 195; E.K. Chambers, *Samuel Taylor Coleridge. A Biographical Study* (Oxford, 1938), p. 176; Wu, *William Hazlitt*, pp. 98–9 • **25**. P. P. Howe, *The Life of William Hazlitt* (London, 1922), p. 130; Richard Holmes, *Coleridge. Darker Reflections 1804–1834* (London, 1998), p. 432; Griggs, *Unpublished Letters of Samuel Taylor Coleridge*, II, 278–9. • **26**. T.W. Kirkbride, rev. Mike Chrimes, 'Aspdin, Joseph (*bap.* 1778, *d.* 1855) cement maker', *ODNB*. • **27**. *A new and general biographical dictionary*, 15 vols. (London, 1798), IV, 516–18; Martin Myrone, 'Grignion, Charles (*bap.* 1753, *d.* 1804), *ODNB*; O. M. Brack, 'Davies, Thomas (c.1712–1785), bookseller and actor', *ODNB*; The National Archives, PROB, 11/1116, 'Will of Thomas Grignion, watch maker of Saint Paul Covent Garden', 6 May 1784. • **28**. Emden, *Gilbert White in his Village*, pp. 12, 20. • **29**. Jeremy Boulton, *Neighbourhood and Society* (Cambridge, 1987), pp. 236–9. • **30**. *Hoby vs Hoby* (1828), in *English Reports*, 162 (London, 1917), p. 537 • **31**. See, for example, OBP, 12 October 1715, John Stapleton et al. (t17151012–34); OBP, 8 December 1742, Michael Bewley (t17421208–5); OBP, 20 October 1779, William Russell (t17791020–32); OBP, 14 September 1791, Thomas Smith (t17910914–15). • **32**. OBP, 24 February 1731, Anne Savage (t17310224–7); OBP, 16 January 1755, Solomon Gabriel (t17550116–26); OBP, 16 January 1766, William, Martha and Anne Higley (t17660116–4); OBP, 28 October 1795, Lucy Hoare (t17951028–32); OBP, 30 October 1816, William Want (t18161030–106). • **33**. OBP, 4 December 1828, James and Rhoda Coleman (t18281204–180). • **34**. Thale, *Autobiography of Francis Place*, p. 126. • **35**. Charles Edward Russell, *Thomas Chatterton* (London, 1909), pp. 221–2. • **36**. Jeremy Boulton, '"It is Extreme Necessity That Make Me Do This": some "survival strategies" of pauper households in London's west end during the early eighteenth century', Lawrence Fontaine and Jürgen Schlumbohn, *Household strategies for survival 1600– 2000* (Cambridge, 2000), pp. 47–70. See also Richard Wall, 'Beyond the Household: Marriage,

Household Formation and the Role of Kin and Neighbours', *International Review of Social History*, 44 (1999), pp. 55–67. • **37**. *Rules of the Friendly Society held at the Angel Inn, Bedford* (Bedford, 1839), p. 3; Elizabeth Kowaleski Wallace, 'The Needs of Strangers: Friendly societies and insurance societies in late eighteenth-century England', *Eighteenth Century Life*, 24 (2000), pp. 53–72. • **38**. OBP, 11 January 1717, Diana Pearse (t17170111–38). • **39**. *Rex vs Byford and Robinson* (1823), *Eng. Rep.*, 168 (London, 1925), p. 929. • **40**. 'News', *London Evening Post*, 27 July 1758, p. 1. • **41**. George, *London Life*, p. 92; OBP, 14 July 1756, Eleanor Fletcher (t17560714–4). See also OBP, 18 April 1798, Mary Brown (t17980418–115). • **42**. OBP, 18 September 1805, Margaret Weaver (t18050918–10); OBP, 20 April 1814, James Stock (t18140420–115). • **43**. OBP, 10 May 1722, James Booty (t17220510–35); OBP, 26 February 1724, William Nichols (t17240226–73). • **44**. OBP, 14 October 1685, Hopeful Hore (t16851014–21); OBP, 10 October 1694, Mary Wilson (t16941010–31); see also OBP, 9 September 1691, Adam Mack Affey (t16910909–27). • **45**. OBP, 5 November 1716, Eleanor Quinby (t17161105–16); OBP, 6 December 1721, Samuel Laws, William Richards (t17211206–12); OBP, 24 February 1742, Elizabeth Carter, Esther Cooper (t17420224–56); OBP, 11 July 1781, Ann Russell (t17810711–38). • **46**. OBP, 19 October 1768, Elizabeth Greaves (t17681019–17). • **47**. OBP, 22 October 1755, Mary and Caleb Smith (t17551022–25). • **48**. OBP, 4 December 1730, William Hollywell, William Huggins (t17301204–22); OBP, 7 September 1737, Frances Marlborough (t17370907–4). • **49**. Charles Allen, *The Polite Lady: or a course of female education*, 2nd edn (London, 1769), p. 108. • **50**. Richard Leppert, *Music and Image* (Cambridge, 1988), pp. 47–8. • **51**. Jane Austen, *Pride and Prejudice* (1813), ed. James Kinsley (Oxford, 2004), p. 278. • **52**. Reeves and Morrison, *The Diaries of Jeffery Whitaker*, pp. xxvii–xxxvii, 3, 20–1, 55–6. • **53**. 'Magistrates Room, Tuesday', *Manchester Guardian*, 23 April 1831, p. 4. • **54**. Reeves and Morrison, *The Diaries of Jeffery Whitaker*, esp. pp. 40, 48–9. • **55**. Erasmus Jones, *The Man of Manners; or, Plebeian Polish'd*, 2nd edn (London, 1737), p. 47. • **56**. Naomi Tadmor, *Family and Friends in eighteenth-century England* (Cambridge, 2001) p. 208. • **57**. 'The Life and Work of John Keates 1795–1821', http://englishhistory.net/keats.html; 'John Keats and Fanny Brawne', http://englishhistory.net/keats.fannybrawne.html; 'Letters to Fanny Brawne, February 1820', http://englishhistory.net/keats/letters/brawnefebruary1820. html; 'Letters to Fanny Brawne, March 1820', http://englishhistory.net/keats/letters/brawnemarch1820.html. • **58**. John Galt, *The Life of Lord Byron*, 4th edn (London, 1832), pp. 35–6. • **59**. Thomas Hood, *Hood's own; or, Laughter from year to year* (London, 1839), pp. 36–9. • **60**. Robert L. Patten, 'Chapman, Edward (1804–1880), bookseller and publisher', *ODNB*. • **61**. Gough, *History of Myddle*, p. 138. • **62**. Barbara White, 'Channing [née Brooks], Mary (1687–1706), murderer', *ODNB*; *Serious Admonitions to Youth, In a Short Account of* the Life, Trial, Condemnation and Execution. Of Mrs Mary Channing (London, 1706), pp. 8–9, 13–14, 22, 28–9. • **63**. 'Fatal consequences of Infidelity', *Observer*, 8 August 1819, p. 2: 'Mrs Stent', *The Times*, 9 August 1819, p. 2; 'Attempted Assassination', *Trewman's Exeter Flying Post or Plymouth and Cornish Advertiser*, 12 August 1819, p. 3; 'Mr and Mrs Stent', *Observer*, 16 August 1819, p. 3; OBP, 15 September 1819, Henry Stent (t18190915–71). • **64**. 'Law Report', *Daily Advertiser*, 6 January 1790, p. 1. • **65**. James Kelly, *A Complete Collection of Scottish Proverbs* (London, 1721), p. 258. • **66**. Reeves and Morrison, *The Diaries of Jeffery Whitaker*, pp. 31, 36, 41. • **67**. Emden, *Gilbert White in his Village*, p. 20. • **68**. John Cordy Jeaffreson, *A Book about lawyers*, 2 vols. (London, 1867), II, p. 375. • **69**. 'City Sessions, Guildhall', *The Times*, 28 September 1802, p. 3. • **70**. Blackstone, *Commentaries of the Laws of England*, III, 216, 218, 220; Real Property Limitation Act, 1833 (3 Will 4 cap 27). • **71**. Brenner, 'Nuisance law and the Industrial Revolution', pp. 405–6. • **72**. Francis Buller, *An introduction to the law relative to trials at Nisi Prius* (Dublin, 1768); see Cockayne, *Hubbub*, pp. 20–1, 214. • **73**. For these, and many other nuisance cases, see Cockayne, *Hubbub*, pp. 141–8. • **74**. Blackstone, *Commentaries of the Laws of England*, III, 217; Cockayne, *Hubbub*, p. 148. • **75**. Cockayne, *Hubbub*, pp. 148, 213. • **76**. Ibid., pp. 195, 245, 248; Blackstone, *Commentaries of the Laws of England*, II, 402–3. • **77**. J. Bold, 'The design of a house for a merchant, 1724', *Architectural History*, 33 (1990), 75–82, p. 76. • **78**. Guillery, *The Small House in Eighteenth Century London*, p. 126. • **79**. LMA, Abstract of Indictment [Henry Kirkham], MJ/SP/1834/08/020 [2]. • **80**. Frederick H. Spencer, *Municipal Origins* (London, 1911), pp. 174–263. • **81**. East Sussex Record Office, Hastings Borough Council, Secretary's Department, Hastings Improvement Commissioners: papers and correspondence, Letter to Rev. Wallinger, 4 May 1832, dhjb/DH/B/182/164; Letter from Edward Burchett, 4 May 1832, dhb/DH/B/182/165; Letter from William Reeves, 7 May 1832, dhbj/DH/B/182/166; Letter about Butchers Buildings, 7 May 1832, dhjb/DH/B/182/107. • **82**. James G. Hanley, 'Demedicalization of Nuisance Law, 1831–1855', *Bulletin of the History of Medicine*, 80:4 (2006), 702–32; p. 707; 'Lancaster Assizes', *The Times*, 13 September 1816, p. 3. • **83**. Russell Ash, *Potty, Fartwell and Knob. Extraordinary but true names of British people* (London, 2007), p. 197. • **84**. Peter Smith, *Blandford* (Blandford, 1968), pp. 30, 46–8, 238. • **85**. 'Police', *The Times*, 28 January 1828, p. 3. • **86**. OBP, 18 September 1811, Edward Phillips (t18110918–159). See also OBP, 17 September 1794, William Molyneux (t17940917–87). • **87**. *The Proceedings at the Assizes of Peace, Oyez, and for the County of Surrey, held at Guildford* (London, 1742), pp. 7–8. • **88**. OBP, 28 June 1769, Susanna Garner (t17690628–61).

3 Face-to-face and Side-by-side in the Back-to-backs (1840–1889)

1. Maurice Beresford, 'The Back-to-Back House in Leeds, 1787–1937', pp. 93–132 of Chapman, *History of Working-Class Housing*; Muthesius, *English Terraced House*, pp. 106, 117. • **2**. Burnett, *Social History of Housing*, pp. 73–5; Wise, *The Blackest Streets*, p. 10. • **3**. Report to Her Majesty's Principal Secretary of State for the Home Department, from the Poor Law Commissioners, on an inquiry into the sanitary conditions of the labouring population of Great Britain, 1842 (006), XXVI.1, p. 11. • **4**. Henderson and Chaloner, *Engels*, p. 62. • **5**. Wohl, 'The housing of the working classes in London', p. 17. • **6**. Mayhew, *London Labour and the London Poor*, II, p. 480. • **7**. Andrew Mearns, *The Bitter Cry of Outcast London* (London, 1883). • **8**. Census returns for 1851. • **9**. Jerome, *My Life and Times*, p. 123; Wright, *The Great Unwashed*, pp. 127–8, 150. • **10**. Wise, *The Blackest Streets*, pp. 11, 19–22; Wohl, 'The housing of the working classes in London', pp. 17–21. • **11**. Edward Cheshire, *The Results of the Census of Great Britain in 1851* (London, 1854), p. 27. • **12**. Leonore Davidoff and Catherine Hall, *Family Fortunes: Men and Women of the English Middle Class, 1780–1850*, rev. edn (London, 2002), pp. xv, 188; Brent Elliot, 'Loudon, John Claudius (1783–1843), landscape gardener and horticultural writer', *ODNB*. • **13**. J.C. Loudon, *The Suburban Gardener, and Villa Companion* (London, 1838), pp. 10, 32. • **14**. Willis, *Peace and Dripping Toast*, pp. 18, 35. • **15**. 'Sheffield – Its town council and its politics', *The Leader*, 5:23, 23 September 1854, p. 901. • **16**. The Metropolitan Office, *Municipality of London Bill. Speech of Mr William Newton at the meeting of the Metropolitan Board of Works, on Friday, 19th March, 1875* (London, 1875), pp. 10–11; Alastair J. Reid, 'Newton, William (1822–1876), trade unionist and journalist', *ODNB*. • **17**. 'Life in London', *London Society*, 14 (1868), p. 298. • **18**. White, *London in the Nineteenth Century*, pp. 120, 122; 'He didn't know his neighbour', *Illustrated Police News*, 14 August 1897, p. 5. • **19**. George Sturt, *A Small Boy in the Sixties* (Cambridge, 1927), pp. 29–30, 32, 34–5. • **20**. Farjeon, *A nursery in the nineties*, pp. 184, 219. • **21**. Ibid., pp. 220, 290, 292, 318. • **22**. 'Old Bailey', *The Times*, 9 January 1832, p. 4; Hole, *Homes of the Working Classes*, p. 129. • **23**. Manchester and Salford Sanitary Association Report, m126/2/3/23, Manchester City Council, 'Learning links: Public Health in 19th Century Manchester Sanitation (Teacher's Notes)', p. 2. http://www.manchester.gov.uk/download/13397/sanitation. • **24**. Hole, *Homes of the Working Classes*, p. 128. • **25**. Metropolitan Sanitary Commission. First Report of the Commissioners appointed to inquire whether any and what special means may be requisite for the improvement of health in the metropolis, 1847–48 [888] [895], XXX II.1, 57, Minutes of evidence, p. 23. • **26**. Bosanquet, *London*, pp. 253–4. • **27**. 'Southampton Police Court', *Hampshire Advertiser*, 2 July 1887, p. 4. • **28**. Manchester and Salford Sanitary Association

Report. op.cit. • **29**. Mayhew, *London Labour and the London Poor*, II, pp. 503–4. • **30**. D'Cruze, *Crimes of outrage*, p. 32. • **31**. 'City Police Court', *Cheshire Observer*, 16 September 1882, p. 6. • **32**. Wright, *The Great Unwashed*, pp. 137–8, 142. • **33**. Burnett, *Social History of Housing*, p. 79. • **34**. Bosanquet, *London*, pp. v, 151–3. • **35**. Willis, *Peace and Dripping Toast*, p. 36. • **36**. D'Cruze, *Crimes of outrage*, pp. 28, 44. • **37**. OBP, 10 June 1844, William Brown, Edward Worley, James Wooderson (t18440610–1630); OBP, 17 September 1877, Robert Cannett (t18770917–683). • **38**. James Weams, *Tyneside Songbook* (Newcastle, 1887), pp. 3–4. • **39**. 'I've cured Our Next-Door Neighbour', *Penny Illustrated Paper and Illustrated Times*, 11 February 1899, p. 82. • **40**. John Johnson Collection, http://johnjohnson.chadwyck.co.uk, A. J. White, London, *Almanac 1889* (1889), p. 3. • **41**. Rowland E. Egerton-Warburton, 'My Neighbour', *Poems, Epigrams and Sonnets* (London, 1877), p. 99. • **42**. Farjeon, *A nursery in the nineties*, p. 290. • **43**. 'Sheffield Town Hall', *Sheffield and Rotherham Independent*, 2 November 1867, p. 11. • **44**. 'Police Intelligence', *Nottinghamshire Guardian*, 22 April 1870, p. 7. • **45**. 'Sheffield Town Hall', *Sheffield and Rotherham Independent*, 29 September 1884, p. 1. • **46**. 'Town Hall, Leicester', *Leicester Chronicle: or, Commercial and Agricultural Advertiser*, 28 November 1846, p. 1. • **47**. Sims, *How the Poor Live*, pp. 122, 143–4, 146, 149. • **48**. 'Attempted murder at Stratford', *Lloyd's Weekly Newspaper*, 21 August 1881, p. 4. • **49**. 'Occasional notes', *Pall Mall Gazette*, 19 December 1870, p. 4. • **50**. Report from the Select Committee on Imprisonment for Debt, 1873 (348) XV.I, Minutes of evidence, p. 95. • **51**. Cited in Davin, *Growing up Poor*, p. 59. • **52**. Sims, *How the Poor Live*, p. 144. • **53**. 'The Barnsley Anthem', in Roy Palmer (ed.), *A Touch on the Times: Songs of Social Change 1770–1914* (Harmondsworth, 1974), p. 160. • **54**. Wright, *The Great Unwashed*, pp. 144–7. • **55**. 'Law & Police Intelligence', *Age & Argus*, 25 January 1845, p. 4. • **56**. 'Guisborough Police Court', *Evening Gazette*, 7 September 1870, p. 4. • **57**. 'Serious fire at Romsley, near Kidderminster', *Birmingham Daily Post*, 29 June 1868, p. 3. • **58**. 'Deaths from burning through crinoline', *Observer*, 28 November 1859, p. 7. • **59**. Sarah Milan, 'Refracting the gaselier: understanding Victorian response to domestic gas lighting', pp. 84–102 of Inga Bryden and Janet Floyd (eds.), *Domestic Space in the nineteenth-century interior* (Manchester, 1999), pp. 84, 93. • **60**. 'Bradford', *Leeds Mercury*, 15 November 1859, p. 3; 'Dreadful Gas Explosion near Bradford', *Manchester Guardian*, 14 November 1859, p. 3. • **61**. 'Metropolis Management and Building Acts (Amendment) Bill, 1890, (245) XV.443, Minutes of evidence, p. 84. • **62**. 'Fatal Gas Explosion', *The Times*, 18 October 1884, p. 7. • **63**. Burnett, *Social History of Housing*, p. 104. • **64**. Metropolitan Sanitary Commission, *First Report. Minutes of Evidence Taken before the Commissioners* (London, 1847), p. 215. • **65**. Henderson and Chaloner, *Engels*, p. 58. • **66**. Thompson, *Street Life in London*, pp. 20–3. • **67**. Gloucestershire Archives, Nuisance & Fire Brigade

Committee, correspondence and related papers, CBR/B2/7/2/7/2, Inspector of Nuisance reports (1865–87). • **68.** Christopher Hamlin, 'Public sphere to private health: the transformation of "nuisance"', in Steve Sturdy (ed.), *Medicine, Health and the Public Sphere in Britain, 1600–2000* (London and New York, 2002), pp. 189–204, esp. pp. 198–9; Edward Smith, *Handbook for Inspectors of Nuisance* (London, 1873), pp. 30–1. • **69.** Maxwell Alexander Robertson (ed.), *English Reports Annotated*, 2 vols. (London, 1866), I, pp. 1016–17; 'Recent English Decisions', *Lower Canada Law Journal*, 2:2 (August 1866), p. 46; Census returns of 1861; National Archives, Kew, Records of the Supreme Court of Judicature and related courts, J 77/62/W190 – Divorce Court File: Appellant: William Penry Williams. Respondent Mary Williams. Co-respondent [. . .] Padfield, 1865. • **70.** 'Sale of a Wife', *Northern Star & Leeds General Advertiser*, 17 October 1840, p. 4. • **71.** 'New form of action for breach of promise – assault by a lady', *Daily News*, 7 May 1857, p. 2; census returns of 1851. • **72.** Gerald Massey, 'My Neighbour', *Manchester Times*, 4 September 1880, supplement, p. 286. • **73.** Jane Garnett, 'Stephen [née Jackson], Julie Prinsep (1846–1895), celebrated beauty and philanthropist', *ODNB*; Alan Bell, 'Stephen, Sir Leslie (1832–1904), author, literary critic, and first editor of the Dictionary of National Biography', *ODNB*. • **74.** Ralph Waldo Emerson, *English Traits* (Boston, 1857), p. 167. • **75.** Cited in Davidoff, 'Separation of Home and Work?', p. 69. • **76.** Willis, *Peace and Dripping Toast*, p. 85. • **77.** 'Chester City Police Court', *Cheshire Observer and Chester, Birkenhead, Crewe and North Wales Times*, 13 November 1869, p. 2. • **78.** Mayhew, *London Labour and the London Poor*, II, p. 504. • **79.** Wright, *The Great Unwashed*, p. 134. • **80.** Jerome, *My Life and Times*, p. 45. • **81.** Seipp, 'English judicial recognition', pp. 325–70. • **82.** Wise, *The Blackest Streets*, p. 131. • **83.** Ashton, *Thomas and Jane Carlyle*, pp. 340, 343, 438, 440. • **84.** Ibid., p. 343. • **85.** Holme, *The Carlyles at Home*, pp. 58–62, 92–3; Ashton, *Thomas and Jane Carlyle*, p. 440. • **86.** Henry C. Lunn, 'Musical Neighbours', *Musical Times*, 1 April 1874, pp. 446–7. • **87.** Holme, *The Carlyles at Home*, pp. 62–4, 71, 75. • **88.** David Wainwright, *The Piano Makers* (London, 1975), p. 83. • **89.** Cited in Ehrlich, *The Piano*, p. 92. • **90.** Thompson, *Street Life in London*, p. 18. • **91.** Ehrlich, *The Piano*, pp. 98–100; Report from the Select Committee on Coal, 1873 (313) X.I, pp. 290–1. • **92.** Daunton, *House and Home in the Victorian City*, p. 279. • **93.** Henry C. Lunn, *Musings of a Musician* (London, 1854), pp. 84–5, 89– 91. • **94.** Jerome, *My Life and Times*, pp. 47–8. • **95.** Thomas Baker, *The Laws relating to Public Health* (London, 1865), pp. 113, 133, 632. • **96.** 'Police', *The Times*, 30 September 1861, p. 9; see also Gerry Kearns, 'Cholera, Nuisance and Environmental Management in Islington, 1830–55', *Medical History*, supplement 11 (1991), pp. 94–124, esp. p. 104. • **97.** LMA, Middlesex Sessions Papers, MJ/SP/1851/01/016, affidavit, Joseph Barnett, butcher (1851). • **98.** 'Sheffield Town Hall', *Sheffield and Rotherham Independent*, 7 August 1869, p.11.

• **99**. 'A popular concert in Crab-Street', *Leicester Chronicle: or, Commercial and Agricultural Advertiser*, 3 June 1854, p. 1. See also 'Local News', *Leicester Chronicle: or, Commercial and Agricultural Advertiser*, 31 March 1860, p. 1. • **100**. Brenner, 'Nuisance law and the Industrial Revolution'. • **101**. Hole, *Homes of the Working Classes*, p. 130. • **102**. Manchester Record Office, Nuisance Committee Draft Book 9, M9/65 1/9, pp. 34–5, 111, 117, 182; Nuisance Committee Draft Book 11, M9/65 1/11, pp. 42–3, 73, 122, 129. • **103**. Manchester Record Office, Nuisance Committee Draft Book 11, M9/65 1/11, pp. 74, 85. • **104**. A.W. Brian Simpson, 'The story of Sturges v. Bridgman: the resolution of land use disputes between neighbors', in G. Korngold and A. P. Morriss, *Property Stories*, 2nd edn (New York, 2009), pp. 9–40. • **105**. 'Topics of the week', *The Graphic*, 5 July 1879, p. 2. • **106**. See James G. Hanley, 'Parliament, Physicians and Nuisances: The Demedicalization of Nuisance Law, 1831–1855', *Bulletin of the History of Medicine*, 80:4 (2006), pp. 702–32. • **107**. 'Spring Assizes', *The Times*, 11 April 1872, p. 10; see also 'Police', *The Times*, 9 October 1886, p. 13. • **108**. For example, see 'Police Intelligence', *Observer*, 14 December 1856, p. 8. • **109**. Charles Richson, *The observance of the sanitary laws Divinely appointed* (London, 1854), p. 12. • **110**. Manchester Record Office, 'Nuisance Committee – Draft Book 9' [June 1881–June 1882], M9/65 1/9, p. 44. • **111**. 'An artful monkey, my next door neighbour', *Illustrated Police News*, 24 August 1872, pp. 1–2. • **112**. Wright, *The Great Unwashed*, pp. 129, 148; 'Dog fanciers and their Neighbours', *Leeds Mercury*, 26 February 1859, p. 7; 'Shooting a neighbour's dog', *Illustrated Police News*, 30 November 1878, p. 2. • **113**. Isle of Wight Record Office, Letter from Gerald Fitzgerald, 1 Lower Belgrave Street, Eaton Square, London, to John H.O. Glynn, 7 October 1871, OG/CC/680. • **114**. 'Pigeon worrying', *Huddersfield Daily Chronicle*, 4 November 1876, p. 8. • **115**. Census returns for 1861; 'The Broadmires Murder', *Lloyd's Weekly Newspaper*, 14 December 1862, p. 5; 'The Plawsworth Murder – Fearful Scene in Court', *Birmingham Daily Post* 12 December 1862, p. 1; 'Conviction for murder', *Liverpool Mercury*, 11 December 1862, p. 5; 'The murder at Broadmires', *Newcastle Courant*, 22 August 1862, p. 2. • **116**. 'Brutal murder in the County of Durham', *Newcastle Courant*, 15 August 1862, p. 2. • **117**. 'Middlesex Sessions', *Reynold's Newspaper*, 11 January 1863, p. 5. • **118**. 'Suspicious Death of a Wife', *Lloyd's Weekly Newspaper*, 21 August 1881, p.4. See also Wright, *The Great Unwashed*, pp. 131–4. • **119**. 'Tunstall', *Birmingham Daily Post*, 9 August 1866, p. 7. • **120**. 'County Public Office', *Leicester Chronicle and Leicestershire Mercury*, 31 July 1880, p. 2. • **121**. OBP, 25 February 1861, Mary Connor (t18610225–283). • **122**. 'Alleged Manslaughter by Cruelty', *Lloyd's Weekly Newspaper*, 16 August 1863, p. 1; *Post Office Bath Directory 1864–65* (Bath, 1864), pp. 77, 161, 244; census returns of 1871. • **123**. White, *London in the Nineteenth Century*, p. 127. • **124**. Ellen Ross, 'Survival Networks: Women's Neighbourhood Sharing in London

Before World War I', *History Workshop*, 15 (1983), 4–27. • **125**. Finn Jenson, *The English Semi-Detached House* (Huntingdon, 2007), p. 78. • **126**. D'Cruze, *Crimes of outrage*, pp. 32, 53, 55. • **127**. Thompson, *Rise of Respectable Society*, pp. 192–3. • **128**. Daunton, *House and Home in the Victorian City*, pp. 12–13.

4 Suburbia Grows Up (1890–1918)

1. Robert Hendrickson, *Dictionary of American regionalisms* (New York, 2000), p. 644. • **2**. Ernest J. Simmons, *Memoirs of a Station Master (1879)*, ed. Jack Simmons (Bath, 1974), p. 83. • **3**. Veblen, *Theory of the Leisure Class*, pp. 71, 86. • **4**. William Godwin, *An enquiry concerning political justice and its influence on general virtue and happiness*, 2 vols. (London, 1793), I, p. 37. • **5**. Cited in Harold Perkin, *The Rise of the Professional Society. England since 1800* (London, 1989), p. 92; census returns for 1901. • **6**. Wohl, 'The housing of the working classes in London', p. 29. • **7**. On p. 168 of *The Rise of Respectable Society*, F.M.L. Thompson throws some doubt on this oft-bandied figure of 10 per cent, but does concede that it is 'possibly true'; Merrett, *Owner-Occupation in Britain*, p. 1; Pawley, *Home Ownership* p. 51; Daunton, *A property-owning democracy?* p. 13. • **8**. Royal Commission for Inquiring into Housing of Working Classes. First Report, 1884–5 [C.4402], XXX.1, 87, 819, pp. 371–5. • **9**. George Gissing, *The Whirlpool*, Everyman edn (London, 1997), p. 342. • **10**. Quoted in Walter Benjamin, *Illuminations*, ed. Hannah Arendt (London, 1973), p. 191. • **11**. Jackson, *Semi-Detached London*, pp. vii, 21. • **12**. W. Thompson, *The Housing Handbook* (London, 1903), p. 219; George E. Arkell, 'Blocks of Model Dwellings (I) Statistics', pp. 3–28 of Booth, *Life and Labour of the People in London*, III, 3. • **13**. Wise, *The Blackest Streets*, p. 178. • **14**. Jackson, *Semi-Detached London*, p. 11. • **15**. Steele, *The Streets of London*, p. 195; census returns for 1901. • **16**. 'Next door neighbours', *Illustrated Police News*, 25 August 1900, p. 8. • **17**. Census returns for 1901. • **18**. Pember Reeves, *Round About a Pound a Week*, pp. 5–6, 30, 32. • **19**. Wohl, 'The housing of the working classes in London', p. 25. • **20**. Steele, *The Streets of London*, p. 19. • **21**. 'Serious Fires', *The Times*, 22 September 1902, p. 9; census returns for 1901. • **22**. Census returns for 1901. • **23**. Metropolitan Sanitary Commission, *First Report, Minutes of Evidence taken before the commissioner appointed to inquire whether any and what special means may be requisite for the improvement of the health of the metropolis* (London, 1847), pp. 23–4. • **24**. Gissing, *In the Year of Jubilee*, p. 334. • **25**. Davidoff, 'The Separation of Home and Work?', p. 89. • **26**. Willis, *A Book of London Yesterdays*, p. 157. • **27**. White, *Rothschild Buildings*, pp. 57–8. • **28**. Hill, 'Blocks of Model Dwellings', pp. 29–36. • **29**. Cited in Gareth Steadman-Jones, *Outcast London* (Oxford, 1971), p. 184. • **30**. 'A Lady Resident', 'Blocks of Model Dwellings (3) Sketch of Life in Buildings', pp. 37–57 of Booth, *Life and Labour of the People in London*, III, 39–42. • **31**. Roberts, *The Classic Slum*, pp. 17, 23, 25, 28, 33. • **32**. Robert R. Hyde, *Industry was my Parish* (London, 1968), p. 5. • **33**. Willis, *Peace and Dripping Toast*, p. 14. • **34**. Booth, *Life and Labour of the People in London*, II, 86. • **35**. Mary Eleanor Benson, *Streets and Lanes of the City* (London, 1891), pp. xv, 21–2. • **36**. Ross, 'Not the sort that would sit on the doorstep', pp. 39–59, esp. pp. 40–3. • **37**. Steele, *The Streets of London*, p. 23. • **38**. CBO, Notebook B351, pp. 234–5 • **39**. Rowntree, *Poverty*, pp. 9–10, 14–17, 31, 49. • **40**. Elizabeth A.M. Roberts, *Working class Barrow and Lancaster 1890–1930* (Lancaster, 1976), p. 33. • **41**. Booth, *Life and Labour of the People in London*, II, 131. • **42**. This is mirrored in his fiction. See, for example, George Gissing, *New Grub Street*, ed. Bernard Bergonzi (Harmondsworth, 1968), p. 269. • **43**. Coustillas, Mattheisen and Young, *Collected letters of George Gissing*, II, pp. 278–9. Bucalossi wrote dance arrangements for Gilbert and Sullivan. • **44**. 'The Accrington Murder', *Manchester Times*, 28 September 1894, p. 3; 'Murder at Accrington', *Leeds Mercury*, 19 September, 1894, p. 2; 'Sad domestic tragedy at Accrington', *Manchester Times*, 21 September, 1894, p. 3; 'Shocking tragedy at Accrington', *Liverpool Mercury*, 19 September 1894, p. 5; A Sad Tragedy at Accrington', *Manchester Guardian*, 19 September 1894, p. 6; 'The Deed of a Lunatic Mother', *Pall Mall Gazette*, 18 October 1894, p. 8; census returns for 1901 and 1911. • **45**. Pember Reeves, *Round About a Pound a Week*, pp. 39–40. • **46**. White, *Rothschild Buildings*, pp. 59, 97, 100. • **47**. Ross, 'Survival Networks' 4–27. • **48**. Englander, *Landlord and Tenant in Urban Britain*, pp. 9–10, 14. • **49**. Report of the Inter-Departmental Committee on Physical Deterioration, 1904, Vol I; [cd.2175], XXXII, p. 127. • **50**. Jane Lewis, *The Politics of Motherhood. Child and Maternal Welfare in England 1900–1939* (London, 1980), pp. 129, 143. • **51**. Booth, *Life and Labour of the People in London*, II, 53–4. • **52**. Davin, *Growing up Poor*, pp. 57–8, 61. • **53**. Hill, 'Blocks of Model Dwellings', 34 • **54**. Gissing, *In the Year of Jubilee*, p. 334 • **55**. White, *Rothschild Buildings*, pp. 96–7; see also Rowntree, *Poverty*, p. 62. • **56**. Report of the Select Committee on Infant Life Protection, 1908 (99), IX. 49. • **57**. Rowntree, *Poverty*, pp. 36, 38. • **58**. White, *Rothschild Buildings*, p. 100; Roberts, *The Classic Slum*, p. 46. • **59**. OBP, 22 October 1894, Walter Rodford, John Edward Naylor (t18941022–858). • **60**. 'Southampton Police Court', *Hampshire Advertiser*, 6 September 1890, p. 8. • **61**. 'Alleged theft by a neighbour', *Leicester Chronicle and Leicestershire Mercury*, 30 May 1891, p. 7. • **62**. 'At the St Pancras Coroner's Court', *The Times*, 5 December 1894, p. 12. • **63**. Steele, *The Streets of London*, p. 275. • **64**. Isobel Falconer, 'Campbell, Norman Robert, 1890–1949', *ODNB*; census returns for 1911. • **65**. Coustillas, Mattheisen and Young, *Collected letters of George Gissing*, II, p. 235; Coustillas, *London and the Life of Literature*, pp. 308–10, 354, 404. • **66**. Steele, *The Streets of London*, p. 82. • **67**. 'Is Flannelette

Dangerous?', *Manchester Guardian*, 20 April 1905, p. 10. • **68**. Roberts, *The Classic Slum*, pp. 22, 43, 47. • **69**. 'County Bench', *Hampshire Advertiser*, 29 June 1895, p. 7. • **70**. 'Amusing police court case', *Huddersfield Daily Chronicle*, 20 August 1896, p. 4; 'Leicester County Police', *Leicester Chronicle and Leicestershire Mercury*, 17 June 1899, p. 2. • **71**. Coustillas, Mattheisen and Young, *Collected letters of George Gissing*, IV, 261. • **72**. Coustillas, *London and the Life of Literature*, pp. 236, 239. • **73**. Coustillas, Mattheisen and Young, *Collected letters of George Gissing*, IV, 302. • **74**. Korg, *George Gissing's Commonplace Book*, p. 52. • **75**. Coustillas, *London and the Life of Literature*, pp. 253–5. • **76**. George Gissing, *To-Day*, issues from 4, 11, 18, 25 May and 1 & 8 June 1895. See also idem, *The Private Papers of Henry Ryecroft* (London, 1903), p. 30. • **77**. Coustillas, *London and the Life of Literature*, pp. 254–5; census returns for 1891. • **78**. Roberts, *The Classic Slum*, p. 23. • **79**. OBP, 7 September 1909, Frederick Charles Sibbe (t19090907–90); census returns for 1901. • **80**. 'Tragedy at Ipswich', *Ipswich Journal*, 17 September 1892, p. 3; 'Suffolk Winter Assizes', *Ipswich Journal*, 10 December 1892, p. 6. • **81**. 'Charge of killing a next door neighbour', *Manchester Times*, 16 September 1892, p. 3; census returns for 1891; 'Tragedy at Ipswich', *Ipswich Journal*, 17 September 1892, p. 3; 'The Ipswich Tragedy', *Ipswich Journal*, 24 September 1892, p. 3. Another case heard during these sessions involved an attack that had taken place two months previously, and nine miles away: 'Fatal assault at Coddenham', *Ipswich Journal*, 23 July 1892, p. 3. • **82**. 'Suffolk Winter Assizes', *Ipswich Journal*, 10 December 1892, p. 6. • **83**. 'Courtesies between next door neighbours!', *Illustrated Police News*, 10 September 1898, p. 10; Herbert Tatton link established by census returns for 1891. • **84**. *Kelly's Directory of Middlesex* (London, 1899), p. 56; census returns for 1901 and 1911. • **85**. David Peter, *In and around Silverdale* (Carnforth, 1984), p. 49. • **86**. Tanis Hinchcliffe, *North Oxford* (London, 1992), p.180; Winchester, *Surgeon of Crowthorne*, pp. 132–3; Winchester, *The Meaning of Everything*, pp. 164–6. • **87**. East Sussex Record Office, Hastings Borough Council, Secretary's Department, Hastings Improvement Commissioners: papers and correspondence, dhbj/DH/B/182, various; Muthesius, *The English Terraced House*, p. 35. • **88**. Henry R. Aldridge, *A Case for Town Planning* (London, 1915), pp. 227, 491. • **89**. 'Facts, Rumours, and Remarks', *Musical Times*, 558, 1 August 1889, p. 471. • **90**. 'This busy world', *Manchester Times*, 3 June 1898, p. 5. • **91**. Merseyside Record Office, 'Letter from W. Moores to Lee Jones', 364 LWD/11/74 (27 November 1891). • **92** Coustillas, Mattheisen and Young, *Collected letters of George Gissing*, II, p. 170; see also IV, 302; Korg, *George Gissing's Commonplace Book*, p. 22. • **93**. 'Noise-makers. The law and the charter', *The Times*, 3 April 1919, p. 15. • **94**. Ehrlich, *The Piano*, p. 221. • **95**. Ansgar Ohly, 'Introduction to English Private Law WS 09/10 III Tort Law, Cases and Materials', www.zivilrecht8.uni-buyreuth.do/do/download/Download-

Archiv/English_Law_WS_09_10, p. 68; 'Noise-Makers. The law and the charter' *The Times*, 3 April 1919, p. 15; census returns for 1891. • **96**. 'Illustrated Humour', *Trewman's Exeter Flying Post or Plymouth & Cornish Advertiser*, 28 June 1894, p. 3. • **97**. John Johnson Collection, http://johnjohnson.chadwyck.co.uk, A. J. White, London, *Calendar 1902. Millionaires how they are made* (1902), p. 5. • **98**. 'Signor Jones', *Pick-Me-Up*, 14 July 1900, p. 229. • **99**. Coustillas, Mattheisen and Young, *Collected letters of George Gissing*, V, 36, VI, 142; Coustillas, *London and the Life of Literature*, p. 442; see also p. 302. • **100**. Coustillas, *London and the Life of Literature*, pp. 352, 354; Coustillas, Mattheisen and Young, *Collected letters of George Gissing*, VI, 5, 7, 189. • **101**. 'Police', *The Times*, 26 October 1868, p. 11. • **102**. *Reinhardt v Mentasti* (1889), *Law Reports, Chancery Division*, 45 vols. (London, 1876–90), XLII, pp. 682–5. • **103**. 'A neighbour's Rights', *Daily News*, 3 August 1889, p. 5. • **104**. 'The rights of Adjoining Owners', *Belfast News-Letter*, 31 December 1889, p. 7; 'Shock to a popular tradition', *Leeds Mercury*, 7 January 1890, p. 3; 'Multiple news items', *Morning Post*, 6 August 1889, p. 4. • **105**. 'Exeter Winter Assizes', *Trewman's Exeter Flying Post or Plymouth and Cornish Advertiser*, 2 February 1895, p. 1; 'Chastey v Ackland', *The Times*, 18 June 1895, p. 13; 'Law Report', *The Times*, 23 February 1897, p. 3. • **106**. Wise, *The Blackest Streets*, p. 254. • **107**. Booth, *Life and Labour of the People in London*, II, 116, 132, 139. • **108**. Wise, *The Blackest Streets*, p. 29. • **109**. Dave Russell, 'Elen, Ernest Augustus [Gus] 1862–1940, music hall singer', *ODNB*; *Kelly's London Suburban Directory*, 2 vols. (London, 1901), II, p. 15. • **110**. 'Police', *The Times*, 29 August 1895, p. 8. • **111**. Daunton, *House and Home in the Victorian City*, pp. 13, 26. • **112**. M.B. Simey, *Charitable effort in Liverpool in the nineteenth-century* (Liverpool, 1951), pp. 119–27; Malcolm Payne, *The Origins of Social Work. Continuity and Change* (Basingstoke and New York, 2005), p. 21. • **113**. Ross, 'Not the sort that would sit on the doorstep', p. 19. • **114**. Harris, *Origins of the British Welfare State* p. 192; Simon Cordery, *British Friendly Societies, 1750–1914* (Basingstoke, 2003), p. 123.

5 Semi-detached Neighbours (1919–1944)

1. Hicks and Allen, 'A century of change', p. 13; Mark Clapson, 'The suburban aspiration in England since 1919', *Contemporary British History*, 14:1 (2000), 151–74, esp. p. 155. • **2**. Jackson, *Semi-Detached London* pp. 57–8. • **3**. J. L. Marshall, 'The pattern of housebuilding in the interwar period in England and Wales', *Scottish Journal of Political Economy*, 15 (1968), pp. 184–205, esp. p. 185. • **4**. J. A. Yelling, *Slums and Redevelopment. Policy and Practice in England, 1918–45, with particular reference to London* (London, 1992), pp. 24, 76, Plate 3. • **5**. Durant, *Watling*. • **6**. 'The Lancashire neighbour', *Manchester Guardian*, 24 March 1931,

p. 6. • **7**. Pawley, *Home Ownership*, pp. 39, 51, 62, 69; Jones, 'This is Magnificent!' p. 100. • **8**. Osbert Lancaster, *Pillar to Post. English architecture without tears* (London, 1938), p. 68. • **9**. Orwell, *Coming Up for Air*, p. 13. • **10**. Jackson, *Semi-Detached London*, p. 99. • **11**. Madge Dresser, 'Housing policy in Bristol, 1919–30', in M. J. Daunton (ed.), *Councillors and Tenants: Local authority housing in English cities, 1919–1939* (Leicester, 1984), pp. 155–216, 214 n96. • **12**. 'Heard his neighbour change his mind', *Manchester Guardian*, 26 April 1920, p. 9. • **13**. 'Room to spread. The old house', *Manchester Guardian*, 23 December 1938, p. 6. • **14**. Peter Collison, *The Cutteslowe Walls* (London, 1963). • **15**. Mass Observation, *Enquiry into People's Homes*, p. 172. • **16**. Davidoff, 'The Separation of Home and Work?', p. 91. • **17**. MOA, 'People's Homes', File Report 1651, p. 375. • **18**. Mass Observation, *Enquiry into People's Homes*, p. 207. • **19**. Cited in Andrzej Olechnowicz, *Working-class housing in England between the wars: The Becontree Estate* (Oxford, 1997), pp. 124–5. • **20**. MOA, 'People's Homes', pp. 242, 373, 376. • **21**. Wilson, *Rich in all but Money*. • **22**. Mass Observation, *Enquiry into People's Homes*, p. 198. • **23**. W.R. Mitchell, *By gum, Life were sparse. Memories of the Northern mill towns* (London, 1991), p. 137 • **24**. MOA, 'People's Homes', p. 231. • **25**. Margery Spring-Rice, *Working-class wives: Their health and conditions* (Harmondsworth, 1939), pp. 146–7. • **26**. Greenwood, *There was a Time*, p. 43. • **27**. Joseph Pearce, *The Unmasking of Oscar Wilde* (London, 2000), pp. 130, 188, 192. • **28**. Richard Cork, 'Stevenson, (John) Cecil (1889–1965), artist', *ODNB*. • **29**. Robert Graves, *Goodbye to All That* (1929), Penguin edn (Harmondsworth, 1960), pp. 238–42, 251–3; Jeremy Wilson, T.E. Lawrence Studies, http://telawrence.net/telawrencenet/index. htm , 'Letter to Robert Graves 21.05.1921', http//telawrence.net/telaw-rencenet/letters/1921/210521_r_graves.htm; David Gervais, 'Masefield, John Edward (1878–1967), poet and novelist', *ODNB*. • **30**. Aldous Huxley, *Point Counter Point* (London, 1928), pp. 73–4. • **31**. Wilson, *Rich in all but Money*, p. 116. • **32**. James Douglas, 'Get To Know Your Neighbour', *Daily Express*, 5 October 1934, p. 12. • **33**. Jennings, *Societies in the Making*, p. 62. • **34**. 'Neighbourliness', *Manchester Guardian*, 2 October 1935, p. 6. • **35**. Seabrook, *City Close Up*, p. 14. • **36**. Hoggart, *A Local Habitation*. • **37**. Davies, *North Country Bred*, p. 57; White, *London in the Twentieth Century*, p. 121. • **38**. White, *Worst Street in North London*, p. 72. • **39**. MOA, 'People's Homes', pp. 378–9. • **40**. Jennings, *Societies in the Making*, p. 62. • **41**. Hoggart, *A Local Habitation*, pp. 74–5. • **42**. 'More neighbourly', *Manchester Guardian*, 20 August 1940, p. 3. • **43**. Cited in Tebbutt, *Women's Talk*, p. 37. • **44**. Davies, *North Country Bred*, p. 63. • **45**. 'The Lancashire Neighbour', 24 March 1931, *Manchester Guardian*, p. 6. • **46**. Keith Laybourn, *Britain on the Breadline* (Gloucester, 1990), pp. 19, 31, 36, 73. • **47**. 'Nurse's claim for her fees', *Manchester Guardian*, 15 February 1927, p. 13. • **48**. Jane Lewis, *The Politics of Motherhood. Child and Maternal Welfare in England*

1900–1939 (London, 1980), pp. 20, 120, 128, 130. • **49**. Harris, *Origins of the British Welfare State*, pp. 232–5 • **50**. 'Readers' Letters', *Picture Post*, 6 November 1943, p. 3 and Lewis, *Politics of Motherhood*, pp. 128, 130. • **51**. 'More neighbourly', *Manchester Guardian*, 20 August 1940, p. 3. • **52**. 'Neighbours fight fire at Chester', *Manchester Guardian*, 30 July 1929, p. 12. • **53**. Durant, *Watling*, pp. 21–2, 25–6, 31. • **54**. Englander, *Landlord and Tenant in Urban Britain*, Chapter 7. • **55**. Bob Graves, *Quinn Square Tenants' Rent Strike Victory*, Communist Party of Great Britain, London District, pamphlet (1938), p. 3. • **56**. Stephen Porter (ed.), *Poplar, Blackwall and Isle of Dogs I. Survey of London*, vol. *43* (London, 1994) p. 116. • **57**. Massingham, *I took off my Tie*, pp. 74–5, 129–30. • **58**. Ibid., p. 195. • **59**. Tebbutt, *Women's Talk*, pp. 89–90. • **60**. Cited in ibid., p. 37. • **61**. Constance Harris, *The Use of Leisure in Bethnal Green. Survey of Social Conditions in the Borough 1925 to 1926* (London, 1927), pp. 15, 33, 35, 54, 62. • **62**. Greenwood, *There was a Time*, p. 29. • **63**. 'Must these things happen?', *Picture Post*, 22 July 1939, p. 73. • **64**. Letters, *Picture Post*, 11 March 1939, p. 77. • **65**. Adrian Glew (ed.), *Stanley Spencer. Letters and writings* (London, 2001), p. 222. • **66**. Fiona MacCarthy, 'What ho, Giotto!', *Guardian*, 11 August 2007, Review, p. 10; 'Royal Academy take back old rebel', British Pathé video newsreel, http://www.britishpathe.com/record. php?id=33360. • **67**. The Stanley Spencer Gallery, http://www.kwantes.com/ SSG%20website/index.html; 'Neighbours', http://www.stanleyspencergallery. org.uk/index.asp?id=97&page=search-item. • **68**. Advert, Rinso, *Picture Post*, 9 September 1939, p. 70. • **69**. Orwell, *Coming Up for Air*, p. 7. • **70**. Paint Marketing Council advert, *Observer*, 20 March 1938, p. 19; also 17 April 1938, p. 7. • **71**. Durant, *Watling*, pp. 7–8. • **72**. Richardson Wright, *The Gardener's Bed Book* (London, 1929), pp. 59–60, 288. • **73**. *Pett and Pott* (1934), dir. Alberto Cavalcanti, Royal Mail Film Classics, *Film and Sound Online* – http://edina.ac.uk. • **74**. Malcolm K. Macmillan, 'Future full of interest for the unseen listeners', *Manchester Guardian*, 23 September 1955, p. 7. • **75**. Geoffrey Lewis, 'Atkin, James Richard, Baron Atkin (1867–1944), judge', *ODNB*; Richard Castle, 'Lord Atkin and the neighbour test: origins of the principles of negligence in Donoghue v Stevenson', *Ecclesiastical Law Journal*, 7:33 (2003), pp. 210–14. • **76**. 'Law Report, July 9', *The Times*, 10 July 1936, p. 4; 'Egham Cockerels new home', *Manchester Guardian*, 15 July 1936, p. 20. • **77**. Durant, *Watling* p. 1. • **78**. Mass Observation, *Enquiry into People's Homes*, p. 198. • **79**. Swan, *We Travel Home*, p. 85. • **80**. Letters, *Picture Post*, 21 September 1940, p. 5. • **81**. Kenneth Pople, *Stanley Spencer. A Biography* (London, 1991), p. 78. • **82**. Ministry of Health, *Construction of flats for the working classes* (London, 1937), appendix III, esp. p. 39. • **83**. MOA, 'People's Homes', p. 379 • **84**. MOA, 'People's Homes', pp. 379–81 • **85**. 'Twice wrongfully imprisoned', *The Times*, 11 August 1921, p. 10; 'Echo of the Gooding Case', *The Times*, 24 October 1921, p. 7; 'Littlehampton Libel Charge', *The Times*, 28 October 1921, p. 7; 'A remarkable libel series', *Manchester Guardian*, 10 December, 1921, p. 10;

'Anonymous letters case recalled', *The Times*, 10 October 1922, p. 9; 'Littlehampton letters mystery', *The Times*, 12 July 1923, p. 9; Travers Humphreys, *Criminal Days* (London, 1946), pp. 124–33; Douglas G. Brown, *Sir Travers Humphreys. A Biography* (London, 1960), pp. 199–202; 'Policewoman hid in a shed', *Daily Mirror*, 28 October 1921, p. 3. • **86**. Correspondence re: proposed new vicarage with neighbour, LMA, DRO/008/A/09/031, Letter from Maud Hatch, 7 August 1937; Letter to C.R. Callard from Mr Hogg, 2 December 1937; Letter to C.R. Callard from Mr Hogg, 13 December 1937; Letter to Rev. Eric Barnes from H[erbert] L. Hatch, 14 April 1939; Letter to J. Hogg from M[aud] E. Hatch, postmark 24 August 1942. • **87**. Advert, Lancaster Blindcloth, *Picture Post*, 16 March 1940, p. 13. • **88**. 'Wartime guide for Battery Users' (Exide Batteries), *Picture Post*, 20 December 1941, p. 2. • **89**. Peter Bowles, *Ask me if I'm happy: An actor's life* (London, 2010), p. 2. • **90**. Cited in Tebbutt, *Women's Talk*, pp. 37, 60. • **91**. 'More neighbourly', *Manchester Guardian*, 20 August 1940, p. 3. • **92**. Letters, *Picture Post*, 19 June, 1943, p. 3. • **93**. 'More neighbourly', *Manchester Guardian*, 20 August 1940, p. 3. • **94**. MOA, Diarist Number 5408 [Amy Riley, b. 1866], 8 April 1942. • **95**. 'The Good Neighbours' Movement', *Manchester Guardian*, 20 April 1934, p. 12. • **96**. 'Hull's wardens and shelters', *Manchester Guardian*, 6 September 1940, p. 4; see also 'Good Neighbours Fund', *Manchester Guardian*, 1 December 1939, p. 12. • **97**. 'Good neighbour panels', *Manchester Guardian*, 12 February 1941, p. 8. • **98**. 'Good neighbour fire squads', *Manchester Guardian*, 23 April 1941, p. 6; 'Help after raids', *Manchester Guardian*, 26 May 1942, p. 3. • **99**. MOA, Diaries 1939–1942, Diarist 5039.9, M, 1921, Civil Servant, Highams Park, London, 5 July 1940. • **100**. James Hinton, *Nine Wartime Lives* (Oxford, 2010), p. 179. • **101**. 'What our readers say', *Picture Post*, 14 October 1939, p. 45. • **102**. Second World War Experience Centre, Leeds, Letter from Derek F. Orchard, 6 January 2003, HF/LEEWW:2003.2076.1. • **103**. Letters, *Picture Post*, 24 May 1941, p. 3. • **104**. 'Three families solve the food problem', *Picture Post*, 22 February 1941, p. 26. • **105**. MOA, 'Impression of exhibition on fuel economy' (1942), File Report 1528, p. 6. • **106**. Letters, *Picture Post*, 19 October 1940, p. 35. • **107**. MOA, 'Fuel Economy' (1942), File Report 1487, p. 13; see also 'Fuel Economy' (1942), File Report 1448, p.16. • **108**. MOA, 'Reconstruction IV' (November 1942), File Report 1485, document between pages 28 and 29. • **109**. Derek F. Orchard, letter. • **110**. 'MOI. Not an OGPU', *Manchester Guardian*, 22 July 1940, p. 5 • **111**. 'Letters', *Manchester Guardian*, 2 June 1941, p. 4. • **112**. 'Readers' Letters', *Picture Post*, 26 November 1949, p. 9.

6 A Separate House for Every Family (1945–1969)

1. Hicks and Allen, 'A century of change', p. 13. • **2**. Jones, 'This is Magnificent!', pp. 99–101. • **3**. For a poignant explanation of the development of estates, see Hanley, *Estates*. • **4**. Pawley, *Home Ownership*, pp. 85, 131, 140. • **5**. University of Liverpool, Social Science Department, *Neighbourhood and Community. An Enquiry into Social Relationships on Housing Estates in Liverpool and Sheffield* (Liverpool, 1954). • **6**. Hodges and Smith, 'The Sheffield Estate', pp. 79, 89. • **7**. 'Before the houses fall down', *Manchester Guardian*, 16 November 1951, p. 10. • **8**. Young and Willmott, *Family and Kinship*' pp. 104–9, 147, 150. • **9**. Maurice Edelman, 'Planning Post-war Britain: The Example of Birkenhead', *Picture Post*, 8 July 1944, pp. 16–20; Wolfe, *The Reilly Plan*, esp. pp. 9–11, 35–6, 40–1, 87–9, 106–7; P. J. Larkham, 'New suburbs and post-war reconstruction: the fate of Charles Reilly's greens', *University of Central England School of Planning and Housing, Working Paper*, 89 (2004). • **10**. Segal, *Home and Environment*, pp. 104–5, 112. • **11**. 'Letters to the Editor', *Manchester Guardian*, 16 August 1950, p. 4. • **12**. Personal correspondence from Jennifer Longford, 28 March 2010; Alan Sillitoe, 'Revisiting Wigan Pier', *Observer*, 18 February 1962, p. 31. • **13**. Lassell, *Wellington Road*, pp. 5, 7, 12–15, 22, 28, 74, 95. • **14**. Kuper, 'Blueprint for Living Together', pp. 9, 11, 114, 134. • **15**. 'Diamond pair mark special day', *Coventry Telegraph*, 23 May 2011, p. 23. • **16**. Kuper, 'Blueprint for Living Together', pp. 18–19, 24, 100–1. • **17**. Hodges and Smith, 'The Sheffield Estate', p. 118; see also Mitchell and Lupton, 'The Liverpool Estate', p. 70. • **18**. Dagenham Municipal Housing Estates, *Tenants' Handbook* (Gloucester, 1949), p. 19. • **19**. Lassell, *Wellington Road*, p. 114. • **20**. Bracey, *Neighbours*, pp. 79, 94. • **21**. Bulwer and Abrams, *Neighbours*, pp. 49, 52. • **22**. Gorer, *Exploring English Character*, pp. 52, 59–60. • **23**. Young and Willmott, *Family and Kinship*, p. 142. • **24**. Wolfe, *The Reilly Plan*, pp. 79, 83. • **25**. Willmott, *Evolution of a Community*, p. 60. • **26**. Roberts, 'Neighbours', pp. 37–45, esp. pp. 38, 41. • **27**. Lassell, *Wellington Road*, pp. 65, 117. • **28**. Mogey, *Family and Neighbourhood*, p. 92; see also Young and Willmott, *Family and Kinship*, p. 107. • **29**. Kuper, 'Blueprint for Living Together', p. 51. • **30**. Gorer, *Exploring English Character*, p. 52. • **31**. Mitchell and Lupton, 'The Liverpool Estate', p. 56. • **32**. Bott, *Family and Social Networks*, pp. 66–9. • **33**. Kuper, 'Blueprint for Living Together', pp. 55–7, 61. • **34**. Hodges and Smith, 'The Sheffield Estate', p. 112. • **35**. Family Allowance Act (1945); Children's Act (1948); National Insurance Act (1946); National Assistance Act (1948); National Health Service Act (1946). • **36**. 'Home Helps: An Experiment Succeeds', *Picture Post*, 2 March 1946, p. 8. • **37**. 'The start of an idea', *Picture Post*, 14 February 1948, p. 25. • **38**. Jennifer Worth, *Call in the Midwife* (London, 2002), pp. 63–4, 127, 142. • **39**. 'A baby is born at home', *Picture Post*, 31 August 1946, p. 8. • **40**. 'Climbed on to roof of outhouse', *Manchester Guardian*, 20 February 1954, p. 10. • **41**. 'Girl saves brothers from fire', *Manchester Guardian*, 2 January 1957, p. 2. • **42**. Evan Green-Hughes, *A History of Firefighting* (Ashbourne, 1979), pp. 118–19, 122–31. • **43**. Leodis, a photographic archive of Leeds, 'Langford Street, 1966', http://www.leodis.net/display.aspx?resourceIdentifier=200365_52262515. • **44**. Lassell, *Wellington Road*, p. 28. • **45**. Gorer, *Exploring English Character*, p. 57. • **46**. Syd Little, *Little by Little* (Norwich, 2004), p. 21. • **47**. 'Couple stay with the good neighbours', *Guardian*, 27 April 1963, p. 3. • **48**. Gorer, *Exploring English Character*, pp. 55–6, 373. • **49**. Hodges and Smith, 'The Sheffield Estate', p. 112. • **50**. Roberts, 'Neighbours', p. 40. • **51**. Peter C. Jupp and Tony Walter, 'The healthy society: 1918–98', in Peter C. Jupp and Clare Gittings (eds.), *Death in England: An illustrated history* (Manchester, 1999), 256–82, p. 263. • **52**. Hodges and Smith, 'The Sheffield Estate', p. 110. • **53**. Stacey, et al., *Power, Resistance and Change*, p. 86. • **54**. Bracey, *Neighbours*, p. 85. • **55**. Mogey, *Family and Neighbourhood*, p. 144. • **56**. Kuper, 'Blueprint for Living Together', pp. 49–50. • **57**. Lassell, *Wellington Road*, pp. 37, 54–5, 57. • **58**. Mitchell and Lupton, 'The Liverpool Estate', pp. 57, 69, 110. • **59**. I expect much advice followed the sugar too, amongst the working classes. Stacey et al, *Power, Resistance and Change*, p. 103. • **60**. 'Christmas shopping already at peak', *Observer*, 11 November 1945, p. 7. • **61**. 'Being a good neighbour', *Observer*, 14 December 1947, p. 5. • **62**. 'Good neighbours to help the elderly', *Guardian*, 30 May 1963, p. 18. • **63**. 'A "good neighbour" for each street', *Guardian*, 16 August 1963, p. 4. • **64**. Cited in 'Guidance for good neighbours', *Guardian*, 10 April 1968, p. 5. • **65**. Nigel Slater, *Toast. The story of a boy's hunger* (London, 2004), p. 79. • **66**. Kuper, 'Blueprint for Living Together', p. 77. • **67**. Seabrook, *City Close Up*, p. 121. • **68**. Mitchell and Lupton, 'The Liverpool Estate', pp. 59–61. • **69**. Hodges and Smith, 'The Sheffield Estate', p. 117. • **70**. West Yorkshire Archive Service, Leodis: 'A photographic archive of Leeds', www.leodis.net, WYAS Abercorn Street, Box I, no. 31. • **71**. Lassell, *Wellington Road*, p. 94. • **72**. Foley, *Shiny Pennies*, pp. 21, 54. • **73**. Lassell, *Wellington Road*, p. 27. • **74**. Mitchell and Lupton, 'The Liverpool Estate', p. 55. • **75**. Neil Innes and Vivian Stanshall, 'My Pink Half of the Drainpipe', on *The Doughnut in Granny's Greenhouse* (1968). • **76**. 'Ogden's Nut Gone Flake Review', BBC Music, www.bbc.co.uk/music/reviews/b3jw. • **77**. Wolfe, *The Reilly Plan*, pp. 70, 78, 131. • **78**. 'A father's love ban', *Daily Express*, 29 November 1965, p. 14. • **79**. 'Dispute about Sycamore', *Manchester Guardian*, 23 May 1951, p. 8. • **80**. A survey from 1948, cited in Ravetz, *The Place of Home*, pp. 121–2. • **81**. Kuper, 'Blueprint for Living Together', pp. 11, 13, 16. • **82**. Advert, GEC, 'The Bride's Iron', *Picture Post*, 11 September 1954, p. 6; advert, Remington, 'Noiseless Portable', *Picture Post*, 16 July 1955, p. 4. • **83**. Kuper, 'Blueprint for Living Together', pp. 14, 16, 135. • **84**. Ravetz, *The Place of Home*, p. 121. • **85**. Kuper, 'Blueprint for Living Together', p. 75. • **86**. 'Readers' Letters', *Picture Post*, 18 May 1957, p. 32. • **87**. Young and Willmott, *Family and Class*, pp. 112–13. • **88**. Young and Willmott, *Family and Kinship*, p. 160. • **89**. Willmott, *Evolution of a Community*, pp. 96–7. • **90**. Kuper, 'Blueprint for Living Together', pp. 46,

71–2. • **91**. Young and Willmott, *Family and Class*, p. 114. • **92**. Young and Willmott, *Family and Kinship*, p. 164. • **93**. John F. Sleeman, 'A new look at the distribution of private cars in Britain', *Scottish Journal of Political Economy*, 16 (1969), pp. 306–78, esp. p. 306. • **94**. 'Contact', *Guardian*, 18 February 1963, p. 6. • **95**. Leodis, a photographic archive of Leeds, 'Meanwood Terrace, 1967', http://www.leodis.net/display.aspx?resourceIdentifier=20021231_21390933. • **96**. Lassell, *Wellington Road*, p. 120. • **97**. Dennis Chapman, *The Home and Social Status* (London, 1955), pp. 100–1. • **98**. Colin McIver, 'How soon will colour reach the masses?', *Guardian*, 7 March 1967, p. 9. • **99**. Avner Offer, *The Challenge of Affluence* (Oxford, 2006), pp. 174, 179, 187. • **100**. Gorer, *Exploring English Character*, p. 58; Young and Willmott, *Family and Class*, pp. 120–1. • **101**. 'Communal isolation for two', *Guardian*, 18 April 1960, p. 2. • **102**. 'Good Neighbour lessons for immigrants', *Guardian*, 22 January 1966, p. 12. • **103**. Clayton Goodwin, 'If you want a nigger for a neighbour', *New African* (October 2004), pp. 40–2; '"Racialism by Tories" attacked', *Guardian*, 13 July 1963, p. 8; 'Immigrants main election at Smethwick', *The Times*, 9 March 1964, p. 6; 'Racial slogans reappear', *The Times*, 7 October 1964, p. 15; 'Vile – It's all in black and white', *The Times*, 13 October 1964, p. 18; Dennis Barker, 'The defeat of Patrick Gordon Walker', *Guardian*, 17 October 1964, p. 8. • **104**. Paul Ward, *Britishness since 1870* (London, 2004), p. 134. • **105**. 'Two more Chinese attacked', *Guardian*, 6 May 1963, p. 1. • **106**. Seabrook, *City Close Up*, pp. 14, 33, 44, 46, 49, 52, 58, 80; Kenneth Leech, *Race* (New York, 2005), p. 71. • **107**. Seabrook, *City Close Up*, pp. 34, 39. • **108**. Nadine Asante, 'A Mixed Marriage', *Guardian*, 18 March 1964, p. 10. • **109**. Kuper, 'Blueprint for Living Together', p. 19. • **110**. F.M. Martin, J.H.F. Brotherston and S.P.W. Chave, 'Incidence of neurosis in a new housing estate', *British Journal of Preventative and Social Medicine*, 11:4 (1957), pp. 196–202.

7 Detached Neighbours (1970–2010)

1. Office for National Statistics, *Social Trends*, 30 (Basingstoke, 2000), p. 166. • **2**. Report of the Committee on Privacy, 1971–2 [Cmnd.5012], XXII.1, p. 24. • **3**. Mark Clapson, *Invincible green suburbs. Brave new towns* (Manchester, 1998), pp. 121–55. • **4**. National Statistics, *Living in Britain. Results from the 2000/01 General Household Survey* (London, 2001), pp. 27–8; Table 1, 'Household type by tenure, 2008–09', *English Household Survey, Bulletin 1*, www.communities.gov.uk/ehs; Office for National Statistics, *Social Trends*, 39 (Basingstoke, 2009), pp. 146, 154. • **5**. www.upmystreet.com/article/local-area/anti-social-behaviour-in-your-neighbourhood.html (uploaded 26/11/2010). • **6**. Oonagh O'Hagan, *I lick my cheese* (London, 2007), esp. pp. 91–2, 135. • **7**. 'Kids' two days with dead mum', *Liverpool Echo*, 13 July 2010, p. 2. • **8**. 'His next-door neighbour', *Reynold's Newspaper*, 8 August 1897, p. 2. • **9**. 'Most young do not know neighbours, study suggests', *BBC News*, 4 December 2009, www.news. bbc.co.uk/1/hi/uk/8393872.stm. • **10**. M. Coulthard, A. Walker, A. Morgan, *People's Perceptions of their Neighbourhood and Community Involvement* (Basingstoke, 2002), p. 27; 'YouGov/Co-operatives UK Survey Results. Neighbours', 2010, http://today.yougov.co.uk/sites/today.yougov.co.uk/files/YG-Archives-Life-Coop-Neighbours-130510.pdf. • **11**. Patrick Kidd, 'Sunny sides of the Street', *The Times*, 8 July 2005, Property Supplement, p. 15. • **12**. 'Sarah Beeny: dates and destiny', *Sunday Herald*, 27 May 2007, 'Seven Days', p. 10. • **13**. *Social Trends*, 39, p. 49. • **14**. Abrams, et al., *Neighbourhood Care*, p. 43. • **15**. 'The good neighbours', *Guardian*, 16 July 1962, p. 2. • **16**. 'Neighbourhood Watch grows', *The Times*, 5 November 1984, p. 4; Trevor Bennett, *Evaluating Neighbourhood Watch* (Aldershot, 1990), p. 11. • **17**. Neighbourhood Watch, http://www.ourwatch.org.uk. • **18**. Francis Fukuyama, *The Great Disruptions: Human nature and the reconstruction of social order* (London, 1999), p. 88. • **19**. 'Why we no longer love thy neighbour', *Daily Express*, 16 August 2005, p. 23. • **20**. 'Item 6/4', Minutes, Dulwich Community Council Agenda Planning Meeting, 19 August 2008, p. 8, http://moderngov.southwarksites.com/Data/Dulwich%20Community%20Council/20081008/Agenda/Agenda.pdf. • **21**. Hanley, *Estates*, p. 25. • **22**. 'Pensioner broke neighbour's arm', *BBC News*, 19 September 2008, www.bbc.co.uk/1/hi/England/Lancashire/7625794.stm. • **23**. 'Neighbours' war over 35cm strip of land sparks five-year legal battle which could cost losers up to £80k', *Daily Mail*, 11 May 2010 (accessed online, http://www.dailymail.co.uk/news/article-1277521/Neighbours-war-35cm-strip-land-sparks-year-legal-battle-cost-losers-80k.html). • **24**. 'Man arrested over garden fence death', *Guardian*, 9 July 2010 (accessed online, http://www.guardian.co.uk/uk/2010/jul/09/neighbour-dead-fence-argument); 'Murder suspect will not be charged', *Independent*, 24 December 2010, p. 18. • **25**. 'Man shot neighbour four times in row over hedge, inquest told', *Independent*, 13 January 2004, p. 6; Esther Addley, 'Real lives: The hedge war', *Guardian*, 25 June 2003, Features, p. 6. • **26**. 'Curse of the Leylandii', *Express*, 8 September 2010; 'See the light; Neighbours happy as trees are axed', *Daily Telegraph*, p. 18. • **27**. Alan Wilson, 'Hedge wars', *Guardian*, 1 July 2003 (accessed online, http://www.guardian.co.uk/money/2003/jul/01/yourrights.legal). • **28**. 'Figures reveal horrifying picture of our yob culture', *Daily Express*, 14 July 2009, p. 7. • **29**. Frank Field, *Neighbours from Hell* (London, 2003); 'Neighbours from Hell', Central Television 1998, Carlton Television 1999–2004. • **30**. Tim Dowling, 'Love thy neighbour?', *Guardian*, 12 April 2007, Features, p. 4. • **31**. 'Neighbours from Heaven', *Guardian*, 8 February 2000, p. D3H. • **32** Elizabeth L. Kenyon, 'Seasonal sub-communities: the impact of student households on residential communities', *British Journal of Sociology*, 48:2 (1997), pp. 286–301. • **33**. Rover 200 Series, advert, *Guardian*, 11 March 1995, p. 8. • **34**. Mazda 323 range, advert, *Observer*, 9 June 2002, p. 16. • **35**. Sam Jones, 'Woman, 22, shot twice in head after dispute with "neighbour from hell"', *Guardian*, 28 February 2008, p. 16. • **36**. 'Golfer attacks neighbour with PUTTER for parking his car "an inch too near" his house', *Daily Mail*, 18 October 2010 (accessed online, http://www.dailymail.co.uk/news/article-1321476/Golfer-attacks-neighbour-putter-parking-car-inch-near-home-Rochdale.html). • **37**. Peter Ito, 'Beaconsfield Road, Ipswich', 14 March 2008, www.flickr.com. • **38**. Letter from L.T. Medcraft, Thimbler Road, Canley, in 'Letters: Your Views', *Coventry Evening Telegraph*, 18 February 2002, p. 12. • **39**. Steven Morris, 'The Lady in the Car', *Guardian*, 8 May 2002, G2, p. 6; Terence Blacker, 'Miss Naysmith steps up the property ladder', *Independent*, 12 March 2002, Comment, p. 4; Laura Smith, 'Heartbreak of the Rag Lady', *London Evening Standard*, 25 October 2002, p. 25. • **40**. Andrew Oldham, *Ghosts of a Low Moon* (Belfast, 2010), p. 25. • **41**. 'Pennine based poet and writer – Andrew Oldham', *Pennine Life*, 29 September 2010, http://www.pennine-life.co.uk/?p=1300. • **42**. 'Dog row shooting neighbour guilty of attempted murder', *BBC News*, Norfolk, 20 January 2011, www.bbc.co.uk/news/uk=england-norfolk-12244361. • **43**. 'Pet puma to stay caged', *The Times*, 17 December 1971, p. 5. • **44**. 'Cockerel owner gets noise asbo', *Guardian*, 16 April 2008 (accessed online, http://www.guardian.co.uk/uk/2008/apr/16/ukcrime). • **45**. 'Worse than her bite? Judge sees red over dog feud', *Guardian*, 15 December 2010, p. 1. • **46**. 'Court hears couples' sex sessions', *BBC News*, 9 November 2009, http://news.bbc.co.uk/1/hi/england/wear/8351405.stm; 'Noisy sex woman loses appeal bid', *BBC News*, 10 November 2009, http://news.bbc.co.uk/1/hi/england/wear/8352729.stm; 'Noisy sex Asbo breach woman Caroline Cartwright avoids jail', *Independent*, 22 January 2010 (accessed online, http://www.independent.co.uk/news/uk/crime/noisy-sex-asbo-breach-woman-caroline-cartwright-avoids-jail-1875870.html) 'Wife says noisy sex conviction breaches rights', *Independent*, 9 November 2009 (accessed online http://www.independent.co.uk/news/uk/home-news/wife-says-noisy-sex-conviction-breaches-rights-1817634.html). • **47**. Bumps in the night from next door', *Guardian*, 4 August 1975, p. 1. • **48**. Edward Pilkington, 'Hoggs and Foggs at loggerheads', *Guardian*, 8 March 1994, p. A6; Ball and Ball, *What the Neighbours say*, p. 52; Bolton Mediation, 'Neighbours', www.boltonmediation.org.uk. • **49**. M. J. Simpson, *Hitchhiker: A biography of Douglas Adams* (London, 2003), p. 262. • **50**. 'Dreaming of a green Christmas', *Daily Mail*, 4 December 2009, (accessed online, http://www.dailymail.co.uk/news/article-1233174/Dreaming-green-Christmas-Neighbours-use-100-000-low-energy-bulbs-transform-cul-sac.html); 'Welcome to Illumination Street', *Daily Mail*, 2 December 2010, p. 7. • **51**. 'The ho-ho-whodunnit; after a mystery vandal strikes, suspicion falls on the king of the fairy lights', *Daily Mail*, 20 November 2007, p. 3. • **52**. Mortimer Whitaker O'Sullivan Ltd, 'Tiscali Broadband, Bob next door' (2008). • **53**. 'Florence and the Machine: my Glasto gig with a Mick Jagger wig', *Daily Mail*, 26 June 2009, p. 7. • **54**. Liz Hodgkinson, 'Confessions of a wife who swapped', *Daily Express*, 6 September 1993, p. 20. • **55**. Brian Viner, 'Tales of the Country; A year in Hertfordshire', *Independent on Sunday*, 18 July 2003, Features, pp. 6–7. • **56**. Mark Brendon, *Swinging: The Games your Neighbours Play* (London, 2008), esp. pp. 58, 90, 118–19, 129, 132. • **57**. 'Neighbours in porn movie protest', *BBC News*, 31 January 2009, *http://news.bbc.co.uk/1/hi/england/bristol/7862721.stm*; 'Neighbours to stage demo outside porn producer's Bristol home', *Bristol Evening Post*, 30 January 2009, p. 3. • **58**. 'Experience: I ran a brothel in a country village', *Guardian*, 5 June 2010, Weekend Pages, p. 12; 'We thought of ourselves as calendar girls', *The Times*, 14 May 2010, Features, p. 63. • **59** David Gray, 'The need for nosy neighbours', *Guardian*, 2 January 1973, p. 11. • **60**. Eric J. Evans, *Thatcher and Thatcherism*, 2nd edn (London, 2004), p. 137. • **61**. Abrams et al., *Action for Care*; Good Neighbours Schemes, www.onesuffolk.co.uk; Springline Good Neighbour Scheme, http://www.ibnl.org.uk/services/help-at-home/home-sitting-service/springline-gns. • **62**. 'Vicar seeks "good neighbours"', *Guardian*, 28 March 1998, p. 15; Pendower Good Neighbour Project, www.pendowergnp.org.uk/history_1.php. • **63**. 'Female Student dies in "frenzied" knife attack', *Press Association*, 11 December 1994. • **64**. 'We shall not be moved! Neighbours hold up £2.3 billion housing project . . . so they can be rehomed next to each other', *(Stoke) Sentinel*, 19 February 2011, p. 1.

8 *If Friends are Electric, are Virtual Neighbours the Future?*

1. Wrightson, *English Society*, pp. 26, 31. • **2**. Introduction, *Neighbourhood and Community. An Enquiry into Social Relationships on Housing Estates in Liverpool and Sheffield* (Liverpool, 1954), p. 70. • **3**. Roberts, 'Neighbours', pp. 40, 44. • **4**. Seabrook, *City Close Up*, pp. 213, 227. • **5**. OBP, 25 October 1852, Richard Garthwaite (t18521025–1054). • **6**. Mitchell and Lupton, 'The Liverpool Estate', p. 71. • **7**. Ball and Ball, *What the Neighbours Say*, pp. 8, 24. • **8**. David Morgan, *Acquaintances: The space between intimates and strangers* (Maidenhead, 2009), pp. 18–19. • **9**. Gorer, *Exploring English Character*, pp. 56, 58. • **10**. 'Mike S-P from Canley', comments after Gerald Nash, 'The Prefab', *BBC News*, South East Wales, www.bbc.co.uk/wales/southeast/sites/cardiff_aberdulaisroad/pages/gerald_nash.shtml. • **11**. Harris, '"Do you live on 'ere?"' p. 56. • **12**. Ball and Ball, *What the Neighbours Say*, p. 8. • **13**. Kuper, 'Blueprint for Living Together', p. 99. • **14**. 'Southampton Police Court', *Hampshire Advertiser*, 19

July 1884, p. 6. • **15**. Mitchell and Lupton, 'The Liverpool Estate', p. 54. • **16**. Ball and Ball, *What the Neighbours Say*, pp. 16, 18. • **17**. Jennings, *Societies in the Making*, p. 133. • **18**. Seabrook, *City Close Up*, p. 53. • **19**. http://twitter. com/XMillyBeiberX/status/56270660242128897 (accessed 08/04/2011). • **20**. Seabrook, *City Close Up*, p. 58. • **21**. Davin, *Growing Up Poor*, p. 59. • **22**. Richard Sennett, *Respect. The formation of character in the age of inequality* (London, 2003), pp. 101, 124. • **23**. Advert, Berhard BM80, *Country Life*, 14 May 1981, p. 1,357. • **24**. *Urban Dictionary*, www.urbandictionary.com, s.v. 'neighbornet'. • **25**. 'Man arrested over wi-fi theft', *BBC News*, 22 August 2007, http://news. bbc.co.uk/1/hi/england/london/6958429.stm. • **26**. Erzo F.P. Luttmer, 'Neighbors as negatives: relative earnings and well-being', *Quarterly Journal of Economics*, 120 (2005), 963–1,002; Christopher J. Boyce, Gordon D.A. Brown and Simon C. Moore, 'Money and Happiness: Rank of Income, Not Income, Affects Life Satisfaction', *Psychological Science*, 21:4 (2010), 471–5. • **27**. 'Beat the neighbours and save energy, say Tories', *Independent*, 17 June 2008, p.8. • **28**. 'Neighbours drive us green with envy in new eco status', *Scotsman*, 23 May 2008, p. 13. • **29**. Louis Simond, *An American in Regency England. The Journal of a Tour in 1810–1811*, ed. Christopher Hibbert (London, 1968), p. 36. • **30**. MOA, 'People's Homes', p. 7. • **31**. Willis, *A Book of London Yesterdays*, p. 158. • **32**. Merrett, *Owner-Occupation in Britain*, p. 5. • **33**. Pawley, *Home Ownership*, p. 140. • **34**. Oscar Newman, *Defensible Space, People and Design in the Violent City* (London, 1972), pp. 2–4, 9, 51. • **35**. Ernst Dückershoff, *How the English Workman Lives* (London, 1889), p. 39. • **36**. Booth, *Life and Labour of the People in London*, II, 92. • **37**. Ministry of Health, *Housing Manual* (London, 1949), p. 85. • **38**. Thompson, *Rise of Respectable Society*, p. 193. • **39**. Harris, '"Do you live on 'ere?"' p. 54. • **40**. J.H. Treble, 'Liverpool Working-class Housing, 1801–51', in Chapman, *History of Working-Class Housing* (pp. 165–220), pp. 214, 217. • **41**. 'Percentage of Households without sole use of a WC 1951–2001', 'A Vision of Britain through Time', www.visionofbritain.org.uk. • **42**. Willmott, *Evolution of a Community*, p. 7. • **43**. Jennings, *Societies in the Making*, pp. 47, 62. • **44**. Gowing, *Domestic Dangers*, p. 129. • **45**. Wolfe, *The Reilly Plan*, p. 14. • **46**. *Living in Britain* (2001), p. 6. • **47**. Mike Biddulph, 'The social life of some streets', *Urban Design*, 118 (2011), pp. 12–14. • **48**. Wolfe, *The Reilly Plan*, p. 155. • **49**. 'Blunkett's blunder', *The Economist*, 23 November 2002, p. 33. • **50**. Deirdre McCloskey, 'Paid work', in Ina Zweinider-Bargie-slowska (ed.), *Women in Twentieth-Century Britain* (Harlow, 2001), pp. 165–79. • **51**. Gina Ford, *The Contented Little Baby Book* (London, 2002), pp. 95–9. • **52**. Jennings, *Societies in the Making*, p. 201. • **53**. News Film Online, www.nfo. ac.uk, 'Cry Baby', *News at Ten* (ITV), 23 April 1993; Paul Tyler, *Hansard*, Session 1992–3, Vol. 224, 14 May 1993, col. 1044. • **54**. Graham Crow, Graham Allan and Marcia Summers, 'Neither Busybodies nor Nobodies: Managing

Proximity and Distance in Neighbourly Relations', *Sociology*, 36:1 (2002), pp. 127–45, esp. p.137. • **55**. Harris, '"Do you live on 'ere?"', p. 55. • **56**. NSPCC Helpline, 'Media briefing April 2010', www.nspcc.org.uk; 'Neighbours' calls to NSPCC help abused children', *Herald Scotland*, 22 September 2008 (accessed online, www/heraldscotland.com/neighbours-calls-to-nspcc-help-abused-children-1.890078). • **57**. Margaret Borkowski, Mervyn Murch and Val Walker, *Marital Violence. The Community Response* (London and New York, 1983), pp. 83–8, 90–3. • **58**. Camilla Cavendish, 'The cries of Baby P must not lead to despair', *The Times*, 14 November 2008, Features, p. 35. • **59**. Seabrook, *City Close Up*, p. 227. • **60**. 'Neighbours from Hell in Britain', www.nfh.org.uk. • **61**. www.valweedon.me; Noise Direct, press release, 21 January 2010, www.noisedirect.co.uk. • **62**. 'Neighbours ignored cries of dying man stuck in drain', *The Times*, 18 November 2009, p. 23. • **63**. Kate Fox, *Watching the English* (London, 2004), pp. 84–7. • **64**. YouGov/Co-operates UK Survey results, p. 1. • **65**. Eli Pariser, 'How the net traps us all in our own little bubbles', *Observer*, 12 June 2011, Review Discovery, p. 20; idem, *The Filter Bubble: What the Internet is hiding from you* (London, 2011). • **66**. East Dulwich Forum, www.east-dulwichforum.co.uk; 'Half Houses' thread, started 17 June 2010. See posting by 'Dorothy', 21 June 2010, 23:47, http://www.eastdulwichforum.co.uk/forum/read.php?30,481819,484035.

Bibliography

ABBREVIATIONS

ASBO   Anti-Social Behaviour Order

CBO   Charles Booth Online Archive, London School of Economics, http://booth.lse.ac.uk

LCC   London County Council

LMA   London Metropolitan Archives

MOA   Mass Observation Archive Online, special collections, University of Sussex

OBP   Old Bailey Proceedings online, www.oldbaileyonline.org

ODNB   *Oxford Dictionary of National Biography* online, http://oxforddnb.com

OED   *Oxford English Dictionary* online, http://dictionary.oed.com

PRIMARY SOURCES

Blackstone, William, *Commentaries of the Laws of England*, 4 vols. (London, 1770)

Booth, Charles, *Life and Labour of the People in London*, 8 vols. (London and New York, 1892–6)

Bosanquet, Charles B.P., *London: Some account of its growth, charitable agencies, and wants* (London, 1868)

Chew, Helena M., and William Kellaway (eds.), *London Assize of Nuisance 1301–1431. A Calendar*, London Record Society (London, 1973)

Coustillas, Pierre (ed.), *London and the Life of Literature in late Victorian England. The Diary of George Gissing, Novelist* (Hassocks, 1978)

Coustillas, Pierre, Paul F. Mattheisen and Arthur C. Young (eds.), *The collected letters of George Gissing*, 9 vols. (Athens, Ohio, 1990–7)

Davies, C. Stella, *North Country Bred. A Working-Class Family Chronicle* (London, 1963)

Farjeon, Eleanor, *A nursery in the nineties* (Oxford, 1980)

Foley, Winifred, *Shiny Pennies & Grubby Pinafores* (London, 2010)

Gissing, George, *In the Year of Jubilee*, Everyman edn (London, 1994)

Gough, Richard, ed. David Hey, *The History of Myddle* (Harmondsworth, 1981)

Gowing, Laura, and Patricia Crawford (eds.), *Women's Worlds in Seventeenth-Century England* (London, 2000)

Greenwood, Walter, *There was a Time* (London, 1967)

Griggs, Earl Leslie (ed.), *Unpublished Letters of Samuel Taylor Coleridge*, 2 vols. (London, 1932)

Hawkins, William, *A summary of the Crown-law, by way of abridgment of Serjeant Hawkins's Pleas of the Crown*, 2 vols. (London, 1728)

Hearnshaw, F.J.C., and D.M. Hearnshaw (eds.), *Court Leet Records, Vol. I, part III, AD 1603–1624*, Publications of the Southampton Record Society, 4 (Southampton, 1907)

Henderson, W.O., and W.H. Chaloner (eds., trans.), *Engels. The Condition of the Working Class in England* (Oxford, 1958)

Hill, Octavia, 'Blocks of Model Dwellings (2) Influence on Character', pp. 30-6 of Booth, *Life and Labour of the People in London*

Hoggart, Richard, *A Local Habitation: Life and times 1918–40* (London, 1988)

Hole, James, *The Homes of the Working Classes with suggestions for their improvement* (London, 1866)

Jerome, Jerome K., *My Life and Times* (London, 1926)

Korg, J. (ed.), *George Gissing's Commonplace Book* (New York, 1962)

Lassell, Margaret, *Wellington Road* (Harmondsworth, 1966)

Loengard, J.S. (ed.), *London Viewers and their Certificates, 1508–1558*, London Record Society, 26 (London, 1989)

Massingham, Hugh, *I took off my Tie* (London, 1936)

Mass Observation, *An Enquiry into People's Homes* (London, 1943)

Matthews, William, and Robert Latham (eds.), *The Diary of Samuel Pepys*, (11 vols., London, 1970–83)

Mayhew, Henry, *London Labour and the London Poor*, 4 vols. (London, 1861)

Orchard, Derek F., Letter, 6 January 2003, Second World War Experience Centre, Leeds

Orwell, George, *Coming Up for Air* (1939), Penguin edn (Harmondsworth, 1962)

Pember Reeves, Maud, *Round About a Pound a Week* (1913) repr. edn (London, 1979)

Reeves, Marjorie, and Jean Morrison (eds.) *The Diaries of Jeffery Whitaker, schoolmaster of Bratton 1739–1741*, Wiltshire Record Society, 44 (1989)

Roberts, Robert, *The Classic Slum* (Harmondsworth, 1973)

Rowntree, B. Seebohm, *Poverty. A Study of Town Life*, 2nd edn (London, 1902)

Schofield, John (ed.), *The London Surveys of Ralph Treswell*, London Topographical Society, 135 (London, 1987)

Sims, George R., *How the Poor Live and Horrible London* (London, 1889)

Steele, Jess (ed.), *The Streets of London: The Booth Notebooks – South East* (London, 1997)

Thale, Mary (ed.), *The Autobiography of Francis Place (1771–1854)* (Cambridge, 1972)

Thompson, John, *Street Life in London* (1877), reprinted as *Victorian London Street Life*, by Dover (New York, 1994)

Tusser, Thomas, *Five hundreth points of good husbandry* (London, 1573)

Willis, Frederick, *Peace and Dripping Toast* (London, 1950)

Willis, Frederick, *A Book of London Yesterdays* (London, 1960)

Wolfe, Lawrence, *The Reilly Plan – a new way of life* (London, 1945)

Wright, Thomas, *The Great Unwashed* (London, 1868)

SECONDARY SOURCES

Abrams, Philip, Sheila Abrams, Robin Humphrey and Ray Snaith, *Action for Care – a review of Good Neighbour Schemes in England* (Berkhamsted, 1981)

Abrams, Philip, Sheila Abrams, Robin Humphrey and Ray Snaith, *Neighbourhood Care and Social Policy* (London, 1989)

Amussen, Susan Dwyer, *An ordered society. Gender and class in early modern England* (Oxford, 1988)

Ashton, Rosemary, *Thomas and Jane Carlyle. Portrait of a Marriage* (London, 2002)

Baer, William, 'Housing for the lesser sort in Stuart London: Findings from certificates and returns of divided houses', *London Journal*, 33:1 (2008), 61–88

Ball, Colin, and Mog Ball, *What the Neighbours Say. A Report on a study of neighbours* (Berkhamsted, 1982)

Bott, Elizabeth, *Family and Social Networks. Roles, Norms, and External Relationships in ordinary urban families*, 2nd edn (London, 1971)

Bracey, H.E., *Neighbours. On New Estates and Subdivisions in England and USA*, repr. edn (London, 1998)

Brenner, Joel Franklin, 'Nuisance law and the Industrial Revolution', *Journal of Legal Studies*, 3:2 (1974), pp. 403–33

Bulwer, Martin, and Philip Abrams, *Neighbours. The Work of Philip Abrams* (Cambridge, 1986)

Burnett, John, *A Social History of Housing 1815–1985*, 2nd edn (London, 1986)

Capp, Bernard, *When Gossips Meet. Women, Family and Neighbourhood in Early Modern England* (Oxford, 2003)

Chapman, Stanley D. (ed.), *History of Working-Class Housing* (Newton Abbot, 1971)

Cockayne, Emily, *Hubbub. Filth, Noise & Stench in England* (London, 2007)

Daunton, M. J., *House and Home in the Victorian City. Working-class housing 1850–1914* (London, 1983)

Daunton, M. J., *A property-owning democracy? Housing in Britain* (London, 1987)

Davidoff, Leonore, 'The Separation of Home and Work? Landladies and Lodgers in Nineteenth- and Twentieth-Century England', in Sandra Burnam (ed.), *Fit Work for Women* (London, 1979)

Davin, Anna, *Growing up Poor. Home, School and Street in London 1870–1914* (London, 1996)

D'Cruze, Shani, *Crimes of outrage. Sex, violence and Victorian working women* (London, 1998)

Durant, Ruth, *Watling: A Survey of Social Life on a New Housing Estate* (London, 1939)

Ehrlich, Cyril, *The Piano. A History* (London, 1976)

Emden, Cecil S., *Gilbert White in his Village* (Oxford, 1956)

Englander, David, *Landlord and Tenant in Urban Britain, 1838–1918* (Oxford, 1983)

George, Dorothy, *London Life in the XVIIIth Century* (London, 1930)

Gorer, Geoffrey, *Exploring English Character* (London, 1955)

Gowing, Laura, *Domestic Dangers. Women, words and sex in Early Modern London* (Oxford, 1996)

Guillery, Peter, *The Small House in Eighteenth Century London* (New Haven and London, 2004)

Hanley, Lynsey, *Estates. An Intimate History* (London, 2007)

Harris, Bernard, *The Origins of the British Welfare State* (Basingstoke, 2004)

Harris, Kevin, '"Do you live on 'ere?" Neighbouring and Respect', pp. 47–71 of idem, *Respect in the Neighbourhood* (Lyme Regis, 2006)

Hicks, Joe, and Grahame Allen, 'A century of change: Trends in UK statistics since 1900', *House of Commons Research Paper*, 99:111 (1999)

Hodges, Mark W., and Cyril S. Smith, 'The Sheffield Estate', in University of Liverpool, Social Science Department, *Neighbourhood and Community. An Enquiry into Social Relationships on Housing Estates in Liverpool and Sheffield* (Liverpool, 1954), pp. 79–143.

Holme, Thea, *The Carlyles at Home* (London, 1965)

Ingram, Martin, *Church Courts, Sex and Marriage in England, 1570–1640* (Cambridge, 1987)

Jackson. Alan A., *Semi-Detached London. Suburban Development, Life and Transport 1900–39*, 2nd edn (Didcot, 1991)

Jennings, Hilda, *Societies in the Making. A study of development and redevelopment within a county* (London, 1962)

Jones, Harriet, 'This is Magnificent!: 300,000 Houses a Year, and the Tory Revival after 1945', *Contemporary British History*, 14:1 (2000), pp. 99–121

Kuper, Leo, 'Blueprint for Living Together', in idem, *Living in Towns* (London, 1953), pp. 1-202

Orlin, Lena Cowen, *Private Matters and Public Culture in post-Reformation England* (London, 1994)

Orlin, Lena Cowen, 'Boundary disputes in Early Modern London', in idem, *Material London c.1600* (Philadelphia, 2000), pp. 344–76

Orlin, Lena Cowen, *Locating Privacy in Tudor London* (Oxford, 2008)

Melville, Jennifer Dawn, 'The use and organisation of domestic space in late-seventeenth-century London' (unpublished PhD thesis, Cambridge University, 1999)

Merrett, Stephen, with Fred Gray, *Owner-Occupation in Britain* (London, 1982)

Mitchell, D.G., and T. Lupton, 'The Liverpool Estate', in University of Liverpool, Social Science Department, *Neighbourhood and Community. An Enquiry into Social Relationships on Housing Estates in Liverpool and Sheffield* (Liverpool, 1954), pp. 15–77.

Mogey, J. M., *Family and Neighbourhood. Two studies in Oxford* (London, 1956)

Muthesius, Stefan, *The English Terraced House* (New Haven and London, 1982)

National Statistics, *Living in Britain. Results from the 2000/01 General Household Survey* (London, 2001)

Pawley, Martin, *Home Ownership* (London, 1978)

Ravetz, Alison, with Richard Turkington, *The Place of Home. English domestic environment 1914–2000* (London, 1995)

Roberts, Elizabeth, 'Neighbours: North West England 1940–70', *Oral History*, 21:2 (1993), pp. 37–45

Ross, Ellen, 'Survival Networks: Women's Neighbourhood Sharing in London Before World War I', *History Workshop*, 15 (1983), pp. 4–27

Ross, Ellen, 'Not the sort that would sit on the doorstep: respectability in pre-World War I London neighbourhoods', *International Labor and Working Class History*, 27 (1985), pp. 39–59

Seabrook, Jeremy, *City Close Up* (London, 1971)

Segal, Walter, *Home and Environment* (London, 1948)

Seipp, David J., 'English judicial recognition of a right to privacy', *Oxford Journal of Legal Studies*, 3:3 (1983), pp. 325–70

Stacey, Margaret, Eric Batstone, Colin Bell and Anne Murcott, *Power, Resistance and Change. A second study of Banbury* (London and Boston, 1975)

Swan, Annie S., *We Travel Home* (London, 1935)

Tebbutt, Melanie, *Women's Talk. A Social history of 'gossip' in working-class neighbourhoods, 1880–1960* (Aldershot, 1997)

Thompson, F.M.L., *The Rise of Respectable Society. A Social History of Victorian Britain 1830–1900* (London, 1988)

Veblen, Thorstein, *The Theory of the Leisure Class*, New American Library edn (New York, 1953)

White, Jerry, *Rothschild Buildings. Life in an East End tenement block 1887–1920* (London, 1980)

White, Jerry, *The Worst Street in North London: Campbell Bunk, Islington between the wars* (London, 1986)

White, Jerry, *London in the Twentieth Century* (London, 2001)

White, Jerry, *London in the Nineteenth Century* (London, 2007)

Willmott, Peter, *The Evolution of a Community. A Study of Dagenham after Forty Years* (London, 1963)

Wilson, Van, *Rich in all but Money: Life in Hungate 1900–1938* (York, 1996)

Winchester, Simon, *The Surgeon of Crowthorne* (London, 1999)

Winchester, Simon, *The Meaning of Everything; The story of the Oxford English Dictionary* (Oxford, 2003)

Wise, Sarah, *The Blackest Streets. The Life and Death of a Victorian Slum* (London, 2009)

Wohl, A.S., 'The housing of the working classes in London 1815–1914', pp. 15–54 of Chapman, *History of Working Class Housing*

Wrightson, Keith, *English Society, 1580–1680* (London, 1982)

Wrightson, Keith, 'The "decline of neighbourliness" revisited', in Norman L. Jones and Daniel Woolf (eds.), *Local identities in Late Medieval and Early Modern England* (Basingstoke, 2007), pp. 19–49

Wu, Duncan, *William Hazlitt: The First Modern Man* (Oxford, 2000)

Young, Michael, and Peter Willmott, *Family and Class in a London Suburb* (London, 1960)

Young, Michael, and Peter Willmott, *Family and Kinship in East London*, rev. edn (Harmondsworth, 1962)

Acknowledgements

Earlier this week, my son Ned bounded into the shed where I work and begged me to play football with him. 'I can't,' I pleaded, 'I have to work.' Ned wailed, 'You are always working.' He played alone, to my occasional chorus of 'MIND THE PLANTS!', and eventually sent his ball over the fence. The ball came back today.

I have moved often and had many neighbours. My twenty-one homes have come in various sorts and sizes, including a tiny caravan in a Yorkshire field (until it blew over one night, strewing the contents of our chemical toilet across the neighbouring plots). I have childhood memories of learning to ride a neighbour's bike, of the taste of raw runner beans fresh from the plant next door (these neighbours might be in the photograph of the Silver Jubilee in Chapter 7), and of the kindly old man who played an accordion in his kitchen, which was opposite ours. Many of their names are hazy, but my memories are happy. Some of my erstwhile neighbours were special, and our relationship has survived the separation (especially Clare and Jason Gibbons, Alison Cowe and Cóilín Nunan, and Elizabeth McKellar and Tony Mitton).

A few neighbours are memorable because of the grief they caused (mentioning no names), but thankfully they are outnumbered by the nice ones. Almost worse than enduring a bad neighbour is being thought to be one. Households with young children, adolescents discovering music or uncontrollably yappy dogs worry about the miseries they might be inflicting. So apologies to Tyson, and El and Derek; we really do *try* to keep the children quiet and their balls on our side of the fence. A survey from the 1950s identified 'shouted directives to children' as a source of neighbourly noise. I shuddered with recognition. I often bellow 'TURN IT DOWN, MAUD!' I promise we will not get them drums.

Kay Peddle and Will Sulkin at Bodley Head have been friendly and helpful, and my agent Clare Alexander has always been one step ahead of me, pushing my ideas in better directions and giving me the perfect title, for a second time. I have been inspired by two Jennifers – Jennifer Longford, who wrote the amazing *Wellington Road* (1962) under an alias, and Jennifer Melville, author of the best PhD thesis I have ever read. I extend a big thanks to people at various libraries and archives, especially Roger Hull at the Liverpool Record Office and Lucy Ashby at the Littlehampton Museum, and the staff at the London Metropolitan Archives and Manchester Record Office. Bill Baer, Andrew Oldham and Richard Grenville all helped me out at a late stage. Stephanie Bolt kindly gave up a Saturday morning to introduce me to a street in Littlehampton, and the neighbours either side of the Silverdale spite wall both responded to my surprise enquiries.

I could not have written this book without the help of two of my current neighbours: Kim Owen, who helped with my shed, and Joe Ozyer-Key, who gave me wise counsel and the slipper quote. Paul Warde has always encouraged me, and helped me through a rough patch early on. My mother Yvonne did some expert genealogical sleuthing and created beautiful drawings, and David, my dad, has shown abundant enthusiasm, taken photographs, undertaken research, read every word and made sensible suggestions. Rachel Smith took good care of Ned while I worked on the book. I have lived with Ben for eighteen years, and for the last two I have been semi-detached, writing at the bottom of the garden while he bore the brunt of the childcare and domestic chores. For this, and for forensically examining the manuscript, I owe him a huge debt of gratitude. I would like to end with a word to Ned and Maud. I hope you will always try to be good neighbours and promise never to keep a monkey in the back garden (or a pig, Maud).

List of Illustrations

1. From Ernest Betham (ed.), *House Building*, 1934-1936 (The Federated Employers' Press London, 1934).

2. Simplified drawing of the lean-to-house depicted in *View of a fragment of London Wall, as it stood in the churchyard of St Giles Without Cripplegate in 1793* depicted by J. T. Smith (1812), redrawn by Yvonne Cockayne (inspired by Elizabeth Baer).

3. How buildings could develop in a piecemeal fashion through encrustations and sag, by Yvonne Cockayne.

4. *The New Art and Mystery of Gossiping* (London, 1760?), © The British Library Board, 11621.e.5.(3).

5. James Gillray, 'Farmer Giles and his Wife showing off their daughter Betty to their neighbours on her return from school', published by Hannah Humphrey in 1809. © Bridgeman Art Library / Courtesy of the Warden and Scholars of New College, Oxford.

6. Diagram from a Manchester and Salford Sanitary Association report. Manchester Archives and Local Studies.

7. The aftermath of a fire in Littlehampton's Western Road, *c.* 1895. Image courtesy of Littlehampton Museum.

8. 'An artful monkey, my next door neighbour', *Illustrated Police News*, 24 August 1872. © The British Library Board.

9. 'During the hot weather the Smythe Robinsons of Tiddlington take their meals in a cool and shady spot of the garden', 1913, by Henry Mayo Bateman © H.M. Bateman Designs www.hmbateman.com / The Bridgeman Art Library.

10. Half-houses in East Dulwich, 2011. Photograph by David Cockayne.

11. 49–53 Whateley Road in 2011. Photograph by David Cockayne.

12. Lambeth house plans, from Maud Pember Reeves' description. Drawn by Yvonne Cockayne.

13. Little Collingwood Street, photograph taken by John Galt, between 1900 and 1907. © Ian Galt/ Museum of London.

14. Housing off Corporation Street, Manchester, 1908. Manchester Archives and Local Studies.

15. Pearson Court, Corporation Street, Manchester, 1908. Manchester Archives and Local Studies.

16. Ruston's Place, off Nottingham's Bellar Gate, 1919. Courtesy of Nottingham City Council Health Department and www.picturethepast.org.uk (NTGM000205).

17. Ruston's Place, off Nottingham's Bellar Gate, 1919. Courtesy of Nottingham City Council Health Department and www.picturethepast.org.uk (NTGM000204).

18. Spite wall, Silverdale. Photograph by Richard Grenville, 2010.

19. Backyards of homes, Spitalfields by John Galt, c. 1900. © Ian Galt/ Museum of London.

20. Wide Yard, York, about 1933. © City of York Libraries, Archives and Local History Department, http://www.york.gov.uk/archives. Imagine York, http://www.imagineyork.co.uk.

21. Washington Street, Nottingham, 1930s. Courtesy of Nottingham City Council and www.picturethepast.org.uk (NTGM002409).

22. Neighbours in Southend, 1941. © Photograph by Fred Morley/ Getty Images.

23. Women knitters in Bayford, Hertfordshire, 1940. © Photograph by Fox Photos/Getty Images.

24. Neighbours erecting Anderson air-raid shelters. © Photograph by Keystone / Getty Images.

25. *The Neighbours* by Siegfried Charoux, Highbury Quadrant Estate, installed in 1959. Photograph by Maud Webster, 2011.

26. *Neighbourly Encounter* by Uli Nimptsch, Silwood Estate. City of London, London Metropolitan Archives.

27. Langford Street, Leeds. The aftermath of a fire in 1966. West Yorkshire Archive Service, Leeds: Reference LC/ENG Clearance Photograph, Box 75, number 60; www.leodis.net (200365_52262515).

28. 'Semi-detached' by Michael Landy, Tate Britain 2004. © Michael Landy / Tate Images, London 2011.

29. Silver Jubilee on Moss Lane, Bramhall, 1977. Photograph by David Cockayne.

30. The Beach Town Community Garden on the corner of Western Road, Littlehampton. 2011. Photograph by Emily Cockayne.

31. The Beach Town Community Garden. Photograph by Emily Cockayne, 2011.

32. Neighbourhood Watch signs in Littlehampton. Photograph by Emily Cockayne, 2011.

33. In the Night Garden. A Ragdoll Production for the BBC.

34. The Golden City on the corner of Whateley Road. Photograph by David Cockayne, 2011.

35. Stocks Street, Leeds. West Yorkshire Archive Service, Leeds: Reference LC/ENG Clearance Photograph, Box 23, number 59; www.leodis.net (592003116_89008731).

Index

Abrams, Philip, 160
access issues, 9–10, 32, 74, 93, 191–2, 212
Accrington, murder overheard in, 102–3
Acts for Local Improvement, *see* Local Improvement Acts
affluence, effect of on neighbouring, 130, 153–4, 161, 166–8, 175, 200, 210–12
air-raid shelters, 148–9
Aldred's Case (1608), 27–8
animals, *see* birds; cats; dogs; donkeys; monkey in the garden next door; pets; snakes
anonymous neighbours: 8, 155, 215; increasingly, 184–6, 189–90, 218, 224; in urban settings, 22, 37, 60
arguments: between neighbours, 18, 74–5, 100, 107, 170–1, 189, 209; over rights of way, 63; overheard by neighbours 3, 74–5, 84, 116, 223
arson, 54–5
assaults: sexual, 41; violent, 54, 62, 108–10, 143, 170, 192–3, 195–7, 209
Assize of Nuisance, 11–12, 24, 30, 49
Austen, Jane, 43

baby crying, 54, 173, 221, 223
back-to-backs: 4, 31, 69, 90, 164, *165*; described 56–7, *57*; shared spaces around, 62–3, 86, 99–100, 121, 127, 216
backyards: 64, 91, 164; private, 56, 61, 118–19, *119*, 220; shared, 86, 191
Ball, Colin and Mog, 198–9, 207–9
balls, thrown into gardens, 7, 61, 108, 110–11, 170
Banbury, 167–8
barrows, problem of storage, 58, 96, 100, 119
Becontree Estate, Dagenham, 126–7, 159–60, 175
Benson, Nellie, 98–9, 120–1, 210
Bermondsey: 31, 55, 70, 110, 155, 162; industry of 51–2, 81
Bethnal Green, 48, 135, 137, 154–5, 161, 217–18; *see also* Collingwood Estate, Bethnal Green; London streets, Little Collingwood Street
birds: macaw, 76; pigeons, 83, 119; poultry, 76–7, 114, 140–1, 172, 178, 197
Birkenhead, 156–7, 214
Blackburn, 169, 178–9, 207, 210, 211, 222
Blackstone, William, 50, 51
Blitz spirit, 189; *see also* World War II, neighbourliness

Bolton Mediation Service, 198–9

Booth, Charles, 91, 94, 97–9, 104, 106–7, 216

borrowing: 22, 38, 64–5, 104, 149, 152, 211–12; becoming less frequent, 166, 211; combs, 133; cookware, 64, 132–3, 134; donkey, 38–9; foodstuffs, 65, 130, 131, 167–8; gardening equipment, 146, 167, 211; hobbling iron, 65; items listed, 38, 134, 167, 211; tools, 38, 65–6; washing paraphernalia, 64, 132–3; see also creditors, neighbours as; lending

boundaries: 14, 171, 225; conflict over, 25, 111, 144, 172, 192–3; ill-defined, 64, 86; see also fences

Bracey, H. E., 160, 167

Bristol: 130, 131–2; 'Wellington Road', 157–8, 160, 162, 165, 167, 170

building work, conflict over, 24–5, 111–13, 118, 143–4, 190; see also Viewers, London

building societies, 90, 124, 214

cars: 182; ownership, 140, 175–6, 189, 190, 195, 213, 220–1; parking issues, 192–3, 195–6, 220

Carlyle, Jane, 8, 76–7

Carlyle, Thomas, 8, 45, 76–7

cats, 83, 196, 197

cesspools, 34, 52, 71, 79, 131

charity, see philanthropy

Chester, 14, 63, 74, 134, 190

child abuse, 84–5, 222

childbirth: 225; assisted by neighbours, 23, 104, 133–4, 164, 165, 219; hospital, 133–4, 291; infanticide at, 34

childcare provided by neighbours:
39, 169, 178, 219; ad hoc, 76, 105, 165–6; adopting, 67; arrangements, 105, 129–30, 157, 161; fostering, 76, 105; wet nursing, 66–7

children as neighbours: 3, 8, 41, 57, 219, 221; memories of being, 60–2, 99, 107, 169, 183–4, 192; noise of, see noises, children; nuisance of, 58, 91–2, 109, 111, 115, 128, 142, 163, 170, 174, 221; playing on streets, 105, 128, 157, 220–1; playing together, 61, 132, 169–70

chimneys: dangerous, 28; smoky, 27, 28, 50, 52–3

cholera, 53, 70–1

Collingwood Estate, Bethnal Green, 123, 179

communication technologies, 2, 224–5

compurgation, 19, 41

conflict, see arguments, between neighbours; assaults, violent; defamation; feuds; fights; nuisance, legal cases; threatening behaviour

Conservatives: 177; Birkenhead Council 156–7; policies and pledges, 153, 212

costermongers, 38–9, 57, 58, 91, 96, 118–20

council housing: 123–7, 153, 154, 156–7, 170, 176, 177; gardens, 159–60, 191; right to buy, 182, 191, 198; see also tower blocks

court dwellings: 10, 32, 36, 62–4, 66–8, 86, 100–1, 100, 101; crowded, 57; insanitary conditions of, 33–4, 57, 71, 99–100, 217; privacy limited in, 26, 31–2, 64, 74–5

Coventry, Thimbler Road: 158,

203–4, 220; borrowing on, 167; children of, 169, 174; display of possessions on, 175; fencing, 159, 191, 192; gardens, 159; love on, 59; noise, 173–4; parking along, 196; privacy on, 158–9; sociability on, 162–3, 174, 209; steel houses, 158–9, 173–4;

creditors, neighbours as: 22–3, 64–5, 104, 167, 170; discouraged, 65–6, 167

cul-de-sacs, 159, 196, 200, 202, 220–1

Cutteslowe Walls, Oxford, 125–6, 213

Daunton, Martin, 78, 86

Debden, Essex, 154–5, 161, 175

defamation: 6, 63; early modern, 20–2, 30; see also Swan, Edith

defensible spaces, 186–9, 214

divided houses, see half-houses; lodgers; sub-divided houses

dogs: 159, 172; barking, 82–3, 114, 116–17, 142–3, 144, 151; feared, 91, 196–7, 198; kennels causing nuisance, 51

domestic abuse, 16–17, 35–6, 75, 84, 221–2

donkeys, 38–9, 96, 119, 120

doorsteps: donkey-stoning, 161; limit of neighbourly communication, 132, 162–3, 208–9; talking at, 20, 162–3, 179, 208–9; sitting on, 99, 179; standing at, 20, 137, 147

drainage, 13, 24, 79, 86; see also cesspools; guttering

dunghills, 26, 50, 79

eavesdropping, 13–15, 19, 20, 30 see also overhearing the neighbours

elderly neighbours: 11, 58, 61, 192, 194, 218; helped by neighbours, 23, 64, 97, 105, 185–6, 168–9, 212; involved, 130, 185, 190; murdered, 83–4; vulnerable, 23, 163, 202–3

emergency, helping in an, 68, 133–4, 146, 163–4, 203–4, 220, 223–4

Engels, Friedrich, 57, 71

estates: 139, 152–60, 167, 179–80, 191–2, 203, 207; new neighbour relationships formed on, 123–4, 153–4, 177, 199–200; privacy on, 159–60, 162–3, 198, 210, 205–6; types of, 123, 125, 159–60, 177; see also Becontree Estate, Dagenham; Collingwood Estate, Bethnal Green; Liverpool, estate; Sheffield, estate; Watling Estate, Barnet

Exeter, 101, 108, 109, 118

Farjeon, Eleanor, 61–2, 66

fences: 4, 82, 90, 138, 159, 171, 191–3, 224; chatting over, 144–5, 150–1, 171, 198, 215, 218; high, 74, 121, 159, 192–3; insubstantial, 159, 191, 209

feuds, 59–60, 93, 110, 171, 172, 192–3, 195–9, 209

fights, 108–11, 127, 141, 170–1, 192–3

fire: 10, 61, 68, 69, 94, 107, 147–8, 150, 166 ; precautions against, 28, 53–4, 57, 113; rescuing neighbours from, 134, 164–5; see also arson

flat dwellings, 91, 109–10, 123, 153, 170, 182; design of, 157; difficulties of, 4, 8, 96–7, 105, 126, 142, 215, 222; sharers of, 183, 200; see also tower blocks; tenements

Foley, Winifred, 8, 170

food sharing: 39, 130–1, 138, 146, 178,

210; communal eating, 64, 150; declining incidence of, 132, 162, 211

football, 127, 156–7, 191

friendly societies, 39–40, 122

friendship between neighbours: 1, 4, 38, 60, 98, 106–7, 112; absent, 54–5, 88, 168–9; abuse of, 47–8, 143; in adversity, 59, 148–51, 168; bounds of, 133, 160, 162–3; conditions for, 57, 60, 63, 85–6, 107, 128–9, 141, 156, 162–3, 204–9, 215; soured, 111, 170, 174, 192, 196–7, 200, 209

fuel sharing, 146, 150

funerals and undertaking, 65, 104, 130, 164, 166–7

gardens: 61, 127, 138, 169, 189; community, 186–9; privacy in, 138, 159–60, 191; shared, 159, 191–2, 198

gas: explosions, 54, 69–70, 154; meter theft, 106

gates, 61, 74, 124, 160, 171

Gissing, George: 90, 213; on lodging, 95, 101–2, 105, 106–7, 108–9, 116; on noise, 114, 116–17

Godwin, William, 7, 88

Good Neighbour schemes, 147–8, 168–9, 177, 180, 203, 219

Gorer, Geoffrey, 160–1, 162, 165, 166, 207–8

gossiping: 63, 68, 72, 139–40, 151; decline of, 218, 224; defined, excessive, 20, 42; forging reputations, 20, 21, 23–4, 108, 109, 162; malicious, 18, 20, 131, 137; salacious, 7, 45; women, 45, 68, 107, 136–7, 145–6, 161–2, 216

Gough, Richard, 28, 46–7

green spaces, 125, 156–7, 158, 191–2, 198, 214, 220

Greenwood, Walter, 128, 137

guttering, 13, 25–6. 172, 217; see also drainage

half-houses, 91–2, 92, 225, 251n66

hanging out washing, 33, 127, 215–16

Harris, Kevin, 208, 216–17, 222

health visitors, 104, 134

hedges: 4, 111, 121, 138, 157; conflict over, 193–4; overgrown, 189; privet, 124, 159–60, 171, 182; theft from, 28

Hell, neighbours from, 194–5, 203; see also nuisance neighbours

Hill, Octavia, 96, 105, 121

Hoggart, Richard, 130–1, 132

home ownership: 74, 89–90, 124–6, 186, 189; affecting neighbourliness, 2, 31–2, 182–3, 214; increasing, 124, 153–4, 182, 214

house sales, see property values

housing types, see back-to-backs; council housing; court dwellings; flat dwellings; half-houses; semi-detached houses; slums; steel houses; sub-divided houses; tenements; terraced houses; tower blocks

hypersensitivity, 8, 115, 142, 198

immigration, see race relations

individualism: increased, causing lessening of social coherence, 21–2, 161; inhibited, 96, 125; opportunities for, 93, 121, 124, 175

infill building, 9–11, 25, 31, 57, 118

Ipswich, Beaconsfield Road, 110, 196

Jerome, Jerome K., 58, 75, 79, 109

Jones, Lee, 114, 121, 223

Joneses, the, 78–9, 88, 116, 121, 138–9, 174, 195, 212

Keats, John, 45–6

keeping oneself to oneself, 98–9, 126, 168, 184–5, 205–8, 210, 220; see also neighbour types, stand-offish; privacy

keeping up with the neighbours, see Joneses, the; one-upmanship

keys, 34, 38, 40, 105–6, 170, 185, 193

knocking on walls, 74, 102, 165, 173–4, 198

Kuper, Leo, 158–9, 162–3, 175

Lambeth, 92–3, 109–10, 121, 132, 136

landladies: 75; caring, 39, 65, 105, 214; privacy of, 95; robbed, 40, 106; as witnesses, 35, 42

landlords: 56, 58, 95, 119, 135; George Gissing on, 106–7, 108–9; as neighbours, 89–90, 106–7, 108–9; privacy and, 33; robbed, 40, 105; see also landladies

Landy, Michael, see 'Semi-detached', by Michael Landy

laundry: 3, 33, 97, 131, 132, 136, 216; compared, 138, 159; spoilt, 50, 53; stolen, 66; see also hanging out washing; washing lines

Leeds: 31, 38, 80, 106, 131, 164–5, 165, 170, 176, 217; back-to-backs, 56, 62, 220

legal action against neighbours, 28, 48–9, 50–2, 75–6, 80, 114–15, 117–18, 174; see also nuisance, legal cases

Leicester, 40, 66, 80, 108

lending, 146, 167; see also borrowing

letters, written to neighbours, 73, 114, 142–4, 182

Liberals, 121–2, 133, 152

light blocking, see windows, blocked

Little Collingwood Street, Bethnal Green, see London streets, Little Collingwood Street

Littlehampton, Western Road: 215–16; community garden, 186–9, 187, 188, 211, 214–15; fire on, 69; poison-pen letter episode, 142–3

Liverpool: 68, 114, 121, 199, 202; estate, 154, 162, 167, 169–71, 207, 209; poor housing in 32, 217

Local Improvement Acts, 33, 52, 58, 79, 113

lodgers: 3, 36, 67, 79, 97, 157–8, 213–14; fluctuating numbers of, 11, 56, 92–6, 126, 179, 214; privacy of, 33, 37, 74, 75, 95–6, 213; theft by, 33, 40–1; as witnesses, 35, 42; see also Gissing, George, on lodging

London: 17, 32, 59, 64, 67, 86, 91, 104–5, 113, 174–5; anonymity of, 37, 60; early modern surveys of, 9–11; see also Assize of Nuisance; Bermondsey; Bethnal Green; Lambeth; London streets; Watling Estate, Barnet; Viewers, London

London streets: Adelaide Street, 61–2, 66; Belgrave Square, 31, 55, 81, 93, 117; Burdock Road, 64, 98; Cheyne Row, 76–7; Ethelm Street, 132, 136; Euston Road, 65, 113; Holborn, 37–8, 41–2; Little Collingwood Street, 58, 62, 68, 70, 94–5, 95, 99, 123; Lock Court,

63–4, 68, 75; Prebend Gardens,
  110–11, 196, 212; Whateley Road,
  91–2, 93, 190–1, 215, 225
Longford, Jennifer, 157–8, 162
love (romantic) between neighbours, 7, 45–8, 72–4, 106, 172,
  201–2, 224
Lunn, Henry, 77, 78–9, 114

Manchester: 133, 147, 150; conditions
  of neighbouring, 57, 57, 62, 71, 99,
  100, 100, 101; nuisances in, 26, 28,
  80–2
Mass Observation, 2, 8, 126–8, 142,
  146–50
material support, see support,
  material
Mayhew, Henry, 57, 63, 75
mediation between neighbours, 38,
  198–9, 206
midwives, 104, 134, 164
Mogey, J. M., 162, 167
monkey in the garden next door, 82
murder: 7, 186; committed by a
  neighbour, 83–4, 110, 195;
  overheard by neighbours, 17,
  34–6, 102–3
music: 3; to humiliate, 80; as noise,
  27, 76–9, 113–17, 173, 194, 223; see
  also pianos
mutual support, see reciprocity

negligence, distinguished from
  nuisance, 24, 49–50, 140
neighbourhoods: 2, 4, 11, 39, 59–60,
  80, 127, 132, 211; divided, 135–6;
  fictional, 1, 199–200; traditional,
  121, 161, 169, 203, 207; working
  class, 109, 131, 203, 211
neighbourhood watch schemes, 190
neighbourliness: 1–4, 19–23, 44–5, 64,
  97, 130, 208; declining, 30, 151,
  168, 178, 182, 205–6, 210–11,
  216–20, 222–3; northern, 124, 132,
  163, 175; rural, 59–60, 67, 131;
  traditional, 16, 42, 64, 124, 178–9,
  203–4, 220, 222
neighbour types: 8–9, 59, 85, 89,
  90–1, 128–9; dirty, 26–8, 33, 71–2,
  99, 131; inquisitive, 20, 22, 45, 85,
  132, 160–1, 170, 202; lonely, 23,
  146, 161, 168, 182, 203; new, 2, 61,
  98, 123–4, 134–5, 139, 140, 153, 155,
  202; quarrelsome, 18–19, 44, 116,
  169–70; standoffish, 44–5, 210;
  suspicious, 16, 18–20, 23, 34,
  102–3, 136, 148, 151, 209–10, 222;
  see also keeping oneself to
  oneself; scolds; snobs; trades as
  nuisance neighbours
neighbours: defined, 6, 32, 61; male,
  148, 162, 175–6, 195, 220; rural, 2,
  6, 9, 22, 31, 44–5, 59–60, 67, 87,
  134, 140–1, 172, 189, 210; see also
  children as neighbours; elderly
  neighbours; social status;
  students; women
night shifts, 58, 144, 158–9, 173
noise insulation, see soundproofing
noises: 8, 141, 158–60, 190; animals
  and birds, 76, 114, 116–17, 140–2,
  144, 196–7; bathroom, 142, 157,
  173; bedroom, 142, 173, 197–8, 223;
  children, 58, 97, 113, 142, 174, 221,
  223; coughs, 79, 173; DIY and
  construction, 2, 77; housework,
  4, 173–4; music and chimes, 27,
  76–9, 113–17, 173, 194, 223; radio,
  125, 144, 173–4, 177; voices, 75,
  115–16, 173, 196, 221; see also baby
  crying
noisy neighbours, see noises

nosy neighbours, *see* neighbour types, inquisitive

Nottingham, 66, 100–1, 102, 136, *137*

Nuisance, Assize of, *see* Assize of Nuisance

nuisance: 50, 140, 223; definition, 50, 140, 223; inspectors of, 71–2, 79–82; legal cases, 49–51, 52–3, 80–1, 118, 120, 140–1, 172, 197–8; legislation, 49–52, 71, 79, 120, 174, 194, 206

nuisance neighbours: 6, 24–6, 113–18, 174; *see also* Hell, neighbours from; neighbour types, dirty; noise; trades as nuisance neighbours

one-upmanship: 43–4, 88–9, *89*; absent in metropolitan neighbourhoods, 60; housework related, 138–9; purchases triggered by, 174–5, 195, 200, 212

Orlin, Lena Cowen, 14, 15

overcrowding: 32, 64, 118, 121; early modern, 11; twentieth century, 91–6, 127, 136; Victorian, 57–9, 71, 119

overhearing the neighbours, 3, 16–17, 34–7, 84–5, 97, 157–9, 197–8, 221–2; *see also* eavesdropping; noises

overlooking the neighbours, 3, 34, 75–6, 88, 157

owner-occupiers, *see* home ownership

Oxford: 49, 111–12, 129, 162, 163, 167; *see also* Cutteslowe Walls, Oxford

pampas grass, 201–2, 205,

parcels taken in for neighbours, 132, 185, 195

parking, *see* car, parking issues; terraced streets, parking along

partitions: 1, 4, 11, 173; substantial, 76–7, 85, 157; thin, 7, 14–15, 20, 34–6, 42, 49, 54, 83–5, 158–9, 173–4, 198, 221, 225; *see also* party walls; peepholes

party walls: 4, 25, 29, 80, 124–5, 157; banging on, 115, 173–4; overhearing through, 84, 173, 198–9, 223; thickness of, 34, 83, 85, 115, 124–5, 158–9, 173–4

Paston family, 9, 28

pawning, 40, 66, 97–8, 106, 211

peepholes, 14, 30, 40, 46

Pember Reeves, Maud, 92–3, 103, 162

Pepys, Samuel, 26, 217

Pets, 132, 149; *see also* birds; cats; dogs; monkey in the garden next door

philanthropy, 64, 67–8, 96, 99, 104, 121, 201, 219

pianos: 43, 77–9, 115, 139; noisy, 76–7, 78–9, 113–15, 173, 223

pigs, 27–8, 49–51, 57, 71, 79, 81–2

Place, Francis, 33, 39

planning, *see* town planning

play areas, 135, 156–7, 220–1

porch sharing, 91, 127

poverty, neighbouring in: 21–2, 64, 87, 91, 98–9, 104, 121; neighbourliness enhanced in, 22–3, 39, 42, 64, 66–8, 105, 122, 124, 129–32, 205, 211, 219–20, 222; nuisances more pronounced in, 53, 55, 71, 80–1, 99–100; privacy elusive in, 32–3, 57–9, 68, 96–7; visible signs of, 70, 98, 107, 132; *see also* slums; overcrowding

practical support, *see* support,
practical
Prebend Gardens, Chiswick, *see*
London streets, Prebend Gardens
Preston, 52–3, 63, 65
privacy: 2–3, 30, 209–10, 220;
balancing with sociability, 3,
44–5, 75, 98–9, 126, 157, 160–1,
208–9, 210, 222; defined, 3;
enjoying, 102, 130, 159–60, 182,
206–7, 210, 213, 216, 219–20;
lacking in slums, 56, 64, 68,
97–101; limited in flats, 97, 126,
157; limited in lodgings, 37, 75, 93,
95, 158, 213; limits to, 3, 14–15, 20,
30–4, 124–5, 139, 159, 173, 192;
seeking, 37, 74; violations to, 13,
16, 75–6, 127–8; *see also* spying on
neighbours
privies: 26, 86, 188, 191; nuisance of,
24, 49, 57, 71, 79; shared, 11–12, 13,
33–4, 62, 100, 217; *see also* toilets
property values, 2, 182–3, 189, 192,
196, 199–200, 202, 214
prostitution, 49, 63–4, 107, 136, 158,
160, 202
public health, 70, 72, 79, 90, 120; *see*
also nuisance, inspectors of
Public Health Acts, 53, 70–1, 90, 120,
174
pumps, *see* water supplies

race relations, 177–9
radios: 139; sounds of, 125, 138, 144,
173–4, 177
railway lines, the cutting of, 58, 89
reciprocity: 64–5, 205–6, 211; and
childcare arrangements, 129–30,
166; declining, 223, 210–11, 220;
and food, 130–3, 210; in traditional neighbourhoods, 103–5, 161

recycling, 3, 212–13
Reformation, 21, 30
Reilly, Charles: 171; Birkenhead
plan, 156–7, 219; green spaces,
156, 214, 220–1; rejects self-
containment, 193–4, 210, 212,
214–15; *see also* Wolfe, Lawrence
relatives: 14, 71, 134, 154, 164, 167,
202; as neighbours, 2, 59, 103, 138,
155, 169, 210
renting privately, 56, 68, 89, 124–5,
135, 182; *see also* landladies;
landlords; lodgers
reputation, 18–20, 47, 179, 186, 216,
218; *see also* compurgation;
witnesses, court
residents' associations, 134–5
respectable neighbours, *see* rough
and respectable neighbours
right to light, *see* windows, blocked
Roberts, Elizabeth, 161, 166–7, 207
Roberts, Robert, 97–8, 107, 109
rough and respectable neighbours:
dichotomy of, 86–8, 98–9, 108,
120–1, 126, 137; respectable, 39, 53,
74, 78, 102, 136, 216; training the
rough to be respectable, 96–7,
98–9
Rowntree, Seebohm, 99, 105
rural neighbours, *see* neighbourliness, rural; neighbours, rural

Salford, 44–5, 97–8, 107, 109, 154
sanctuary, neighbours providing, 67,
84
sanitary legislation, *see* public
health; Public Health Acts;
nuisance, legislation
scolds, 18–19, 23, 36, 48
Seabrook, Jeremy, 169, 178–9, 207,
211

Segal, Walter, 3, 157
semi-detached houses: 77, 176, 193; competitiveness of residents, 138–9, 152; post-war, 152–3, 171, 173–4, 182, 205; pre-war, 4, 90, 120, 123–5; sounds heard in, 114–15, 198–9
'Semi-detached', by Michael Landy, 181–2, *181*
settlement movement, 98, 203
sex: hearing a neighbour having, 3, 197–8, 223; seeing a neighbour having, 14–16, 197; with a neighbour, 48, 72, 210–2
shared facilities, 56, 96, 100–1, 156–7, 171–2, *see also* toilets, shared; privies, shared; water supplies
shared outdoor spaces: 64, 118, 127, 220–1; *see also* back-to-backs, shared spaces around; backyards, shared; gardens, shared; green spaces
Sheffield: 59–60, 66, 79–80; estate, 154, 159, 163, 166–7, 170
Silverdale, spite walls, 111
Sims, George, 66–7, 68, 120
slaughterhouses, 11, 71–2, 79, 80, 127
slums: *100, 101,* 121, 136; caring relationships in, 67–8, 130–1; clearances, 59, 71, 123–4, 153–5; conditions, 99–102; conflict in, 74–5, 107; individualism in, 92–3; overcrowding in 93–5, 119–20; privacy issues, 68, 136; reputations forged in, 97; solidarity in, 68
Small Faces, The, 171, 223
Smethwick, 177–8
snakes, 120
snobs, 88, 126, 176–7, 199–200, 210; *see also* neighbour types, stand-offish

soap operas, 1, 199–200, 218
socialising, *see* doorsteps; food sharing; gossiping; street parties; streets, as venues for socialising; swinging; tea, cups of; visiting
social status: differences, 33, 81, 88–91, 123–4, 129–32, 160–2, 176–7, 219–20; middle class, 43, 86, 165, 169, 182, 203; upper class, 55, 59, 64, 66, 128; working class, 58, 67, 86–7, 97–9, 109–10, 156–7, 177, 179, 203; *see also* snobs
social work, 98, 120–2, 133, 152, 163–4, 219, 222
soundproofing, 76–7, 142, 157–8, 182, 206, 225
Southampton, 24, 26, 62, 108, 209
Spencer, Stanley, 138, 142
spite walls, 111, 193
spying on neighbours, 14–16, 22, 30, 44–5, 151, 161; *see also* eavesdropping
stealing, *see* theft from neighbours
steel houses, 158–9, 173–4, 208; *see also* Coventry, Thimbler Road
street parties, 7, 183–4
streets: as venues for work, 33, 64, 86, 99, 100; as venues for socialising, 62–4, 100, 105, 136, 139–7, 145–6, 162, 179, 187–8, 215–17, 220–1; *see also* street parties
students, 194–5
sub-divided houses, 9–11, 32–3, 35–6, 74, 91, 213; *see also* half-houses
'suburban neurosis', 180, 182
suburbs: 72, 141, 156–7, 195, 199–200, 202; conflict in, 110–11, 114–15, 125–7; Edwardian, 89–91, 98; interwar, 123–4, 138; post-war, 168, 171–2, 174–5, 180, 182;

Victorian, 59, 87, 101, 120–1;
wartime, 146
support: 7, 22–3, 39, 86, 129–33, 166,
205, 208–11, 223; emotional, 66–8,
103–4, 133, 166; material, 2, 22, 58,
151–2; mutual, *see* reciprocity;
practical, 23, 64, 104, 151–2; *see
also* borrowing; childcare
provided by neighbours; creditors, neighbours as
Swan, Edith, 69, 142–3
swinging, 201–2

tea, cups of, 131, 146–7, 162, 170, 188
Tebbutt, Melanie, 20
telephones, 139–40
television, neighbours depicted on,
199–200, 205–6, 218–19
tenements: 1, 30, 32, 36, 41–2, 99–101,
104–5; in blocks of model
dwellings, 96–7, 105, 121, 135
terraced houses: 3, 4, 54–6, 176, 199,
204; periods of development, 4,
31, 55–6, 64, 90, 123; sounds heard
in, 4, 77, 125, 173, 221, 225;
through terraces, 56, 64, 90; *see
also* back-to-backs
terraced streets, parking along,
195–6
Thatcher, Margaret, 203
theft from neighbours: 28–9, 40–2,
66, 106; from a neighbour's land,
28, 142
Thimbler Road, Coventry, *see*
Coventry, Thimbler Road
thin partitions, *see* partitions, thin
threatening behaviour, 108, 110
toilets: 11, 159, 217–18; shared, 4, 11,
86, 99–100, 127–8, 131, 135–6,
217–18; *see also* privies
tower blocks, 153–4, 183

town planning, 112–13, 123, 174,
190–1, 206
trades as nuisance neighbours:
51–3, 80–1; armourer, 26–7;
artificial manure factory, 81;
butchers, 79; confectioners,
80–1; fish shops, 80; forges,
26–7; pickle factory, 80; rubber
works, 80; smiths, 27, 52–3;
tallow-chandlers, 27, 51, 54–5, 80;
tripe dresser, 80; *see also* slaughterhouses
trees, 61, 142, 144, 172, 193, *see also*
hedges
Treswell, Ralph, 9–11
trust: 22–3, 38–9, 41, 185, 210–11;
abuse of, 41; mistrust, 190, 193;
see also keys; theft from neighbours
Tusser, Thomas, 19, 20, 22, 23, 45

unemployment benefit, 122, 133,
137–8, 163

Viewers, London, 24–6, 30, 194
visiting, 6, 35, 43–5, 106, 131–2, 158,
160, 162, 176, 185, 208–9, 218, *see
also* doorsteps; tea, cups of

walls, *see* Cutteslowe Walls, Oxford;
knocking on walls; partitions;
party walls; spite walls
washing lines: 3, 33, 131, 137, 171, 216,
217; clues gathered from, 3, 159,
213; cluttering shared spaces, 33,
99, 127, 136; lessening visibility of,
127, 216; items stolen from, 66;
see also laundry
water supplies: 70, 86, 99–100, 135;
conflict over, 62–3; gathering
points at, 4, 86, 88, 215

Watling Estate, Barnet, 123–4, 134–5, 139, 141
Weedon, Val, 223
welfare state, 2, 121–2, 163–6, 168, 179–80, 219
Western Road, Littlehampton, *see* Littlehampton, Western Road
Whateley Road, East Dulwich, *see* London streets, Whateley Road
Whitaker, Jeffrey, 44, 45, 48–9
White, Jerry, 104, 131
wife-beating, *see* domestic abuse
Willis, Frederick, 59, 64–5, 74, 95–6, 98, 131
Willmott, Peter, 154–5, 161, 174–5
windows; 14, 26, 27, 75–6, 88, 124; blocked, 9, 25–6, 50–1, 75, 111, 144, 206; broken, 99, 178; coverings, 98, 132, 139, 144, 175, 195; open, 64, 100, 174; overlooking neighbours, 30, 34, 157, 214; positioning of, 24, 30, 143–4, 214
wine, spoiled, 27, 117
witchcraft, 18, 23–4, 30

witnesses: character statement providers, 19–20, 41–3; court, 16, 30, 34–7, 47, 54–5, 60, 63, 83–5, 140–1, 185; to wills, 38
Wolfe, Lawrence, 157, 171, 193–4, 210
women as neighbours: 37, 131–2, 141, 159, 161, 169; exposed to more neighbouring, 36, 162, 177, 189–90, 203, 221; fighting, 62–3, 75, 110–11, 170–1; gossiping together, 7, 45, 63, 107, 131, 136–7, 144–6, 145, 171; knitting together, 146–7, 147; reputations of, 45, 75, 99, 107, 218; supporting each other, 23, 104–5, 131, 134, 161
World War II, neighbourliness, 144–51
Wright, Thomas, 58, 63, 68, 75
Wrightson, Keith, 6, 22, 131, 169

York, 105, 127–8, 130
Young, Michael, 126, 154–5, 161, 174–5